הרב אברהם יצחק הכהן קוק

הנשמות של עולם התהו

RABBI ABRAHAM ISAAC HAKOHEN KOOK

THE SOULS OF THE WORLD OF CHAOS

TRANSLATION, INTRODUCTION
AND NOTES

BEZALEL NAOR

אורות
OROT

KODESH PRESS

OROT/KODESH

5783/2023

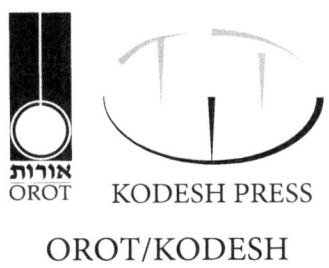

הַנְּשָׁמוֹת שֶׁל עוֹלַם הַתֹּהוּ

Ha-Neshamot shel 'Olam ha-Tohu

The Souls of the World of Chaos

This volume includes two book reviews
by Bezalel Naor:

Yehudah Mirsky,
Towards the Mystical Experience of Modernity:
The Making of Rav Kook, 1865-1904

Ḥagay Shtamler,
Eight Letters from Rabbi Zvi Yehuda Kook

Cover illustration:
Tree of Life by Shem Tov Ben Shlomo

Corrected version April 2023

Hardcover ISBN : 979-8-88894-002-0
Paperback ISBN: 979-8-88894-006-8

For permission requests, write to the publisher.
Published and distributed exclusively by:

Kodesh Press L.L.C., New York, NY
www.kodeshpress.com

Orot, Inc., Monsey, NY
www.orot.com

Printed in the United States of America

מכתב ברכה

בהופעת הספר הנשמות של עולם התוהו

יג כסלו, תשפ"ג

אין דור שאין בו בעיות ציבוריות, מְתָחִים ולחצים. כך ייסד ה' את עולמו שיהיו תמיד מלחמות הדיעות, והתנגשויות בין תרבויות שונות. זה מיוסד בכוונה תחילה כדי שהאדם יצטרך להתמודד, להתאמץ, ולהתגבר בכל יכולתו להביא ברכה לעולם. המחסומים נבראו כדי שהאנושות תטפס עליהם, לקראת הקידמה הנכספת. לְמַה הדבר דומה? הרופא מחדיר בגוף האדם חומר-חיסון נגד מחלות. החיסון מורכב מחיידקים מומתים או מוחלשים. בתחילה החיסון מחליש את האדם, אבל סופו לטובה, יהיה חסון יותר, בריא יותר.

הגאון הגדול, הצדיק המופלא, החסיד העליון, מעמיק-חקר הרב אברהם יצחק הכהן קוק זצ"ל היה אלוף האמונה, כמו שיווכח כל הלומד באוסף מאמריו שבספר **אורות האמונה**. אין כמוהו שחקר ובדק ועיין בכל הנושא של אמונה. והוא ידע בבירור גמור אמיתות דברי נחום איש גם זו "גם זו לטובה" (תענית כא, א) על כל המתרחש למראה עינינו. המרד-בדת שהתאושש בימינו, החוצפא להכחיש מציאות הבורא, ההתקפות התמידיות נגד קיום המצוות, אלו לא הרפו את רוחו של הרב. כי "האדם יראה [רק] לעיניים" אבל היודעים פנימיות התורה, העוסקים ברזי עולם, יסירו את המסך וידעו שכל אשר עשה ה', גם הנראה כאי-סדרים, הכל מכוון למעלה. וביודעו שאין דבר בטל בעולם שה' ברא, הבחין הרב מה המתניע "נשמות של תוהו" בפעלן.

הרב הגדול, המלומד והבקי במאות ספרי הגות וספרי היסטוריה, ספרי חסידות ואף ספרי חוקרים רבים, ר׳ בצלאל נאור שליט״א, כבר העשיר את עולמנו בעשרות ספרים חשובים. אמנם רבים מאד הם אחרים שכתבו אודות הרב קוק ופעלו. בספרי **אוצרות הראי״ה** (חלק רביעי עמ׳ 439) שכתבתי עוד בשנת תשס״ב, יש רשימה של 426 מחברים שכתבו למעלה מ-1200 מאמרים וספרים אודות הרב קוק והגותו. ומאז התעשרנו פי כמה במאמרים נוספים. אבל הבעיה הזו שמחבר **הנשמות של עולם התוהו** עוסק בה היא מן ״האגוזים הקשים״ שבכתבי הרב קוק. לומר שנשמותיהם של האפיקורסים האלו הן גבוהות מנשמותיהם של שומרי-דת פשוטים, הוא מהחידות הגדולות. מי יכול לפענח? כמה יפה עשה הרב המחבר שהביא מקורות נאמנים לדברי הרב, וכדרכו בכל ספריו הביא בסוף ספרו מאות הערות המרחיבות את היריעה ומוסיפות פרטים חשובים לכל הרוצה הבנה נוספת.

גם הוסיף נספחים חשובים בהערכה של ספרים נוספים שיצאו לאור זה עכשיו, בעניני הראי״ה ובעניני הרב צבי יהודה קוק, זצ״ל.

הספר **הנשמות של עולם התוהו** מוסיף פנינה יקרה לעטרת הספרים שהרב המחבר החשוב העניק לעולמנו. אשרינו.

משה צוריאל

מלקט סדרת שבעת הכרכים **אוצרות הראי״ה**

Table of Contents

Foreword 7

Introduction 11

The Souls of the World of Chaos

Hebrew Text 23

English Translation 27

Appendix A: The Transition from *Tohu* to *Tikkun* 33

Appendix B: Beyond *Tohu* and *Tikkun* 39

Appendix C: The Binary Universe 43

Appendix D: Defining *Yetser ha-Ra‘* and *Yetser ha-Tov* 46

Appendix E: *Tsurat ha-Adam:* A Philological Study 49

Appendix F: Rabbi Menashe of Ilya and Rav Kook 57

Appendix G: The *Leshem* and Luzzatto 68

Book Reviews

Yehudah Mirsky, *Towards the Mystical Experience of Modernity: The Making of Rav Kook, 1865-1904* 85

Ḥagay Shtamler, *Eight Letters from Rabbi Zvi Yehuda Kook* 93

Endnotes 103

Bibliography 195

הרב אברהם יצחק הכהן קוק
בגימטריא אהבת ישראל

Foreword

THIRTY YEARS AGO, when I first undertook the translation of Rav Kook's seminal work, *Orot*, I restricted myself to the first edition which appeared in Jerusalem in 5680 AM (1920 CE).[1] This editorial decision was motivated by the desire for historical accuracy. I wanted the reader to have in hand the text which so sparked controversy in the Land of Israel and throughout the Jewish world. In this way, the reader would be able to formulate an independent, objective judgment concerning the issues raised. Including extraneous pieces that were appended to the later 1950 edition of *Orot*, would only have clouded matters.[2]

Since then, from that later edition I translated separately Rav Kook's historical essay, "*Le-Mahalakh ha-Ide'ot be-Yisrael*" ("To the Process of Ideas in Israel").[3]

Today, I present yet another piece from the later edition of *Orot*, "*Ha-Neshamot shel 'Olam ha-Tohu*" ("The Souls of the World of Chaos").[4]

*

This *pensée* of Rav Kook takes us back to what many view as the most creative period of his life, the decade that he served as Rabbi of Jaffa. But he was not only the

Rabbi of Jaffa. He was the "Rabbi of Jaffa and the colonies (*moshavot*)," as stated boldly on his letterhead stationery. And while Rabbi Tsevi Yehudah Kook recreated for me some of the atmosphere in the Kook home at the Third Meal of the Sabbath, when the intelligentsia of Jaffa gathered to thirstily drink in the Rav's words of wisdom, another, less known, figure recounted for me Rav Kook's interaction with the agriculturalists of Reḥovot, the settlement where Rav Kook would summer.[5] I am indebted to Amihud Naḥmani (1899-1985), one of the first children born in Reḥovot, for sharing with me the memories of his youth.[6] Amihud's first language was Modern Hebrew. Yiddish was a second, acquired language. And so when Rav Kook, a visitor to the Naḥmani home, asked the precocious youngster in Yiddish, "*Wie alt bist du, yingel?*" ("How old are you, child?"), Amihud, improvising, responded, "*A halb nokh sieben*" ("Half past seven"). (He had heard his elders telling time in Yiddish.) This repartee made the rounds of the village for some days.

According to Amihud, Rav Kook greatly esteemed the friendship of his father, Mordechai Halevi Naḥmani (Gorodinsky), for both men had studied in the Volozhin Yeshivah. (However, Amihud confided to me that it was his father's wont to study Talmud bareheaded, citing Onkelos' Aramaic translation of the verse, "And the Children of Israel went out with a high hand" [Exodus 14:8]—"*be-reish gelei*," "with an uncovered head.")

Amihud remembered vividly Rav Kook standing in the middle of the dance circle, eyes closed, surrounded by the *ḥalutsim*, idealistic young pioneers who had left European exile to settle in the ancestral land. Even as a child, it was apparent to him that Rav Kook was in some extraordinary state of ecstasy—*deveikut*—as he stood there transfixed.

*

In closing I should like to address a complaint concerning Rav Kook's writings that has gained some currency of late. Before I enter into the fray, I must preface my remarks by stating that I sat at the feet of both Rabbi Yosef Dov Soloveitchik of Boston and Rabbi Tsevi Yehudah Kook, of blessed memory, and consider both men my teachers.

Recently, there has circulated a recording of Rabbi Soloveitchik, in which he states categorically that Chief Rabbi Avraham Yitzḥak Kook was not a philosopher. Rabbi Soloveitchik, one of the great Jewish thinkers of the twentieth century, was not able to find in Rav Kook's writings a coherent philosophy. Instead, he assigned to Rav Kook the role of a "religious personality." In his recorded talk, Rabbi Soloveitchik then goes on to recount how when he visited Erets Yisrael in the summer of 1935, he experienced first-hand the impact of Rav Kook's charismatic personality on anti-religious kibbutzniks.[7]

Evidently, Rabbi Soloveitchik was not the first to throw up his hands in frustration, unable to discern in Rav Kook's aphoristic writings a distinct method or a systematic philosophy. In a recently released journal of Rav Kook, we come across this paragraph:

It is folly to search in thought for exact order. In general, that order comes about from imitating small matters, totally inappropriate for a broad spiritual thought, such as that created by a liberated soul.[8]

BN

Introduction

THIS CLASSIC PIECE, a chapter of the collection *Zer'onim* ("Seeds"), first appeared in 1913, in the short-lived journal *Ha-Tarbut ha-Yisraelit* (*The Israelite Civilization*), edited by Tsevi Yehudah Kook.[1] Since 1950, it has been included in standard editions of *Orot*, Rav Kook's seminal work.[2]

"The Souls of the World of Chaos" speaks specifically to the soul of the Second Aliyah, the second wave of immigration to Erets Yisrael in modern times. Typically, these founders of the kibbutz movement were young Russian Jews who espoused ideals of Socialism while rebelling against the traditional Jewish lifestyle and mores.[3] Like any classic work of literature, this essay is of perennial value and continues to resonate throughout the ages, whenever there is a concerted breakdown of the established order and a new world order, yet hazy and ill-defined, looms on the horizon.

Though Rav Kook witnessed a total shattering of the old and familiar, he remains resilient and uncannily optimistic—in stark contrast to most of his rabbinic peers. "But in truth, there is nothing to fear; only sinners, weak souls and flatterers fear and tremble." Rav Kook is confident that this very revolutionary power, a cause of consternation to many, will be appropriated by "the righteous, strong as lions, who will reveal the truth of the *tikkun* and the building."

Our essay draws on the Lurianic trope of the World of Chaos (*'Olam ha-Tohu*) which preceded the World of Establishment (*'Olam ha-Tikkun*). That kabbalistic motif, in turn, echoes the ancient Midrash that before *Bereshit*, God was "building worlds and destroying them."[4] What typifies the World of Chaos and brings about its destruction, is that the "vessels" (*kelim*) cannot contain the "lights" (*'orot*), which prove overwhelming and cause the shattering of the vessels. (In the succinct formulation of ḤaBaD Ḥasidism, *Tohu* represents a state of "plurality of light and paucity of vessels" [*"ribbui 'or u-mi'ut kelim"*], and *Tikkun*, a state of "paucity of light and plurality of vessels" [*"mi'ut 'or ve-ribbui kelim"*].)[5]

HORIZONTAL AND VERTICAL AXES

In his notes published at the conclusion of *Orot*, the author's son, Rabbi Tsevi Yehudah Kook, sources the crucial term, *"neshamot shel 'Olam ha-Tohu"* ("souls of the World of Chaos"), in the commentary of the Vilna Gaon to *Sifra di-Tseni'uta*.[6] There, the Gaon wrote:

> And in those years [of the exile since the destruction of the Temple] there reincarnate all the nine hundred and seventy-four generations,[7] which are the Mixed Multitude (*'Erev Rav*);[8] which are the souls of the World of Chaos (*ha-*

> *neshamot me-'Olam ha-Tohu*), as it states, "[The Holy One, blessed be He] planted them in every generation, and they are the brazen-faced of the generation,"[9] and they said, "In the footsteps of Messiah, impudence (*ḥutspah*) will increase," and, as it states in *Ra'aya Mehemna*, *Naso*, "the *'Erev Rav* have become the [spiritual] shepherds over Israel."[10]

Thus, having sourced his father's notion of the contemporaneity of the "souls of the World of Chaos" in the writings of the Vilna Gaon,[11] Rabbi Tsevi Yehudah next located the notion that the "souls of Chaos" (*"neshamot de-Tohu"*) are higher than the "souls of Establishment" (*"neshamot de-Tikkun"*) in the teachings of ḤaBaD. Rabbi Dov Baer Shneuri of Lubavitch (the *"Mitteler Rebbe,"* or "Middle Rabbi") taught that Jacob's humbling himself before Esau was reflective of the fact that at their root, the "lights of Chaos" (*'orot de-Tohu*) of Esau are higher than the "lights of Establishment" (*'orot de-Tikkun*) of Jacob.[12]

In order to map out Rav Kook's ideas, his son (and editor) Tsevi Yehudah turned to the two kabbalistic worlds that his father inhabited: the *"beit midrash"* (studyhouse) of Rabbi Elijah of Vilna and the *"beit midrash"* of Rabbi Shneur Zalman of Lyady.[13]

The spiritual heirs of Rabbi Elijah of Vilna provided the horizontal coordinates along the timeline of cosmic history.[14] The two millennia of *Tohu* of the *Tanna de-Vei Eliyahu*[15] were wedded to the *'Olam ha-Tohu* of Rabbi Isaac

Luria,[16] and then catapulted through time to emerge once again (somewhat softened) in the era of the "footsteps of Messiah."[17]

The spiritual heirs of Rabbi Shneur Zalman of Lyady assigned vertical coordinates. The "root" of the souls of *Tohu* is higher than the "root" of the souls of *Tikkun*. In Esau, there are enormous energies that transcend, in some sense, the straight and narrow path of Torah and commandments associated with Jacob.[18]

RESONANCES

A century after Rabbi Isaac Luria, Nathan of Gaza would shift the nomenclature, writing of the infinite "light that does not contain thought" (*'or she-ein bo maḥshavah*) and the finite "light that contains thought" (*'or she-yesh bo maḥshavah*). The former "seeks destruction" (*mehader batar ḥurbana*), while the latter "seeks construction" (*mehader batar binyana*).[19]

Rabbi Eizik of Homel (1770-1857), a master of ḤaBaD Hasidism, ventured into the field of developmental psychology, finding a parallel to the schema of *Tohu* in children's need to break vessels as part of their development. As reported in the Talmud, "Rabbah bought broken clay vessels for his children and they broke them."[20]

Drawing on a passage in the Talmud concerning the creation of the world, Rabbi Gershon Ḥanokh Leiner of Radzyn envisions *Tohu*, not as a world order that has been phased out altogether by a new world order of *Tikkun*, but as an ongoing process, whereby *Tohu* and *Tikkun* represent two tracks of creation that are contemporaneous and complimentary.

The passage in the Talmud reads:

> When the Holy One, blessed be He, created the world, it continued to expand like two balls of a warp [whose cord lengthens as they unravel], until the Holy One, blessed be He, rebuked it and made it stand still ... What is the meaning of that which is written: "I am the Almighty God [*El Shaddai*]"[21]? I am He Who said to the world, "Enough!" (*Dai!*).[22]

There follows the Radzyner's reading, striking in its profundity:

> In truth, those energies from "the worlds that were destroyed" (*'almin de-'itḥaravun*) are very precious, for they extend yet from that saying that was expanding constantly like [the thread of] two unravelling balls of a warp, until the Holy One, blessed be He, said to His world, "Enough!" The whole creation stands between these two sayings, between the first saying which was without limit, and the saying "Enough!" This first saying was not stopped, God forbid, by the saying "Enough!" Rather, this first saying still continues to expand without limit. The second saying that the LORD set up—"Enough!"—was only in order that there be limits as well. Indeed, the limits themselves are

> also in His hand, blessed be He, and to the extent that man restricts himself within the limits of the saying "Enough," so the LORD expands his limit to grant him possession of the first saying that still continues to expand without limit ... Those energies from "the worlds that were destroyed," the LORD created them too, and they are very precious.[23]

It seems that in Lubavitch, the kabbalistic terms "*Tohu*" and "*Tikkun*" were actually invoked in regard to certain individuals. Rabbi Joseph Isaac Schneersohn quoted his great-grandfather, the *Tsemaḥ Tsedek*, as saying: "Mikhel Opotzker was a *tohu'diker*, and Grandfather's direction and blessing made Reb Mikhel into a *tikkun'nik*."[24]

Lastly, the novelist Shmuel Yosef Agnon—a key figure in the literary movement of the Second Aliyah and a great admirer of Rav Kook during his days in Jaffa[25]—casts certain characters as "souls of chaos,"[26] but this most likely should be attributed to Agnon's own fascination with the kabbalistic theory of reincarnation,[27] rather than to arcane wisdom imbibed from Rav Kook.

VARIANTS

Having access now to the hitherto unpublished journals of Rav Kook, we are able to see how an editor (presumably the Rav's son, Tsevi Yehudah) stitched together four *pensées* to produce our piece, "The Souls of the World of Chaos."[28] There are slight variants, but for the most part they are of little consequence, with one notable exception. Toward the conclusion of "The Souls of the World of Chaos," we read:

> But warriors know that this show of strength is one of the visions that come for the need of perfecting the world, for the need of fortifying the powers of the nation (*ha-'ummah*), man and the world.

The final words, "man and the world" (*ha-adam ve-ha-'olam*), are not found in the manuscript version.[29] In its final incarnation, "The Souls of the World of Chaos" addresses not only the nation of Israel, but also the individual and the world at large.

"A LAW THAT IS ABOVE LAWS"

Most intriguing is Rav Kook's cryptic allusion that we are on the threshold of a higher law. The exact quote reads: "before the birth of a law that is above laws." What are we to make of this prophetic statement?

Shortly before penning these lines in the first of his Jaffa journals, earlier, back in Boisk, Rav Kook wrote a parallel passage in a full-length work, only recently published, that has come to be known as *Li-Nevukhei ha-Dor* (*For the Perplexed of the Generation*).[30] That paragraph merits our scrutiny:

> Therefore it should come as no wonder to us if there are found thinkers capable of finding

> within themselves the temerity to engage in the destruction of general morality—which is the foundation of the present world—to undermine the laws of compassion that proceed from them; to nickname these lights of the world—that are the salvation of the human species, psychically and physically, generally and specifically—"slave morality,"[31] and all kinds of derisive names. We well recognize from whence flows this malady, this megalomania.[32] They are tributaries of high souls of the World of Chaos (*neshamot gevohot shel 'Olam ha-Tohu*), that break out to receive a light exceeding the measure of their vessels (*'or merubeh 'al middat ha-kelim*), and they fall into the depths of evil and the *kelipot*.[33] This is the interpretation that the Wisdom of Israel[34] gives us concerning the strange spectacle of "those who lift themselves up to establish a vision but stumble" [Daniel 11:14].[35]

After this first salvo which confronts the iconoclasts of humanity in general (*kelal ha-'enoshut*), Rav Kook restricts his remarks to the renegades of the Jewish People.[36] Once again, he will draw on the apocalyptic verse in Daniel while wedding it to the cosmogony of Lurianic Kabbalah:

> From the general we shall come to the specific. From the rebels of the human species in general, we shall understand the psychic[37] disposition of the rebels of our people in particular....[38]

> And the arrogant rebels (*ve-ha-mitpartsim ha-mitnas'im*)[39] from the foundation of the Kings of *Tohu*, who aspire to reign "before the reign of a king to the Children of Israel,"[40] shall wither like a wilting flower, "He reigned… and he died,"[41] until they reach [as far as] the rejection of the laws of the LORD and a hatred of the sages, and after, denial of Torah and the fundament.[42]

But deep down, in depths plumbed perhaps only by Rav Kook,[43] the root of the rejection of conventional morality consists of a longing for a higher morality, an autonomous morality, as opposed to one enforced by religious coercion.[44] And here,[45] Rav Kook invokes the verse, "[For the ways of the LORD are straight,] the righteous shall walk in them, and the sinners shall stumble in them."[46] In the right time and place (and with halakhic sanction), the transition from heteronomy to autonomy can take the righteous to the level of the Patriarchs, "who performed the entire Torah before its giving [on Mount Sinai]."[47] In the wrong time and place, and in the wrong hands, this aspiration, as noble as its root, will prove destructive.[48]

In that passage, Rav Kook conjures up the distant past, holding up as an example ancestors who acted autonomously. Elsewhere, Rav Kook fixes his sight on the future:

> Certainly, in regard to the life of morality, as well, we are forever looking to a lofty height *which is above every law and statute*, which are but the

> garments of happiness. But the future orders of life certainly stand to be perfected on their own, and "commandments are nullified in the future."[49]

Some years later, in a discourse at the Third Meal of the Sabbath in Jerusalem, Rav Kook would revisit these themes, explaining that the commandments performed by the Patriarchs (which were unmandated) are likened by the Midrash to "scents" (*reiḥot*),[50] because they were a natural extension of their personalites, and speculating that the nullification of the commandments in the future signifies a return to the natural state of the Patriarchs, symbolized by "scent."[51]

Though unstated and unnamed, these passages in Rav Kook's *oeuvre*, which valorize autonomous over heteronomous morality, seem to be some form of engagement with the "categorical imperative" of Immanuel Kant, though Rav Kook might bristle at the suggestion.[52]

THE RECEPTION OF "THE SOULS OF THE WORLD OF CHAOS"

Rav Kook was targeting a specific audience, a younger generation who, in their wild idealism and relentless search for unbridled freedom, had thrown off what they perceived as the shackles of religion. By a show of empathy, of which only a kindred spirit is truly capable, Rav Kook, a loving leader, thought to gently nudge his wayward flock to the path of Torah.[53] One asks: How was this empathic essay received by the members of that generation?

Perhaps the most eloquent response was that of the iconoclast Yosef Ḥayyim Brenner (1881-1921), a radical thinker who, having rejected the religion of his youth, emerged as the strident voice of avant-gardist Hebrew literature:

> The thoughts of the authors of this journal are not our thoughts, and the ways of the authors of this *Tarbut Yisraelit* (*Israelite Civilization*) are not our ways.... Even the *exalted* Weltanschauung (we stress the word *exalted* fully conscious of the gravitas) expressed in all the "seeds" (*zer'onim*) of our teacher, Rabbi Abraham Isaac Hakohen Kook, that appear in this book—is unfounded for us, who descend to dwell and to see.
>
> "Our resting place" is not "only in God,"[54] and, in general, we know no resting place, and have even ceased to seek it. "The driven madness (*ha-teiruf ha-kal'i*) acts" upon us "with all its power"[55].... Beyond this, there is the fact that we do not believe in [Rav Kook's] own rest. He who wrote the chapters "The Souls of the World of Chaos" and "Purifying Tribulations,"[56] bears witness that the soul-wrestling of the disbelievers and the "destroyers" is not foreign to him, quite the contrary....
>
> In any event, as for the literary aspect... The speech of the author of *Zer'onim*, of the poem "*Laḥashei ha-Havayah*" ("The Whispers of

> Being"), of the overture to *Ha-Tarbut ha-Yisraelit*... this is the culture of true literature. Of this, there can be no doubt. Men of the marketplace do not speak so. So speak deep thinkers![57]

Rav Kook's impassioned writing was not lost on Brenner. The doyen of young writers sensed that here was an old-school rabbi who shared in common with the rebels a certain restlessness of spirit; who, in his own way, was searching for authenticity and was intolerant of sham. Yet, Brenner could not follow Rav Kook even as he stormed the heavens above. He found Rav Kook's vision unrealistic "for us, who descend to dwell and to see."

Rabbi Tsevi Yehudah Kook related to this writer (BN) that "Brenner was one of our *Shalosh Se'udot* Jews." Rabbi Tsevi Yehudah was referring to the intelligentsia of Jaffa who were wont to participate in Rav Kook's *tisch* (table) at the conclusion of the Sabbath. Though they might be alienated from their Jewish roots, they nonetheless relished the Rav's scintillating intellect and wisdom. On one of those occasions, Brenner cornered young Tsevi Yehudah in the kitchen and confronted him: "Your father speaks of *'or, 'or, 'or* (light, light, light). And I see only darkness."[58]

When I recalled to Rabbi Tsevi Yehudah that Brenner was killed in a pogrom in Jaffa in 1921, his response was: "A martyr (*kodosh*)."

הַנְּשָׁמוֹת שֶׁל עוֹלַם הַתֹּהוּ

הַנְּשָׁמוֹת שֶׁל עוֹלַם הַתֹּהוּ

הַהַדְרָכָה הָרְגִילָה שֶׁל תּוֹם וְיוֹשֶׁר, בִּשְׁמִירַת הַמִּדּוֹת הַטּוֹבוֹת וְכָל דָּת וְדִין, זֶהוּ עִנְיַן תַּהֲלוּכוֹת עוֹלַם הַתִּיקּוּן. וְכָל הַהִתְפָּרְצוּת מִזֶּה, בֵּין מִצַּד קַלּוּת דַּעַת וְהֶפְקֵרוּת וּבֵין מִצַּד עֲלִיַּת דַּעַת וְהִתְעוֹרְרוּת רוּחַ עֶלְיוֹן, הוּא מֵעִנְיַן עוֹלַם הַתֹּהוּ; אֶלָּא שֶׁיֵּשׁ הֶפְרֵשׁ גָּדוֹל בַּפְּרָטִים שֶׁל עוֹלַם הַתֹּהוּ עַצְמוֹ וּבִנְטִיּוֹתָיו לִשְׂמֹאל אוֹ לְיָמִין. הָאִידֵיאָלִיסְטִים הַגְּדוֹלִים רוֹצִים בְּסֵדֶר יָפֶה וְטוֹב, מוּצָק וְאַדִּיר כָּזֶה, שֶׁאֵין בָּעוֹלָם לוֹ דֻּגְמָא וִיסוֹד, עַל כֵּן הֵם מְהָרְסִים אֶת הַבִּנּוּי לְפִי מִדַּת הָעוֹלָם. הַמְּעוּלִּים יוֹדְעִים גַּם לִבְנוֹת אֶת הָעוֹלָם הַנֶּהֱרָס, אֲבָל הַגְּרוּעִים, שֶׁהַנְּטִיָּה הָאִידֵיאָלִית הַיּוֹתֵר עֶלְיוֹנָה נָגְעָה בָּהֶם רַק נְגִיעָה כָּל שֶׁהִיא, הֵם רַק מְחַבְּלִים וּמְהָרְסִים, וְהֵם הֵם הַמְּשָׁרְשִׁים בְּעוֹלַם הַתֹּהוּ בְּעֶרְכּוֹ הַנִּשְׁפָּל.

נְשָׁמוֹת דְּתֹהוּ גְּבוֹהוֹת הֵן מִנְּשָׁמוֹת דְּתִיקּוּן. גְּדוֹלוֹת הֵן מְאֹד, מְבַקְּשׁוֹת הֵן הַרְבֵּה מִן הַמְּצִיאוּת, מַה שֶּׁאֵין הַכֵּלִים שֶׁלָּהֶן יְכוֹלִים לִסְבּוֹל. מְבַקְּשׁוֹת הֵן אוֹר גָּדוֹל מְאֹד, כָּל מַה שֶּׁהוּא מֻגְבָּל, מְקֻצָּב וְנֶעֱרָךְ, אֵינָן יְכוֹלוֹת לְשֵׂאתוֹ. הֵן יָרְדוּ מִמַּעֲלָתָן מֵרֵאשִׁית הַנְּטִיָּה שֶׁל הַהֲוָיָה לְהִוָּלֵד, הִתְרוֹמְמוּ כְּשַׁלְהֶבֶת וְנִדְעֲכוּ. שְׁאִיפָתָן הַבִּלְתִּי סוֹפִית לְלֹא תִּכְלֶה, הִנָּן מִתְלַבְּשׁוֹת בְּכֵלִים שׁוֹנִים, שׁוֹאֲפוֹת הַרְבֵּה יוֹתֵר וְיוֹתֵר מֵהַמִּדָּה, שׁוֹאֲפוֹת וְנוֹפְלוֹת. רוֹאוֹת שֶׁהִנָּן כְּלוּאוֹת בְּחֻקִּים, בִּתְנָאִים מוּגְבָּלִים שֶׁאֵינָם נוֹתְנִים לְהִתְרַחֵב לְאֵין קֵץ, לִמְרוֹמִים אֵין דַּי, וְהִנָּן נוֹפְלוֹת בִּתְוּגָה, בְּיֵאוּשׁ, בְּחָרוֹן, וּמִתּוֹךְ קֶצֶף - בְּרֶשַׁע, בְּזָדוֹן, בְּשִׁפְלוּת, בְּכִיעוּר, בְּתִיעוּב, בְּהִירוּס, בְּכָל רַע. הַתְּסִיסָה הַחַיָּה שֶׁלָּהֶן אֵינָהּ שׁוֹקֶטֶת – מִתְגַּלּוֹת הֵן בְּעַזֵּי-פָּנִים שֶׁבַּדּוֹר. הָרְשָׁעִים בַּעֲלֵי הַפְּרִינְצִיפִּים, הַפּוֹשְׁעִים לְהַכְעִיס וְלֹא לְתֵאָבוֹן, נִשְׁמָתָם גְּבוֹהָה מְאֹד – מֵאוֹרוֹת דְּתֹהוּ. בָּחֲרוּ בְּהֶרֶס וְהִנָּם מְהָרְסִים, הָעוֹלָם מִתְטַשְׁטֵשׁ עַל יָדָם וְהֵם עִמּוֹ. אֲבָל תַּמְצִית הָאֹמֶץ שֶׁיֵּשׁ בִּרְצוֹנָם הִיא הַנְּקֻדָּה שֶׁל קֹדֶשׁ. שֶׁכְּשֶׁהִיא נִסְפֶּגֶת אֶל הַנְּשָׁמוֹת

הַמְשֻׁעָרוֹת בְּמַהֲלָכָן, הִיא נוֹתֶנֶת לָהֶן אֶת עֹז הַחַיִּים. בְּיוֹתֵר הֵן מִתְגַּלּוֹת בְּאֵיזֶה אַחֲרִית יָמִים, בַּתְּקוּפָה שֶׁלִּפְנֵי הֲרַת עוֹלָם, שֶׁקֹּדֶם לַהֲוָיָה יְצִירִית חֲדָשָׁה וְנִפְלָאָה, בַּתְּחוּם שֶׁעַל הִתְרַחֲבוּת הַגְּבוּלִים, בְּטֶרֶם לֵדַת חֹק שֶׁמִּמַּעַל לַחֻקִּים.

בְּעִתּוֹתֵי גְּאֻלָּה מִתְגַּבֶּרֶת חֻצְפָּה. וְסַעַר מִתְחוֹלֵל הוֹלֵךְ וְזוֹעֵף, פְּרָצִים אַחַר פְּרָצִים יִפְרְצוּ, חֻצְפָּה מֵחֻצְפָּה תִּגְדַּל, מֵאֵין קֹרֶת רוּחַ בְּכָל הָאוֹצָר הַטּוֹב שֶׁל הָאוֹר הַמֻּגְבָּל וְהַמְצֻמְצָם מִפְּנֵי שֶׁאֵינֶנּוּ מְמַלֵּא אֶת כָּל הַמִּשְׁאָלוֹת כֻּלָּם, מִפְּנֵי שֶׁאֵינֶנּוּ מְסַלֵּק אֶת כָּל הַמַּסֵּכוֹת מֵעַל כָּל פְּנֵי הַלּוֹט, שֶׁאֵינֶנּוּ מְגַלֶּה אֶת כָּל הָרָזִים וְאֵינֶנּוּ מַשְׂבִּיעַ אֶת כָּל הַמַּאֲוַיִּים. בּוֹעֲטוֹת הֵן בַּכֹּל, בַּחֵלֶק הַטּוֹב, בְּגַרְעִינֵי הָאֹשֶׁר הַמּוֹבִיל אֶל הַמְּנוּחָה וְשַׁלְוַת הָעוֹלָמִים, הַמּוֹבִיל אֶל עֶדְנֵי עַד, אֶל רוֹמְמוּת נִצְחֵי נְצָחִים. בּוֹעֲטוֹת וְזוֹעֲפוֹת, מְשַׁבְּרוֹת וּמְכַלּוֹת, יוֹרְדוֹת לִרְעוֹת בִּשְׂדֵי זָרִים, מַשְׂפִּיקוֹת בְּיַלְדֵי נֵכָר, מְחַלְּלוֹת גְּאוֹן כָּל צְבִי וְאֵין נַחַת. מַרְאוֹת הֵן הַנְּשָׁמוֹת הַלּוֹהֲטוֹת הָאֵלֶּה אֶת כֹּחָן, שֶׁשּׁוּם סְיָג וְהַגְבָּלָה לֹא יוּכַל לַעֲצוֹר בַּעֲדָן, וְהַחַלָּשִׁים שֶׁבָּעוֹלָם הַבָּנוּי, בַּעֲלֵי הַשִּׁיעוּר וְהַנִּימוּס, מִתְבַּהֲלִים מִשֵּׁאתָם. "מִי יָגוּר לָנוּ אֵשׁ אוֹכֵלָה, מִי יָגוּר לָנוּ מוֹקְדֵי עוֹלָם?!". אֲבָל בֶּאֱמֶת לֹא הָיָה פַּחַד, רַק חַטָּאִים בַּעֲלֵי נְפָשׁוֹת חֲלוּשׁוֹת וַחֲנֵפִים הֵם פּוֹחֲדִים וּרְעָדָה אֲחָזָתַם. אֲבָל גִּבּוֹרֵי כֹּחַ יוֹדְעִים, שֶׁגִּלּוּי כֹּחַ זֶה הוּא אֶחָד מֵהַחֶזְיוֹנוֹת הַבָּאִים לְצֹרֶךְ שִׁכְלוּלוֹ שֶׁל עוֹלָם, לְצֹרֶךְ אִמּוּץ כְּחוֹתֶיהָ שֶׁל הָאֻמָּה, הָאָדָם וְהָעוֹלָם. אֶלָּא שֶׁבַּתְּחִלָּה מִתְגַּלֶּה הַכֹּחַ בְּצוּרַת הַתֹּהוּ, וּלְבַסּוֹף יִלָּקַח מִידֵי רְשָׁעִים וְיִנָּתֵן בִּידֵי צַדִּיקִים, גִּבּוֹרִים כַּאֲרָיוֹת, שֶׁיְּגַלּוּ אֶת אֲמִתַּת הַתִּקּוּן וְהַבִּנְיָן, בְּעֹז רוּחַ שֶׁל שֵׂכֶל צָלוּל וְאַמִּיץ וּבְאֹמֶץ נֶפֶשׁ שֶׁל הַרְגָּשָׁה וְהִתְגַּלּוּת מַעֲשִׂית קְבוּעָה וּבְרוּרָה.

הַסּוּפוֹת הַלָּלוּ יְחוֹלְלוּ גִּשְׁמֵי נְדָבָה. עַרְפִלֵּי חֹשֶׁךְ אֵלּוּ יִהְיוּ מַכְשִׁירֵי אוֹרִים גְּדוֹלִים. "וּמֵאֹפֶל וּמֵחֹשֶׁךְ עֵינֵי עִוְרִים תִּרְאֶינָה".

English Translation

The ordinary direction of simplicity and rectitude, along with observance of good character traits and religious law—this is the way of the World of Establishment (*'Olam ha-Tikkun*). And any breach of this—whether brought about by lightheadedness and wantonness, or by intellectual ascent and higher inspiration—belongs to the World of Chaos (*'Olam ha-Tohu*), except that there is a great difference when it comes to the details of the World of Chaos itself and its tendencies to the right and to the left.

The great idealists want a beautiful and good order, so firm and mighty, that it has no comparison or foundation in the world—therefore they destroy that which is built in conformity to the world. The better [idealists] know also to [re]build the world [that they have] destroyed, but the worse [idealists], who have been touched ever so lightly by the higher idealism, they only damage and destroy. The latter are rooted in the World of Chaos at its lowest.[1]

Souls of chaos (*neshamot de-tohu*) are higher than souls of establishment (*neshamot de-tikkun*).[2] They are very great; they seek much of existence, that which their vessels (*kelim*) cannot support. They seek a very great light; they cannot tolerate whatever is finite, defined and estimable. They descended from their elevation, from the beginning of the birthing of existence; they rose up as a flame and were extinguished.[3] Their infinite longing will not end.

They are garbed in various vessels; they aspire way beyond the measure[4]; they aspire and fall. They see that they are imprisoned in laws, in circumscribed conditions that do not allow [them] to expand beyond limit to unstoppable heights, and they fall into depression, into resignation, into anger, and from rage—into wickedness, malice, lowliness, ugliness, abomination, destruction, and all manner of evil. Their agitation (*tesisah*) will not be quiet (*shoketet*).[5]

They [i.e., the souls of chaos] are revealed in the brazenfaced of the generation (*'azei panim she-ba-dor*).[6] The principled wicked (*ha-resha'im ba'alei ha-printsipim*), the sinners who flaunt their sins (*le-hakh'is ve-lo le-tei'avon*),[7] their soul is very high—from the lights of chaos (*'orot de-tohu*). They have chosen destruction and they destroy; the world is rubbed out[8] by them, and they with it. But the essence of courage contained in their will is the point of holiness (*nekudah shel kodesh*). When that [point] is absorbed into the souls that are limited in their approach, it gives them the strength of life.

[The souls of chaos] are especially revealed at an end-of-days, at a period before the birth of a world; preceding a new and wonderful creative existence; on the verge of the expansion of borders; before the birth of a law that is above laws.

In times of redemption, *ḥutspah* (impudence) waxes.[9] A storm brews and continues to rage; breach after breach; *ḥutspah* greater than *ḥutspah*; dissatisfaction with the entire store of goodness of the limited, finite light, because it fails to satisfy all the wants; because it does not remove all the masks covering all the faces;[10] [because] it does not reveal all the mysteries and does not satiate all the desires. [The souls of chaos] kick it all: the good portion, the grains of happiness that leads to rest and eternal calm; that leads to eternal pleasure, to everlasting uplift. They kick and rage, break and destroy, go down to pasture in foreign fields "and are contented with alien ideologies."[11] They desecrate all glorious beauty,[11] and there is no satisfaction.

These fiery souls show their strength, that no fence or limit can restrain them, and the weak in the world that has been built,[13] masters of manners and measures, are terrified by them. "Who of us can dwell with a devouring fire? Who of us can dwell with a never-dying blaze?"[14] But in truth, there is nothing to fear; only sinners, weak souls and flatterers fear and tremble. But the "mighty in strength"[15] know that this show of strength is one of the visions that comes for the need of perfecting the world, for the need of fortifying the powers of the nation, man and the world.[16] Just that at the beginning, the strength is revealed in the form of chaos (*tohu*), and at the end, it will be taken from the hands of the wicked and given over to the hands of the righteous,[17] strong as lions, who will reveal the truth of the *tikkun* and the building,[18] with a mighty spirit of strong and clear intellect, with the courage of feeling, and with the revelation of permanent, decisive deed.[19]

These storms will yield bounteous rains; these dark clouds will be the preparation for great lights. "And from darkness and obscurity the eyes of the blind shall see."[20]

Appendix A

THE TRANSITION FROM *TOHU* TO *TIKKUN*

The World of *Tohu* (Chaos) is schematized as a series of *sefirot* (attributes) that do not interact with one another.[1] They are depicted as self-contained *nekudot*, or points, perhaps reminiscent of monads. There is, as it were, an egotism, whereby each "king" declares, irrespective of the other: "I shall reign!" ("*Ani emlokh!*").[2] Thus, in this scheme, the *Ḥesed* (Love) is pure *Ḥesed*, untempered by the opposite *sefirah* of *Gevurah* (Judgment); and the *Gevurah* is pure *Gevurah*, unmitigated by its opposite *sefirah* of *Ḥesed*. Needless to say, what results from such a scenario in which each of the members is off on a tangent with total disregard for the overall state of affairs, is—*Tohu*, Chaos.

The world that replaces the World of *Tohu* is the World of *Tikkun* (Establishment). What allows this new world order to succeed where the previous one failed, is that the monadology of the individual *sefirot* has been replaced with a new model of holographic *partsufim* (figures, or literally, "faces"), which is to say, each *sefirah* contains every other *sefirah*.[3] From a simple linear model, we now have a complex three-dimensional model which allows a level of cooperation and interaction hitherto impossible.

The key word, the operative principle, is: *hitkalelut* (integration).[4] For a rather obvious reason, this world is sometimes referred to as "'*Olam ha-Mitkala*,'" "the World of Balance."

This transition from *Tohu* to *Tikkun* can be understood on many different levels. It can be understood on the level of the microcosm in terms of individual psychology,[5] or on the level of the macrocosm in terms of collective sociology.[6]

On the individual level, it would refer to the transition from infantile narcissism and ego gratification to an adult altruism and sense of communal responsibility.

The divine names associated with *Tohu* and *Tikkun* are instructive in this regard. *BaN* is emblematic of *Tohu*; *MaH* is emblematic of *Tikkun*. There is a certain paradox here. The name *BaN* means at its root, "build." Yet it is associated with *Tohu*, with worlds destroyed, worlds in ruins.[7] At the other extreme, *MaH* means literally, "What?" It is an expression of utter humility and self-effacement. In a word, *bittul*, or abnegation. This was the famous response of Moses and Aaron: "*Ve-naḥnu mah?*" "And we are what?"[8] And yet, this is the name associated with the World of *Tikkun* that endures and survives. The paradox is best summed up by the Sages of the South's responses to Alexander the Macedonian (i.e., Alexander the Great). When asked by Alexander what a man should do to live, they responded: "He should kill himself." And when asked by him what a man should do to die, they responded:

"He should live himself."[9] The commentary explains: "*Kill himself*—lower himself; *live himself*—raise himself up."

On the level of the macrocosm, the tension between *Tohu* and *Tikkun* is the conflict between two divergent visions of reality and two opposing lifestyles. *Tohu* represents an atomistic, ruggedly individualistic, and when carried to an extreme, antisocial lifestyle; *Tikkun*, a collectivist, relational, society-oriented lifestyle. Played out in the arena of world politics, this might translate to the struggle between capitalism and communism (or in its milder form, socialism). A time is foreseen when there will be revealed a rapprochement, a third way beyond *Tohu* and *Tikkun*. In the arcane language of the Kabbalists, this will be the world of *'Akudim*, beyond the worlds of *Nekudim* and *Berudim*; it shall be known by the name of *SaG*, beyond the names of *MaH* and *BaN*.

Rav Kook translates the tropes of *Tohu* and *Tikkun* to the realm of epistemology. In a letter to his fellow Kabbalist, Rabbi Pinḥas Hakohen Lintop, he writes:

> Those opposing differences that cause each particular to block the other; each thought to demolish the other; each human collective to oppress the other; each individual to boast, saying, "I shall reign,[10] no other"—this [state of] *Tohu* too shall certainly return to [a state of] *Tikkun* through the shining of objectivity,[11] and the "damagers of the world" (*mazikei 'alma*),[12] "the workers of iniquity, who are scattered,"[13]

> cannot look into the "encompassing light" (*'or ha-makif*), and they are broken by the rigor of their [own] destruction.[14]

Rav Kook's strategy for conflict resolution consists of prevailing upon the combatants to transcend their particularistic subjective narratives (*Tohu*) to overview from the perspective of the "surrounding light" the objective reality (*Tikkun*).

In a *pensée* probably reflective of the conflagration of World War One, which might very well have been written during his sojourn in St. Gallen, Switzerland, Rav Kook explained the necessity of "*nekudatiyut*" (atomism) preceding the *kavim* (lines), which is to say, the overall Gestalt of *Yosher*, just as the rind must precede the fruit:

> We understand the completion of existence in its entirety by this principle: that every point (*nekudah*) of existence be actualized in all its fullness, in disregard of the fact that the realization of the other points (*nekudot*)—and of the collective—opposes the actualization of this particular point. Nonetheless, precisely this isolated independence will enhance the collective as well. As a result of this, the rind must precede the fruit; the points (*nekudot*) and the circles (*'Iggulim*) [must precede] the lines of *Yosher*.[15] "We shall not fear when the earth is changed, when mountains topple into the heart of the seas,"[16] when the quarrels of peoples rise up, nor

during the sound of mighty wars. These atomistic ferments, which wickedness precipitates, arise without any intention—and against their [stated] intention—to the heights of the higher purpose. "He is capable of all and includes them together."[17] This rule applies to the fullness of the worlds; to the celestial hosts; to the epochs of human history; to the cycles of life, material and spiritual; and to all the moral values of the individual on life's ways. "Your eyes saw my unformed limbs, and in Your book they were all written; in due time they were formed, to the very last one of them."[18]

The way of life of the righteous who sustain the world, is to constantly strengthen the longing for universalism (*kelalut*), that it not disintegrate and not be blurred by the aggression of the atomistic ambitions. And since the eyes and the heart of the righteous forever turn upward, even the particular points draw their inner happiness from the source of whole life, through their [i.e., the righteous'] good will. But until the endtime, wickedness asserts its might; makes the separations more pronounced; empowers atomism. Rather than [focusing on] the universal and the encompassing wholeness (*ha-hashlamah ha-makefet*), wickedness maximizes the exterior over the interior; the outer garment over the inner content. In the glory (*tif'eret*) of the world by the light of Torah,[19] all is included: the atomistic

> attributes inasmuch as they are actualized and integrated, and the overall encompassing attribute. "Everything is prepared (*metukkan*) for the banquet."[20]

Undoubtedly, by way of this last quote (from the Mishnah), Rav Kook is alluding to the Lurianic kabbalistic concept of *Tikkun*, whereby the disparate, even antagonistic, elements, the *nekudot* (points) of *Tohu*, are organized into a harmonious world order, symbolized by the *se'udah*, or future banquet of the righteous.

Appendix B

BEYOND *TOHU* AND *TIKKUN*

IN HIS ESSAY, Rav Kook exposes the reader to the opposition of two kabbalistic schemata, *Tohu* and *Tikkun*. When one delves further into the intricacies of Kabbalah, one discovers that this standoff awaits its *dénouement* in an eschatological future.

This vision of the future is expressed in various ways. In Lurianic Kabbalah, Jacob's sheep, "streaked, speckled, and mottled" ("*'akudim, nekudim u-verudim*"),[1] become tropes for three worlds: *'Olam ha-'Akudim*, *'Olam ha-Nekudim*, and *'Olam ha-Berudim*.[2] *'Akudim* represents an undifferentiated unity in which all the lights are "bound" (*'akudim*) in a single vessel.[3] In *Nekudim*, there occurs a breakdown, a disintegration, a pointillist fragmentation ("*nekudot*," or points), as the lights are distributed in several vessels. In *Berudim*, unity and integration are restored, albeit not the original, undifferentiated unity, but a unity distributed through the plurality of vessels.[4] In the eschaton, reality will return to the realm of *'Akudim*.[5]

Another way in which this dialectic is expressed is in terms of the divine names, *SaG*, *BaN*, and *MaH*.[6] *BaN* is associated with the by now familiar *'Olam ha-Tohu*

(World of Chaos); *MaH* with *'Olam ha-Tikkun* (the World of Establishment). Translated into psychology, *BaN* is the primitive, the bestial; the "new name of *MaH*" that issues from the forehead (*metsaḥ*) of *Adam Kadmon* is the recent human level that clarifies (*mevarer*).[7] But there will yet come a time when the struggle of the human and animalistic elements within, will cease. At that time, mankind shall ascend to the level of *SaG*, beyond the binary of *MaH* and *BaN*.[8] On that day, there will be revealed new souls that transcend the bipolarity of *Tohu* and *Tikkun*.

Rabbi Shneur Zalman of Lyady, founder of the ḤaBaD school of Ḥasidism, unpacked the prophecy of Isaiah (66:22), "For as the new heavens and the new earth, which I make, stand before Me, says the LORD, so shall your seed and your name stand":

> Then there will be a shining of new souls, who require no clarification (*birur*). Behold, all the souls from eternity, are those that were included in Adam, which require clarification and correction (*tikkun*)[9].... That which was already arranged in the order of devolution (*seder ha-hishtalshelut*), is nothing new. But the innovation of souls (*ḥiddush neshamot*) is from above the devolution, that which has not yet descended and devolved.... And in the future, there will be the revelation of this new light that is above the order of devolution, and that is *'Olam ha-'Akudim*....

> And this revelation is called "the new heavens and the new earth which I make."[10]

One may chalk it up to coincidence (something Jewish mystics are loath to do), but the very year in which Rav Kook's essay, "The Souls of the World of Chaos," appeared in print (1913), there was published in Berdichev a prayerbook with kabbalistic commentary composed by Rabbi Isaac Dov Baer Schneerson of Lyady (1835-1910), *Peirush MaHaRID*, which would many times over harp on the theme of achieving *'Akudim*, beyond *Nekudim* and *Berudim*; beyond *Tohu* and *Tikkun*.[11] In truth, the theme is not new. As we have seen, it crops up in the teachings of the founder of the Schneerson dynasty, but it is definitely a trenchant theme in the *Peirush MaHaRID*.[12]

Though ḤaBaD may have portrayed the theme in a more dramatic manner, virtually the same idea—the resumption of *'Akudim*—occurs earlier in the writings that emanated from the school of the Paduan Kabbalist, Rabbi Moshe Ḥayyim Luzzatto. In *KaLaḤ Pitḥei Ḥokhmah*, we read that the six millennia correspond to *'Olam ha-Nekudim*, and their complete *tikkun*, destined for the seventh millennium, will correspond to the *'Olam ha-'Akudim*.[13] In *Kelalim Rishonim*, Luzzatto speaks of the return of the name *SaG*. And in the seventh millennium, when "the Holy One, blessed be He, makes wings for the righteous and they fly over the surface of the water,"[14] the sanctity of the soul will carry the corporeal weight of the body. That situation is rooted in the *'Olam ha-'Akudim*, when a single vessel—as opposed to multiple vessels—is supported by the power of the lights.[15] In *Iggerot Pitḥei Ḥokhmah va-Da'at*, Luzzatto relies on the introduction to the anonymous medieval work of Kabbalah, *Berit Menuḥah*, which traces ten millennia (not stopping at the seven millennia of *b. Sanhedrin* 97a).[16] In the seventh millennium, the wings by which the righteous soar above the waters covering the planet, symbolize the soul's ability to carry the body, which, in turn, corresponds to the one vessel of *'Akudim*.[17]

In the different eschatology of the Vilna Gaon, after the seven millennia of this world order ("six thousand years the world exists and one [thousand] it is destroyed")[18] there will be three more millennia, for a total of ten (as spelled out in *Berit Menuḥah*),[19] corresponding to the three brains (*moḥin*) after the *'Olam ha-Tohu*.[20]

Finally, in his first published work, *Hakdamot u-She'arim*, Rabbi Shelomo Eliashov (like Luzzatto) invokes the authority of the anonymous author of *Berit Menuḥah*, that "man cannot know what will be in the tenth millennium,"[21] "for then there will be the rule of *Arikh Anpin* itself, called *moḥa stima'ah* (hidden brain), for it is hidden, and all the more so after, higher and higher, in the rule of *Ayin*, and *Reisha de-lo' 'ityada'* ("unknown head"), and *'Akudim*, and *Adam Kadmon*, and so higher and higher, until *Malkhut* of *Ein Sof* itself, blessed be its name."[22]

Appendix C

THE BINARY UNIVERSE

The universe of Rabbi Isaac Luria (ARI) is a binary universe in search of unity. As the cosmic drama unfolds, at every stage, the masculine and feminine principles reassert themselves. The *Tree of Life* (*'Ets Ḥayyim*) manifests itself as a series of binaries. From the initial act of *Tsimtsum* (Cosmic Contraction) and the thrust of the shaft of light (*kav*) into the chasm of the *Ḥalal* (Vacuum) or *Makom Panui* (Empty Space);[1] through the configuration of concentric circles (*'Iggulim*) versus the linear model of *Yosher*; continuing through the different arrangements of the ten *sefirot*—*Nekudim*, disjoint points (*nekudot*),[2] that are eventually reconfigured as *Berudim*, finally producing five *partsufim*,[3] or personae, that are overtly gendered: *Arikh Anpin* (*Long Face*), *Abba* and *Imma* (*Father* and *Mother*), *Ze'ir Anpin* and *Nukva* (*Short Face* and *Female*)—we are treated to set after set of binaries. And we are left by Luria with the takeaway that it is the moral imperative of mankind to clamp together this cleft in the cosmos by a process of theurgic *birurim* (clarifications)[4] and *yiḥudim* (unifications).

*

To illustrate the point, I will share with the reader an anecdote told to me half a century ago by a dear friend, a college professor to whom I had the privilege of teaching Talmud.

This professor was raised in a secular Yiddish-speaking household. His grandfather, born in Brisk, had emigrated from Poland to Cuba between the two World Wars. Eventually, the family found its way to New York City.

As a young man, my friend set out on a sea voyage to France, his final destination Paris, then the mecca of the alternative lifestyle. The boat embarked from the port of New York.

On board, he struck up a conversation in Yiddish with an older man. The next day, the man brought him word that the Bobover Rebbe wished to speak to him. On that same ship, Rabbi Shelomo Halberstam, the Rebbe of Bobov, was traveling to *Erets Yisrael*, the Holy Land.

My friend thought it strange that the great Ḥasidic Rebbe would wish to speak to him, a secular Jew and total stranger. Nonetheless, he proceeded to the Rebbe's cabin. The Rebbe—renowned for his *hadrat panim* (beautiful face)—greeted him warmly and invited him to sit at the table with him.

On the table was a *Ḥumash*, the Five Books of Moses. The Bobover opened the book and pointed to the first letter, *Beit*.

"Do you know why this letter *Beit* is bigger than the other letters?" (In the Torah, the first *Beit*, known as a *Beit Rabbati*, is traditionally written large.)

My friend admitted his ignorance.

The Rebbe explained that *Beit* is the number "two."[5] "In this world of ours," he went on, "everything exists in twos." The Rebbe provided numerous examples: the north and south poles of magnets; the positive and negative charges of electricity; and—the two sexes, male and female.[6]

Never once did the Rebbe raise his voice or admonish, but his guest got the message. Evidently, the other man who acted as their go-between had divulged to the Rebbe his plan. Paris remained "the elephant in the room."

I asked my friend if the Rebbe's words had deterred him from pursuing his goal.

"Not in the least. I was determined to follow my dream." He disembarked in Marseilles and continued on to Paris.

"What struck me about the Rebbe's conversation was not the content *per se*, but the method in which it was conducted. Such paternal love. I was very moved that a man would care so deeply about a fellow Jew who was far from a *Ḥasid*."

Appendix D

DEFINING *YETSER HA-RA‘* AND *YETSER HA-TOV*

THERE IS a famous passage in the writings of Rabbi Israel Salanter (a.k.a. Lipkin), the founder of the Lithuanian Mussar movement, as to the definition of the *yetser ha-ra‘* (evil inclination) and *yetser ha-tov* (good inclination) of which the Sages spoke. (See, e.g., *m. Berakhot* 9:5.)

One medieval school defined the *yetser ha-ra‘* as a mystical force of impurity (*ko'aḥ ha-tum'ah*) and the *yetser ha-tov* as a mystical force of holiness (*ko'aḥ ha-kedushah*); another school identified the *yetser ha-ra‘* with man's base desires (*ta'avot*) and the *yetser ha-tov* with man's reason. Rabbi Israel Salanter created a compromise (*pesher*): The *yetser ha-ra‘* is both a spirit of impurity and man's innate desires; the *yetser ha-tov* is both a spirit of sanctity and man's rational self.[1]

Earlier, this same compromise was reached by Rabbi Samuel Yaffe Ashkenazi of Constantinople.[2] He wrote that the *yetser ha-tov* is the rational component of man as well as an angel appointed over reason; conversely, the *yetser ha-ra‘* is both man's material component and an angel appointed over the bodily aspect. Yaffe discusses the medieval controversy. Representative of the philosophic tradition is Maimonides; of the kabbalistic tradition, Naḥmanides. Crucial to the controversy are their respective interpretations of the rabbinic maxim, "It is Satan; it is the Angel of Death; it is the *yetser ha-ra'*."[3] Maimonides adopts a rationalistic, naturalistic reading of the statement; Naḥmanides opts for a supernatural, angelogical reading.[4]

Predictably, Rabbi Ḥayyim Vital, the authoritative amanuensis of Rabbi Isaac Luria, equates the *yetser ha-tov* with the good angels that accompany man, and the *yetser ha-ra'* with the bad angels that accompany him.[5]

Rabbi Shneur Zalman of Lyady may have also attempted a synthesis when he posited that the "bestial soul" (*nefesh ha-behemit*) resides in the heart, the center of desires (*ta'avot*), and the "divine soul" (*nefesh ha-elohit*) resides in the brain, the center of reason (*sekhel*).[6]

Likewise, Rabbi Menashe Ben-Porat of Ilya wrote: "The emissary of the *yetser ha-tov* is reason, and the emissary of the *yetser ha-ra'* is ephemeral desire."[7]

Consistent with kabbalistic tradition, Rabbi Yitzḥak Eizik Ḥaver concluded "that the *yetser ha-tov* in him [i.e., man] is from the Side of Holiness (*Sitra di-Kedushah*) and the *yetser ha-ra'* is from the Other Side (*Sitra Aḥera*)."[8] And yet, the Kabbalist took cognizance of the base of the *yetser ha-ra'* in primitive physical desire (*ta'avah*) and its overcoming by the civilizing effect of Torah.[9]

Finally, Rav Kook believed that both the forces of good (*Tikkun*) and evil (*Tohu*) are found in existence. Man's material side naturally gravitates to the evil in existence. "For the inclination (*yetser*) of man's heart is evil from his youth."[10] But, by virtue of his spiritual aspect, man has the ability to overcome his natural disposition and gravitate to the good.[11]

Appendix E

TSURAT HA-ADAM / THE HUMAN FORM: A PHILOLOGICAL STUDY

MAHARAL AND RADZYN

SEVERAL YEARS AGO, I ventured the guess that the term "*tsurat ha-adam*" ("the form of man")[1] which occurs frequently in the writings of Rabbi Ya'akov of Izhbitsa (Polish, Izbica) and Radzyn, and his son, Rabbi Gershon Ḥanokh of Radzyn, can be traced back to the titan of Jewish thought, MaHaRaL of Prague.[2]

Speculation that MaHaRaL contributed to the Ḥasidic thought of Izhbitsa-Radzyn is not wild at all.[3] It is well known that the original thought of the sixteenth-century Rabbi of Prague was "rediscovered" by Rabbi Simḥah Bunem of Pshysucha (Polish, Przysucha), the master of Rabbi Mordechai Yosef Leiner (author of *Mei ha-Shilo'aḥ*), founder of the Izhbitsa dynasty of Ḥasidism.

As another disciple of Rabbi Simḥah Bunem, Rabbi Isaac Meir Rothenburg of Gur (Polish, Góra Kalwaria) remarked:

> "In the books of MaHaRaL are found precious words spread about in hidden places."

> [Rabbi Isaac Meir] quoted Rabbi Bunem of Pshysucha (who had visited the grave of MaHaRaL) as saying: "Know that I publicized his words."
>
> "And the truth is, that previously the world did not sense taste in the words of MaHaRaL, and the holy Rabbi of Pshysucha, in his learning of the books of MaHaRaL, would provide taste to his words."[4]

So, coming out of the studyhouse of Pshysucha as Rabbi Mordechai Joseph did,[5] it is not unreasonable to assume that some of the terminology of MaHaRaL rubbed off on him and found its way into the works of his successor, his son Rabbi Ya'akov (author of *Beit Ya'akov*), and his grandson, Rabbi Gershon Ḥanokh (author of *Sod Yesharim*).

It is curious then, that the name of MaHaRaL does not surface in the writings of Izhbitsa and Radzyn. This is especially surprising when we contrast these writings to those of Gur and Sochatchov. In the aforementioned Gur dynasty there are sporadic references to MaHaRaL. (Witness *Sefat Emet*, by Rabbi Judah Aryeh Leib Alter, the grandson of Rabbi Isaac Meir.)[6] And in *Shem mi-Shemuel* by Rabbi Samuel Bornstein of Sochatchov (Polish, Sochaczew)—the grandson of Rabbi Menaḥem Mendel of Kotzk (Polish, Kock), the premier disciple of and successor to Rabbi Simḥah Bunem of Pshysucha — references to MaHaRaL abound.[7]

MAHARAL, VITAL AND THE *SHI'UR KOMAH* TRADITION

Rabbi Judah Löw, popularly referred to as MaHaRaL of Prague (1520-1609), and Rabbi Hayyim Vital, known by his initials as MaHaRḤU[8] (1543-1620), were contemporaries, yet the reception of their respective teachings could not have been more different. Until rather recently, the thought of MaHaRaL did not become mainstream.[9] On the other hand, Vital's teachings (a channeling of the Kabbalah of his master, Rabbi Isaac Luria, the ARI, or "Lion") quickly conquered the Jewish world. While both dwell on the word "*adam*" (in MaHaRaL, the prevalent term is "*tsurat ha-adam*"; in Vital, "*tikkun ha-adam*"),[10] they come out of vastly different milieux. While MaHaRaL is generally viewed against the background of European humanism and the Rudolfine Renaissance, Lurianic Kabbalah is traditionally attributed to transmission from the mouth of Elijah the Prophet.[11]

It would be appropriate at this point to discuss this term "*tsurat ha-adam*" in the larger context of Lurianic Kabbalah.

It must be stated that the Kabbalah of the ARI is the latest development of the ancient *Shi'ur Komah* tradition which images the deity as a *macroanthropus*.[12] It is this "humanizing" tendency that gives ascendency to the anatomical structure of *Yosher* over the astrophysical spheres of *'Iggulim*,[13] and that later in *'Ets Ḥayyim*, raises from the chaos and destruction of

Nekudim/nekudot (points), the beauty (Hadar) of the human figure, "Adam" being the numerical equivalent of the new name of *MaH* (45).[14]

PARTSUFIM

And now, a word about the *partsufim*, the five personae (literally "faces")[15] to emerge in this recent *'Olam ha-Tikkun*, that arises on the ruins of the previous *'Olam ha-Tohu*. From whence derived the Lurianic term *"partsufim"*?

I believe that it too can be traced back to the *Shi'ur Komah* tradition. There was preserved in our literature a *gematria* (alphanumerical value) that originated with Rabbi El'azar ben Judah (Roke'aḥ) of Worms (d. 1238): "*Temunah* (Picture) = *Partsuf Adam* (Face of Man)." (They share the exact numerical value of 501). In a letter to the sages of Northern France, intended to defend the anti-anthropomorphism of Maimonides' philosophical works, Rabbi Moses ben Naḥman quoted a chunk from a work by Rabbi El'azar ben Judah of Worms entitled, *"Sha'ar ha-Sod ve-ha-Yiḥud ve-ha-Emunah."* In that lengthy quotation, there occurs our *gematria*.[16] The *gematria* was also recorded later by the anonymous author of *Ma'arekhet ha-Elohut*, who first quotes it in the name of his teacher, Rabbi Isaac,[17] and adds, "and so I found in the words of Rabbi El'azar of Worms."[18] This same *gematria* is to be found in the Ba'al ha-Turim's commentary to Exodus 20:4. The author, the renowned halakhist Rabbi Jacob ben Asher (late 13th century-early 14th century), attaches a pejorative meaning. *Tout court*, we are forbidden to fashion a human face.[19] Contrariwise, it appears that the Jewish mystics named above interpreted this *gematria* in a positive sense. (One must concede, at least, that their presentation is nuanced, and not black and white as that of the Ba'al ha-Turim.) Behold the words of *Ma'arekhet ha-Elohut*:

> And now that you know the construction of the form of man (*binyan tsurat ha-adam*), you can make intelligible—if you received mouth to mouth—the truth of the prophetic vision seen by the prophets. The Rabbis, of blessed memory, called that vision "*Shi'ur Komah*".... And that is the secret [of their saying] "One who knows the measure (*shi'ur*) of the Creator (*Yotser Bereshit*), etc."[20] And in this regard, it was said: "Let us make man in our image, in our likeness" [Genesis 1:26]. And in regard to the vision, it was said: "And I stirred the imagination of the prophets" [Hosea 12:11]. And Rabbi Isaac said by way of a sign: "*Temunah be-gematria Partsuf Adam.*" ("Picture = The Face of Man.") And so I found in the words of Rabbi El'azar of Worms.[21]

Going back to the *Shi'ur Komah* tradition, the mystics glimpsed the divinity in human guise.[22] And while the exact combination of *Partsuf Adam* is, admittedly, rare in the Lurianic corpus,[23] the different personae that constitute the macroanthropus are designated precisely as *partsufim*.

RABBI NAḤMAN OF BRESLOV AND THE *SHI'UR KOMAH* TRADITION

From the hand of Rabbi Naḥman we have a single poem, which goes by the name of *Shir Na'im*. Rabbi David Sears believes that it is a summary work, intended to encapsulate all the teachings of this enigmatic master. The final stanza could come right out of the *Shi'ur Komah* tradition:

> Let us bring a heart of wisdom to understand the dimension of our bodies and the distances of its joints and the arrangement of its limbs.
>
> The obligation of its understanding[24] abets the knowledge of the Creator Who designs all of these creations.[25]

RAV KOOK ON ANTHROPOMORPHIC IMAGERY

It may be said that for Rav Kook, the great divide between the philosopher and the mystic is the issue of anthropomorphic imagery.[26] In an important entry in his journal, Rav Kook refers to Maimonides (RaMBaM) and Naḥmanides (RaMBaN) as "two good leaders" ("*shnei parnasim tovim*") of Israel, and drawing on the Lurianic genealogy of souls, situates Maimonides in the "left corner" (*pe'ah ha-semolit*) and Naḥmanides in the "right corner" (*pe'ah ha-yemanit*) of the Godhead.[27] As always, Rav Kook's language is allusive and aphoristic. The upshot is that Maimonides, the rationalist philosopher bequeathed the *via negativa* (negative attributes, or as they are referred to in Hebrew, "*to'arei shelilah*"), while Naḥmanides, the Kabbalist, bequeathed the *via positiva* (positive attributes, or in Hebrew, "*to'arei ḥiyyuv*").[28] To use technical jargon, Maimonides' theology is apophatic, while Naḥmanides' is cataphatic.

What stands out in the piece in bold relief, is the quote from *Genesis Rabbah* (27): "Great is the power of prophets who liken the creature (*tsurah*, literally "*form*") to its Creator (*Yotser*)." This statement of Rabbi Yudan, which refers to anthropomorphic passages in Daniel 8:16 and Ezekiel 1:26 ("and upon the likeness of the throne was a likeness as the appearance of a man upon it above"), becomes the topic of heated debate between the rationalist and the mystic. Maimonides read Rabbi Yudan as remarking on the audacity of the prophets. "Great is their boldness!"[29] MaHaRaL, on the other hand, took Rabbi Yudan's statement at face value.[30] By juxtaposing Rabbi Yudan's statement to his portrait of Naḥmanides, Rav Kook has placed anthropomorphic imagery at the center of the mystic's quest.[31] Most telling is his update to Rabbi Yudan's original statement: "… the equation of the creature to its Creator, by the great power of the prophets *that does not cease from the sons of prophets from generation to generation*."[32]

PAḤAD YITZḤAK

Recently, there appeared in print a series of lectures by Rabbi Isaac Hutner (1906-1980) on the topic of "*Binyan Tsurat ha-Adam*" ("The Construction of the Form of Man").[33] These talks, delivered at the Third Sabbath Meal in the winter of the year 5727 (1966-1967), were written by a student after the Sabbath.[34] Truthfully, the writings of Rabbi Hutner (entitled "*Paḥad Yitzḥak*") are replete with references to the "*tsurat ha-adam*."[35] Most likely, this was a conscious imitation of (or identification with) MaHaRaL. As is famous, Rabbi Hutner was extremely fond of the works of MaHaRaL,[36] and like Rabbi Bunem of Pshysucha, he too visited the MaHaRaL's grave in the old Jewish cemetery of Prague.[37] But Rabbi Hutner was also enamored of the works of the Radzyner dynasty, as attested to both by his disciples and by Rabbi Mordechai Yosef Leiner (son of Rabbi Yeruḥam Leiner, the nephew of Rabbi Gershon Ḥanokh of Radzyn).[38] Elsewhere, I documented that a neologism of the Radzyner Rebbe showed up in Rabbi Hutner's vocabulary.[39] Is it possible that Rabbi Hutner's adoption of the term "*tsurat ha-adam*" was also inspired by the example of the Radzyner Rebbe?[40] Finally, there is no denying that "*tsurat ha-adam*" may have been a carryover of the teachings of Rabbi Hutner's own master in the Mussar-oriented Slabodka Yeshivah, Rabbi Nathan Tsevi (Nota Hirsch) Finkel, who harped on the theme of "*Gadlut ha-Adam*" (the Greatness of Man).

Appendix F

RABBI MENASHE OF ILYA AND RAV KOOK

THOUGH SEPARATED in time by a couple of generations, it would seem that in many important respects Rabbi Menashe Ben-Porat of Ilya (1767-1831) and Rav Kook (1865-1935) were "kindred spirits," with the former serving as a role model and intellectual hero to the latter. Rav Kook's biographer, his disciple, Rabbi Moshe Tsevi Neriyah, already noted the affinity between the two men, but this avenue deserves further exploration.[1] What makes the researcher's job especially difficult is the fact that Rabbi Menashe's portrait was deliberately distorted by his putative biographer, the *Maskil*, Mordechai Plungian. Plungian's biography of Rabbi Menashe, *Ben Porat* (Vilna, 1858), with its not so hidden modernist agenda, led astray many a well-meaning researcher.[2]

Rabbi Menashe Ben-Porat was born in Smorgon. Most of his mature life was spent in Ilya, after which he is generally referred. Although not a formal student of the Vilna Gaon, he had some personal acquaintance with the Gaon. Evidently, the Gaon had great impact upon him, for Rabbi Menashe refers to him in the most glowing terms possible, even describing him as a Godsend to the generation to impart the correct way to study Torah.[3] Like the Gaon, Rabbi Menashe strove for *peshat*, or the simple meaning of the text.[4]

Plungian read into Rabbi Menashe's work *Pesher Davar* a fondness for the new Beshtian Ḥasidism,[5] but as Rabbi David Kaminetsky has shown by careful textual analysis, this is clearly a misreading.[6]

Another myth spread by Plungian is that Rabbi Menashe, with his supposed Maskilic leanings, aroused the ire of Rabbi Saul Katzenellenbogen of Vilna, who ordered that Rabbi Menashe's works be burnt on the pyre. Again, there is no historical record of any persecution of Rabbi Menashe or his works. Their scarcity is due rather to the fact that they were printed in very limited editions.[7]

Most of his life was spent as a private individual, although in 1827-1828 he served for a year as Rabbi of his birthplace, Smorgon. Subsequently, he turned the rabbinate of Smorgon over to his illustrious student, Rabbi Aryeh Leib Shapira, who went on to become Rabbi of Kovno (and thereafter became known as "Reb Leibeleh Kovner").[8]

Aged eighteen, Rav Kook spent the year 1883 studying in Smorgon—known as a city of sages[9] — under Rabbi Leibeleh's son, Rabbi Ḥayyim Abraham Shapira, the rabbi of Smorgon.[10] Though half a century had transpired since Rabbi Menashe's passing, there were elders who retained his legacy, which the young Abraham Isaac Kook eagerly imbibed.

Rav Kook transmitted various traditions that he heard from the elder sages of Smorgon:

> There was a time that Rabbi Menashe would deliver a *shi'ur* (lecture) in *Gemara* before an elite group of scholars. The day before, Rabbi Menashe would stand in his corner of the study-hall and cry while reciting several Psalms, imploring that his teaching be "*Torah li-shmah*" ("Torah for its own sake"), and that he not stumble into an interpretation that was not true Torah.[11]

> "The LORD is good to all and His compassion is upon all His works."[12] But due to sins, the conduits of goodness have been stopped up, and calamities abound in the world. Yet we all await the correction of the world (*tikkuno shel 'olam*) and the revelation of full goodness. That fullness will encompass not only human life but animal life as well.

> Even if the entire world should arrive at wholeness, with goodness and love ruling throughout, if there should be found at the end of the world one worm in a crevice of a rock, oppressed and suffering—the world will not yet have arrived at wholeness, and man, who is aware of this, must feel that his goodness is still incomplete.[13]

The very graphic description of a worm suffering in a crevice of a rock at the end of the earth, tallies with something that Rabbi Menashe wrote in the recently discovered introduction to his work *Peiruka li-Tekanta*. The introduction, titled *Sidrei Ḥokhmah*, is found in a manuscript (evidently in Rabbi Menashe's own hand) in Israel's National Library (*Sifriyah Le'umit*).[14]

There Rabbi Menashe writes:

> ... All the creations in the world, from the most exalted to the coarse and corporeal material, are not separate creations, but all is one creation composed of parts that appear separate. The complete, final correction (*tikkun*) of all creation depends on the correction of the entire creation, *and it cannot be corrected as long as some sentient life* (ḥai margish)[15] *has not arrived at its perfection which awaits actualization of its potential.* But because life is divided into separate bodies, it appears to each individual, through his corporeal senses, that he is a separate entity, and [therefore] each individual strives only for his own private good—and this causes the destruction of the collective. For example, if a vessel composed of many parts should come apart—though none of its parts are broken—the vessel would cease to be of use. The fruit of reason that has been endowed to humankind, is the ability to understand the unity of things, for the senses feel only particulars. The greater the intellect, the greater the ability to include in the brain particulars and separate issues, to understand their unity which subsumes all the particulars.[16]

Besides the concern for every "sentient being" (*ḥai margish*) and the global consciousness (in Rabbi Menashe's terminology, *"tikkun kelali,"* "collective correction"),[17] that Rabbi Menashe and Rav Kook shared in common—as noted by Rabbi Neriyah—there may be two other areas of overlap.

First, both Rabbi Menashe and Rav Kook had a keen sense of the fluidity of the halakhic process.

At the beginning of his work *Alfei Menashe*, Rabbi Menashe provided a word of clarification concerning one of the more provocative statements in the book:

> It is not my intention that the *beit din* (court) rule according to the time. Rather, when the LORD put in the mind of the *beit din* that they agree with a minority opinion, certainly from heaven they agree that this is correct according to the time, and it does not contradict the fact that previous generations ruled the opposite, for "God stands in the congregation of God" [Psalms 82:1], and it was correct then according to the time, according to the generation.[18]

In a somewhat similar vein, Rav Kook wrote:

> In Torah, there are these two categories: Things that are worthy of enduring forever, so there are found many *halakhot* that will not change from their fixed state, for thus were they established, to be an eternal covenant. [Then] there are

> *halakhot* that change in their rulings from one generation to the next, depending on its leaders and what seems appropriate to the "judge who is in your days."[19]

Second, both Rabbi Menashe and Rav Kook advocated for individuals rising above their subjective viewpoints and differences, in order to arrive at the objective overview.[20] Thus, both Rabbi Menashe and Rav Kook aspired to the role of peacemaker.[21]

*

On a Wednesday evening, January 4, 1978 (by the Hebrew reckoning, the 26th of Tevet, 5738), I met for the very first time Rav Tsevi Yehudah Kook, the only son of Rav Abraham Isaac Kook. The meeting took place in Rav Tsevi Yehuda's home at 30 Ovadiah Street in the Ge'ulah section of Jerusalem.

On that occasion, I remarked to Rav Tsevi Yehudah how incredibly much *Ahavat Yisrael* (love of the People of Israel) his father had.

Rav Tsevi Yehudah's response was an outburst of hearty laughter. Containing himself, he explained what he found risible in my statement. "*Ahavat Yisrael*? My father loved the whole world, even *tsome'aḥ* (the vegetable kingdom), even *domem* (the mineral kingdom)!"[22]

Rav Kook's empathy for all existence and its exigencies is borne out in this passage from his *Letters*:

> Blessed is the LORD who made for me this soul—a spirit alive[23] and feeling (*u-margeshet*) all the various movements and shocks, with all their pangs, but also with all the mighty strength of life and faith of salvation.
>
> All those things meet me in a sensate manner, and I must deal with them in deed and action, to suffer all the crises of the various currents and their crashes, and to listen to the voice within them, revealed and hidden.[24]

In his seminal work, *Orot* (1920), Rav Kook allows us a peek into the consciousness of "the lofty souls, who sense the majesty of the mysteries of the Torah, and the precious inner flow of the divine service in the beauty of its greatness; who listen to the sound of sanctity of life and the tunes of *Pirkei Shirah*[25] from the heavens and the earth and all contained therein, from seas and depths and all their plenitude, the soul of every creation, the feelings of every sentient being (*u-margashei kol margish*),[26] who ascend to the higher unity, with its great, esteemed, brilliant richness."[27]

Of late, a passage in Rav Kook's writings that speaks of the evolution of human consciousness, has come into vogue. Rav Kook describes ever-widening concentric circles, starting with egocentricity or narcissism, proceeding through phases of nationalism and humanism, to what one might term "cosmic consciousness."[28] "*Shir Meruba*," or "A Fourfold Song," has undergone several

English translations. (Momentarily, I shall offer my own rendition.) What is not known, is that Rav Kook was preceded in this outook by—Rabbi Menashe of Ilya!

Here is Rav Kook's *pensée*, culled from one of his journals (St. Gallen, Switzerland, circa 1915):

SHIR MERUBA' / A FOURFOLD SONG

There is one who sings *the song of his soul*, and in his soul he finds all, full spiritual satisfaction.

And there is one who sings *the song of the nation*. He goes out of the circle of his individual soul, which he does not find capacious enough, nor in a state of ideal composure. He aspires to mighty heights, and cleaves with a delicate love to the totality of *Knesset Yisrael* (Ecclesia Israel). With her, he sings her songs, suffers her troubles, and delights in her hopes, thinks lofty and pure opinions about her past and her future, and investigates with love and wisdom of the heart the inner content of her spirit.

And there is one whose soul broadens even more until it goes out and expands beyond the boundary of Israel, to sing *the song of man*. His spirit stretches to the genius of mankind and the majesty of its image. He aspires to its overall destiny and looks forward to its perfection. From this source of life, he draws the totality of his thoughts and researches, his ambitions and his visions.

And there is one who broadens even beyond this, until *he unites with all of existence*, with all the creatures, with all the worlds, and with all of them he utters song. This is the one who every day delves into *Perek Shirah*, who is assured the World to Come.[29]

And there is one who ascends with all of these songs together in one symphony. All lend their voices, all harmonize together. Each contributes to the other vitality and life, the sound of joy and the sound of happiness, the sound of jubilation and rejoicing, the sound of gladness and the sound of sanctity.

The song of the soul, the song of the nation, the song of man, and the song of the world—all together constantly combine in his midst.

And this perfection evolves to a holy song, the song of *El*, the Song of Israel,[30] in the might of her strength and glory, in the might of her truth and greatness. *Yisrael—Shir El, a simple song, a twofold song, a threefold song, a fourfold song. The Song of Songs of Shelomo, of the King that peace* (shalom) *is his.*[31]

Compare this to the outlook of Rabbi Menashe of Ilya:

> It is known that there are many variables in regard to human nature.
>
> At one extreme, there is an individual who cares only about his own wellbeing; he has no compassion upon his own son and daughter.
>
> Then there is one who is concerned also for the welfare of his children and the members of his household; this is the extent of caring of everyman.
>
> Then there is one who cares also for the good of his relations and friends.
>
> Now the enlightened one, who imagines to himself the benefit of the good and how it is difficult to suffer pain, God preserve us, wishes the good and benefit of every sentient being (*kol ḥai margish*), and "prevention of cruelty to animals is from the Torah."[32] Such an individual imitates his Creator; he equates his will to the will of the Creator, blessed be He, Who wishes the good of all His sentient creatures (*ha-margishim*).
>
> Now, for example, in the case of one who cares only for his own wellbeing, if all his needs, including all manner of pleasures, be satisfied, no more good can be added.
>
> However, one who cares also for the welfare of his sons and daughters, his benefit is multiplied when they too benefit.

> By the same token, one who wishes the good of every sentient being (*kol ḥai margish*)—his reward is multiplied exponentially when the totality of creation is corrected. If good be extended to all sentient beings (*le-khol ha-margishim*), the joy of this individual is inestimable, for all his days he was looking forward to this event.[33]

This scheme of Rabbi Menashe of Ilya (with its four levels of caring) bears an uncanny resemblance to Rav Kook's famous "*Shir Meruba*." They are identical in terms of their innermost circle (egomania) and outermost circle (cosmic consciousness). Where they differ is in the intervening levels. Where Rav Kook has Israel and mankind as a whole, Rabbi Menashe of Ilya has the nuclear family ("sons and daughters") and extended family and friends. As this passage from Rabbi Menashe's writings was published in Vilna in 1905, it is not unreasonable to assume that Rav Kook read it before he penned his own reflection. Even if the book was unread by Rav Kook, a generation earlier, as a youngster, he had breathed in the air of Smorgon, yet electrified by the sparks of its most famous son, Rabbi Menashe Ben-Porat.

(In a letter penned in 1908, Rav Kook speaks of extending self-love outward to the family, to the nation, to mankind, to all life forms, and finally, beyond global, planetary concern to concern for all of existence. See *Iggerot ha-RAYaH*, vol. 1, pp. 174-175 [Letter 140].)

Appendix G

THE *LESHEM* AND LUZZATTO

INTRODUCTION

One of the great ironies of recent kabbalistic history is the fact that the man responsible for the publication of the works of Rabbi Moshe Ḥayyim Luzzatto (RaMḤaL) in Eastern Europe at the end of the nineteenth century, later stated in no uncertain terms his rejection of Luzzatto's novel approach to Lurianic Kabbalah.

In an incendiary passage, Rabbi Shelomo Eliashov (known as the *Leshem*, after his work, *Leshem, Shevo ve-Aḥlamah*) (1841-1926), begins by criticizing the futile exercise of "some authors in our generation who went too deeply into the words of RaMḤaL, of blessed memory, and multiply explanations and concepts in these matters [i.e., the *partsufim*, or divine personae], for no creation can comprehend them."[1]

And then Rabbi Eliashov confesses:

> Though the books of RaMḤaL, of blessed memory, are very dear, and contain many pearls and much gold, *and most of his books available today (Rosh Ḥodesh Adar 5658* [i.e., 1898]) *were printed as*

> *a result of my initiative*, and though I did not merit to study his books, and looked into them but little, nevertheless, I drew from him some foundations pertaining to the fundamentals of the wisdom [i.e., Kabbalah]. May his memory be a blessing for eternal life among all the saints who are with the LORD God. Nevertheless, I declare that RaMḤaL, of blessed memory, combined the words of the holy *Zohar* and the ARI [i.e., Rabbi Isaac Luria], of blessed memory, with prophetic vision (as it says, "and in the hand of the prophets I stirred imagination"[2]) and attributed to them visions and imaginings.[3]—I cannot subscribe to this at all.
>
> None of the early or late interpreters said something of this sort; the words of the holy *Zohar* and the ARI, of blessed memory, do not support his contention at all.... No one ever said that they were only visions akin to the prophetic visions. Rather, they are absolute, everlasting existents from the time that the Emanator, blessed be His name, emanated them.... Heaven forfend thinking up explanations and conceptualizations about their essence![4]

After distancing himself from RaMḤaL per se, the *Leshem* returns to lambasting those who would take Luzzatto's conceptual method up to the next level:

> I am especially nauseated by the words of some of the Kabbalists of our generation who went too deeply into his [i.e., Luzzatto's] words, of blessed memory, their only desire being to turn around this entire learning, this sacred teaching, [interpreting] solely by means of the methods of RaMḤaL, of blessed memory. They went even farther than he intended, until they took sacred supernal secrets on high and made them codes (*kinuyyim*) for the process of governance of this world. As if above, God forbid, there is nothing other than the process of governance that they arrived at by their intellect.
>
> Heaven forfend that anyone called by the name of "Israel" entertain this thought! This is but the way of the philosophers upon whom the light of Kabbalah never shone.[5]

Let us analyze the *Leshem*'s litany. The proximate cause of his grievance is the method of "*hasbarah*," or the conceptual, rational approach to Kabbalah, which gained traction in his day. But upon deeper inspection, this methodology was founded on the premise that the various metaphors of the Kabbalah were the products of prophetic visions on the part of the *Ba'al ha-Zohar* or later Rabbi Isaac Luria. And, as the visions of the ancient prophets, they were given to decoding, to interpretation, and ultimately, to ratiocination.[6] Both of these complaints the *Leshem* lay at the doorstep of Luzzatto. If, on the other hand, the many metaphors of the Kabbalah are not a figment of the imagination, but real existents, then the entire enterprise of *hasbarah*, of drawing nigh to reason, founders. The *Leshem* took the kabbalistic elements at face value. The proof he mustered is that before RaMḤaL came along, no one ever cast these elements in a visionary light.

Did the *Leshem* have anyone specific in mind when he penned these lines in 1898? Until recently, this was purely a matter of speculation. Various candidates suggested themselves. Rabbi Isaac Ḥaver's *Pitḥei She'arim* (Warsaw, 1888) abounds with various *hanhagot*, "governances," or modes in which the world is conducted. Rabbi Aryeh Leib Lipkin's *Kelalei Hatḥalat ha-Ḥokhmah* (Warsaw, 1893), even more so. And both reference RaMḤaL.[7] It is only today, with the publication of the letters of the *Leshem* to Rabbi Naftali Herz Halevi (1883-1884), that we are able to pronounce with certainty the name of the *Leshem*'s ideological opponent.

Rabbi Naftali Herz Halevi (Weidenbum) (1852-1902) was a formidable adversary. A native of Bialystock who later became Rabbi of Jaffa, he had distinguished himself as an expert in the Kabbalah of the Vilna Gaon. He published from manuscripts the Gaon's commentary to the *Zohar* (Vilna, 1882).[8] Though the *Leshem* was not one to remain silent when he had grave misgivings, in the presence of greatness he wrote in a deferential tone. Even after Rabbi Naftali Herz asked that they address one another as equals, for the most part the *Leshem* kept the discourse civil. (Fifteen years later, the *Leshem*'s tone became belligerent, as we have seen.)

In 1883, the *Leshem* wrote to Rabbi Naftali Herz the following, by now familiar, critique:

> However for the sake of truth and righteousness which he loves, I shall not keep from my master what is in my heart concerning something of his words that in my humble opinion is totally incorrect. And that is what he wrote concerning the hairs of *Arikh Anpin*, "that it is a prophetic vision, etc. etc."
>
> It appears to me that his honor has invested himself very much in such rationales. Though they seem to be words of wisdom and are sweet to the palate, to the limit of my understanding and knowledge, I have found no basis for such rationales—neither in the words of the Rav [i.e., Rabbi Isaac Luria] nor in the words of the Gaon [i.e., Rabbi Elijah of Vilna]. In my opinion, they are simply speculations and rationalizations that flow only from human reason. And there is no end to such speculations. In my opinion, any rationale that is not taken from the words of the *Zohar* and *Tikkunim*, from the words of the Rav and the Gaon, through whom the spirit of the LORD spoke, and which, as is known, are real *ru'aḥ ha-kodesh* (divine inspiration), but determined purely by reason—in my opinion, it is forbidden to make any use at all of such rationales in the Wisdom of Truth [i.e., Kabbalah], for the investigative intellect is free and there is no end

to its thoughts, and at times it wallows in wind. Heaven forfend to make use of speculations in the Wisdom of Truth! This I discerned from the wise, i.e., our Master and Rabbi, the Gaon, of blessed memory, who great as were his accomplishments, we see clearly that all his words are taken from the *Zohar* and *Tikkunim*, so that all that the Kabbalists drew from the words of the ARI, of blessed memory, [the Gaon] drew from the Midrash of Rabbi Shim'on ben Yoḥai.

That which he said about prophetic visions. It certainly is incomparable. All the prophetic visions were below [in our realm] by accident, but all the matters of the Wisdom of Truth are below [in our realm] essentially. Also, though it is true that all the visions and pictures and imaginings are by way of [the *sefirah* of] *Malkhut*[9]... nonetheless, certainly above, all these matters exist in reality, as the *Zohar* and the Rav say that [our] thought cannot grasp them at all. And if it were as he contends, that all the matters are like prophetic visions given to interpretation, is it possible that the Rav did not let us hear this small introduction? On the contrary, we always find in the words of the Rav that they [i.e., the kabbalistic metaphors] are spiritual lights. And it sounds from all [of the Rav's] words that they are real existents. The upshot is that neither in the words of the Rav nor in those of the Gaon have I found any hint to this.[10]

The correspondence between the two Lithuanian Kabbalists was conducted in the years 1883-1884. We have four letters from the *Leshem*, who resided in Shavel,[11] Kovno Gubernia (Government of Kovno). Though we are missing Rabbi Naftali Herz's half of the exchange of letters, we get the sense that he too was not one to mince words or shy away from frank confrontation. By no means, a milquetoast.

The stage for the *maḥloket le-shem shamayim* (controversy for the sake of Heaven) was set in the second letter (excerpted above). In the ensuing two letters, no one backs down; each stands his ground. Rabbi Naftali Herz would not abandon RaMḤaL's *"mar'ot ha-nevu'ah,"* his theory that the kabbalistic metaphors such as *Tsimtsum*, *ḥalal* and *kav* (Cosmic Contraction, vacuum and ray of light), and *'Iggulim* and *Yosher* (Circles and Straightness), appeared in vision and are in need of interpretation.[12] Neither would the *Leshem* concede this point.[13]

A particular focus of the second letter is the significance of *'orot* (lights) and *kelim* (vessels). Rabbi Naftali Herz adopted the interpretation found in the *Collectanea* of the Vilna Gaon published at the conclusion of the Gaon's commentary to *Sifra di-Tseni'uta* in Samuel Luria's edition of Warsaw 1882, whereby the lights symbolize will (*ratson*), and the vessels, ability (*yekholet*).[14]

While the *Leshem* does not deny the attribution to the Gaon, he vehemently disagrees with the interpretation that Rabbi Naftali Herz gives to the Gaon's statement.[15] (Later, in *Ḥelek ha-Be'urim*, published in Jerusalem in 1935, the *Leshem* will disavow the Gaon's authorship of that *Likkut*, supposing that it was penned by an unidentified student of the Gaon.)[16]

What caused the tone of the *Leshem*'s discourse to turn from courteous to outrightly combative? I believe that what triggered the *Leshem*'s outburst in 1898 was the appearance that year of Rabbi Naftali Herz's *Siddur ha-GRA*, a prayerbook with the kabbalistic *kavvanot* of the Vilna Gaon.

RABBI NAFTALI HERZ HALEVI'S *SIDDUR HA-GRA*

The *Leshem* had good reason to be upset about the *Siddur ha-GRA*. Splashed all over it were Luzzatto's alleged *mar'ot ha-nevu'ah* (prophetic visions), as well as the dreaded accompanying *hanhagot* (governances).[17]

The tone is set at the very beginning of Rabbi Naftali Herz's commentary:

> And in truth, *Malkhut* is one of His attributes, blessed be He, in which there are pictured, as it were, all the deeds of the [creatures] below, according to what they are. And so, all His governances (*hanhagot*), blessed be He, and His attributes are pictured there by way of

> prophetic vision (*mar'eh ha-nevu'i*). And this is one of His powers that has this gift. See *KaLaḤ Pitḥei Ḥokhmah.*[18]

One imagines that the *Leshem* blanched reading in the *Siddur* Rabbi Naftali Herz's portrayal of the "shattering of the vessels" (*shevirat ha-kelim*)—a staged manifestation of God's inability. Why would God wish to give the impression of impotence? This ostensible breakdown was designed to promote the appearance of human ability. The façade of divine incapability and human capability was necessary in order for there to be free will, and in turn, reward and punishment, essential for the governance of this world. At the eschaton, there will be no more free will; on the contrary, at that time there will be revealed how in truth there never was any divine insuffiency and dependence upon human capability.[19]

Besides whatever ideological differences separated the two men, the *Leshem* might have felt that in loading such rationalistic explications of kabbalistic arcana onto a prayerbook for public consumption, Rabbi Naftali Herz had crossed a line.[20]

"NEVERTHELESS, I DREW FROM [RAMḤAL] SOME FOUNDATIONS OF THE WISDOM" *(LESHEM)*

There seems to be in the writings of the *Leshem* a fusion of two mystical motifs: One, common to various

Kabbalist authors; the other, peculiar to Rabbi Moshe Ḥayyim Luzzatto (RaMḤaL).

The theme that is common to various authors is the opposition of *hanhagah tiv'it* (natural governance) and *hanhagah nissit* (miraculous governance).[21] Where the Kabbalists differed, is in the placement of these two governances in terms of the kabbalistic tree.

Rabbi Meir Leibush Malbim (Wisser) expressed the difference in terms of *sefirot*. In his commentary to the Book of Kings, he wrote that the two columns that Solomon erected at the entrance to the Temple in Jerusalem, Yakhin and Boaz, symbolized the two governances. The left column, Boaz, symbolized the stable, natural state of affairs. The right column, Yakhin, symbolized the fluid, miraculous state, subject to improvisations and sudden incursions. Translated into *sefirot*, Yakhin becomes *Netsaḥ* (the right hip), and Boaz, *Hod* (the left hip). Alternatively, Yakhin represents *Yesod* (the masculine, the *mashpi'a* or donor) and Boaz, *Malkhut* (the feminine, the *mekabel* or recipient).[22]

For Rabbi Isaac Ḥaver, author of *Pitḥei She'arim*, the two governances are symbolized by the Lurianic opposition of *'Iggulim* (Circles) and *Yosher* (Lines) (the very first *derush* in Vital's *'Ets Ḥayyim*). The circles upon circles are a trope for the encumberances of nature; the straight line bespeaks the directness of the miracle that cuts through all the conventions.[23]

In keeping with this tradition, the *Leshem* assigns to the miraculous governance the *ʾor makif* (surrounding or transcendent light) of Lurianic Kabbalah; to the natural order, the *ʾor penimi* (inner or immanent light).[24] (Alternatively, he assigns the miraculous to *Arikh Anpin*, and the natural to *Ze'ir Anpin*.)[25]

Yet, to this common opposition of the natural order versus the miraculous order, the *Leshem* has fused an element of teleology—and theodicy—that could come only from Luzzatto.[26] So, while the *Leshem* distanced himself from Luzzatto, he imbibed from him a very significant teaching, perhaps Luzzatto's most significant teaching.

Yosef Avivi has tracked throughout the literary *oeuvre* of RaMḤaL two governances: *hanhagat ha-mishpat* (the governance of law) versus *hanhagat ha-yiḥud* (the governance of unity).[27]

The former revolves on the principle of reward and punishment (*sakhar ve-ʿonesh*). Eventually, good deeds get rewarded and bad deeds punished. In this scheme, everything fits neatly.

And then the problem of evil rears its ugly head. "*Mi-p'nei mah yesh tsaddik ve-raʿ lo; rashaʿ ve-tov lo?*" "Why is there a righteous man who has it bad; a wicked man who has it good?" So Moses inquired of the Master of the Universe.[28] The entire Book of Job is an attempt to come to grips with theodicy.[29] (One opinion in the Talmud ascribes authorship of the book to Moses.)[30] In the sagacious and succinct words of the Mishnah: "We have no explanation, neither for the prosperity of the wicked, nor for the suffering of the righteous."[31]

Luzzatto's revelation was that all of the unexplained and inexplicable events come under the rubric of *Sod ha-Yiḥud*, the Secret of God's Unity.[32] In the final *dénouement* of history, all the polarized elements of light and darkness, good and evil, will come together in a retrospective of divine unity.

The *Leshem*'s interpretation of *'or makif* and *'or penimi*, of the transcendent and the immanent, is designed not only to play the miraculous and natural against one another (as in MaHaRaL, et al.), but also to address the "*kavshei de-Raḥmana*,"[33] "the hidden matters of God"; the question of undeserved human suffering that has gnawed at religious man since time immemorial. And the *Leshem*'s "solution" to the problem—as that of Luzzatto—is eschatological in nature. At some undisclosed date, all of history will pass before the collective eye of humanity, and there will be revealed the One.[34] "All will be returned and rectified to the secret of the hidden unity (*ha-aḥdut ha-ne'elamah*), the end of all ends, which has no end."[35] "Then they will know that the entire governance (*hanhagah*) brought about by the fall of the sparks and their descent into the World of Chaos (*'Olam ha-Tohu*)... was all for a good that is unsurpassed."[36]

In the words of the Talmud:

> "On that day the LORD shall be one and His name one" [Zechariah 14:9].
>
> Is He not one now?
>
> Said Rabbi Aḥa bar Ḥanina: The World to Come is not like this world. In this world, on good tidings one blesses, "Who is good and benefits," and on evil tidings one blesses, "Blessed is the Judge of Truth." In the World to Come, it is all "Who is good and benefits."[37]

CONCLUSION

The battle lines have been drawn between eighteenth and nineteenth-century Kabbalists. There were those such as Rabbis Moshe Ḥayyim Luzzatto, Naftali Herz Halevi Weidenbaum, and Zadok Hakohen Rabinowitz of Lublin who posited *mar'ot ha-nevu'ah*, visionary experiences, as responsible for Lurianic Kabbalah. Others, such as Rabbis Tsevi Hirsch Eichenstein of Zydaczów, Isaac Safrin of Komarno, and Shelomo Eliashov (the *Leshem*) were vehemently opposed to this novel theory of Luzzatto, maintaining the literal existence of the various metaphors.

If I am allowed to contribute to this "conversation of the holy seraphim" ("*si'aḥ sarfei kodesh*"), I should like to offer the following insight. Is it possible that Rabbi Isaac Luria's visions were predisposed by his intellectual pursuits? "A man is shown [in dream at night] only his thoughts [of the preceding day]."[38] Many great sages practiced what has come to be known as "*she'elat ḥalom*," a dream inquiry. This technique was practiced by the medieval halakhist, Rabbi Jacob of Marvège, yielding the work *She'elot u-Teshuvot min ha-Shamayim* (*Responsa from Heaven*), a compendium of halakhic decisions revealed in dream. Before retiring for the night, the sage would pose a specific problem that was bothering him. In dream, he would receive a response solving the problem. The most famous of these heavenly responsa addressed the controversy between Rashi and his grandson Rabbeinu Tam (i.e., Rabbi Jacob of Ramerupt) regarding the proper placement of the Biblical passages within the *tefillin* (phylacteries).[39]

I humbly submit that elements of Lurianic Kabbalah were transmitted in somewhat similar circumstances. This is not to suggest that Rabbi Isaac Luria's visions (assuming they were visions) were the result of a specific technique of *she'elat ḥalom*. I am suggesting that the images that appeared to him did not arise in an intellectual vacuum but as a response to intellectual probing.

Leor Holzer wrote an unpublished dissertation in which he made a case for Rabbi Isaac Luria having studied Ḥasdai Crescas's work *'Or Adonai* that discusses space.[40] (See Harry Austryn Wolfson, *Crescas' Critique of Aristotle*.) Later, Rabbi Isaac Luria might have been shown in a vision the *Tsimtsum* (Cosmic Contraction) and the *ḥalal* (vacuum) or *makom panui* (empty space).

By the same token, Rabbi Isaac Luria was obviously bothered by the discrepancy between *'Iggulim* and *Yosher*, the two conflicting models by which Kabbalists had traditionally configured the *sefirot*: concentric circles versus the human form (*tsurat ha-adam*). And as later, Kekule (1865) beheld in a dream the solution to the problem of the ring structure of benzene (in the form of a serpent biting its own tail), so in a vision, Rabbi Isaac Luria might have been shown the reconciliation of the two schemes of circles and lines.

Book Reviews

Yehudah Mirsky. *Towards the Mystical Experience of Modernity: The Making of Rav Kook, 1865-1904*

Boston: Academic Studies Press, 2021. xvi, 392. ISBN 978-1-61811-955-1

> **Rava said to Bar Hedya, "I saw in a dream that my mansion had fallen, and all came and took it away brick by brick."**
>
> **Bar Hedya said to him, "Your teachings will spread throughout the world."**
>
> **The great sage has a distinct, organized system in which all the specific opinions are interwoven with his permanent inner theory, just as parts of a building relate to the structure as a whole. However, people of smaller stature cannot absorb the overall theory and greatness of spirit of the sage; they are unable to recognize how all these specifics flow from the general theory and how they are interrelated. They receive each specific as a separate entity....**
>
> **So for the generation, there is no "mansion" here, no palace of wisdom, but rather "brick by brick," a collections of opinions, laws and ethics that all appreciate, though they do not recognize their value as parts of the palace.**

> **"Through wisdom a house is built" (Proverbs 24:3).**
>
> **"The mansion fell, the teachings spread throughout the world." Each lovingly grabs a piece, though by doing so, one is unable to encompass the overall theory that produced this specific. Nevertheless, even in their state of disarray, the pieces are dear. They attract attention because of the greatness of their author and recognition of his value in his generation and in generations to come.**
>
> **(Rabbi Abraham Isaac Hakohen Kook, *'Eyn AYaH* commentary to *Berakhot* 56a)**

Rav Kook's interpretation of Rava's dream (channeled through Bar Hedya, a professional dream interpreter) best describes the state of Rav Kook's spiritual legacy today, nearly a century after his passing. In what reads almost as an autobiography, Rav Kook accurately predicted the state of disarray, whereby various students grab pieces of the *Nachlass*, even as the totality, the *Gestalt* of the great man's teaching, disappears beyond the horizon. And though Bar Hedya sought to assuage the sage's anxiety, the frustration remains palpable.

Nowhere is the fragmentation of Rav Kook's literary estate felt more keenly than in the great divide between the *yeshivah* and the academy. While academicians might relegate the late Rabbi Moshe Tsevi Neriyah's many biographies of the Rav to the realm of hagiography, *ḥovshei beit ha-midrash* might tend to dismiss Professor Mirsky's biography as a secularization. A great *"yiḥud"* (a term Rav Kook borrowed from the Kabbalistic tradition), a great "unification" is called for. Attempts in this direction have been made in the past and one hopes that further overtures will be made in the future. And maybe, just maybe, the outline of the elusive palace will once again appear on the horizon.

*

This is Mirsky's second book on Rav Kook. The first, *Rav Kook: Mystic in a Time of Revolution*, appeared in Yale University Press's Jewish Lives series. The present work, based on Mirsky's doctoral dissertation, is restricted to the four decades of Rav Kook's life in Eastern Europe before his arrival in Jaffa in 1904. Geared to a general audience and enveloping an entire lifetime, the biography had a lyrical quality to it. The present study reads more like a textbook for specialists in the field. Prepare for a "hard landing"—and a "deep dive" into *Lita*, Lithuanian Jewry.

The book belongs to the genre of literary biography. By juxtaposing biography and textual analysis, the author aims to trace Rav Kook's intellectual development.

The reader may find fascinating how Abraham Isaac Kook, living at the intersection of the Ḥasidic, Mitnagdic and Haskalah movements that competed for the minds and hearts of young Lithuanian Jews, integrated elements of all three traditions in his being and in his *oeuvre*.

We are introduced to a figure such as Rabbi Yosef Zechariah Stern of Shavel, a member of Rav Kook's extended family, having married the daughter of Rav Kook's great uncle Rabbi Mordechai Gimpel Jaffe. The Rabbi of Shavel, famed for his prodigious memory and breathtaking command of Talmud, displayed in his works Maskilic tendencies, especially fondness for the writings of Naphtali Hirz Wessely and Moshe Mendelssohn.[1] Mirsky speculates that he influenced young Rav Kook in this respect (p. 123, n. 140).

If Rav Kook's father's family were staunch Mitnagdim with roots in the Volozhin Yeshivah (and perhaps mild Maskilic tendencies), Rav Kook's mother's people were devout ḤaBaD Ḥasidim. In fact, it was Rav Kook's maternal grandfather, Refael Felman, who established the Kopyster *shtiebel* in Rav Kook's birthplace of Grieva (a suburb across the river from Dvinsk), Latvia, and brought there Rabbi Yeḥezkel Yanover as *mashpi'a*.[2]

In his youth, Rav Kook studied under the Rabbi of Dvinsk, Rabbi Reuven Levin (known as "Reb Reuvaleh Denaburger," Denaburg being the previous Germanic name of Dvinsk). Mirsky rightly bestows upon him the accolade "a Talmudist's Talmudist" (p. 57). According to a tradition preserved by the Soloveichik family of Jerusalem, the *baḥur* from Grieva conveyed a specific halakhic query from the sages of Volozhin to Reb Reuvaleh.[3] In this country, the adherents of the *"Mal'akh,"* a.k.a. Rabbi Abraham Dov Baer Hakohen Levin of Kurenets and Ilya, recorded that as a young man, he studied Talmud and Codes under "Reb

Reuvaleh Amchislaver." (Before Denaburg or Dvinsk, Reb Reuvaleh served as Rabbi of Amchislav.) As is well known, the Mal'akh was singlemindedly anti-Zionist. He thought heavenly invoked death a suitable punishment for Chief Rabbi Kook![4]

Mirsky devotes an entire Chapter Four to *'Eyn AYaH*, Rav Kook's voluminous commentary to the *'Eyn Ya'akov* Legends of the Talmud, undoubtedly his most important work from this early period. In discussing the emerging importance of the faculty of imagination in Rav Kook's thought, Mirsky provides helpful comparisons to the Kabbalah of Rabbi Menaḥem Mendel of Shklov (a disciple of the Vilna Gaon) and to the Ḥasidic thought of Rabbi Naḥman of Breslov (although to the best of my knowledge, Rav Kook engaged with Breslov Ḥasidism only after his arrival in Jaffa). See Mirsky, pp. 204-205.

One must complete the picture by adding the importance of imagination in the Kabbalah that arose in Volozhin. Recently Yosef Yitzḥak Lifshitz has shown how Rabbi Ḥayyim of Volozhin's *Nefesh ha-Ḥayyim* drew on the *Ḥasidei Ashkenaz*, inasmuch as they sought to bridge the gap between the infinite incorporeal deity and finite man by way of imagery.[5] This involvement with imaging of the divine becomes all the more pronounced in the son, Rabbi Isaac (Itzeleh) of Volozhin.[6] Long after the passing of Reb Itzeleh, his Bible commentaries, preserved by the students of Volozhin, continued to exercise them, and it is not unreasonable to assume that Rav Kook was exposed to them. (Rabbi Naftali Tsevi Yehudah Berlin [NeTsIV],

Rav Kook's mentor in Volozhin, was the son-in-law of Reb Itzeleh.)

In that chapter (p. 225), Mirsky assumes that Rav Kook's coinage "*ahavat 'atsmo*" or "self-love" is a Hebrew translation of the French *amour propre*, somehow coopted from Rousseau. However, an entire section on "*Ahavat 'Atsmo*" occurs in Rabbi Eliezer Papo's ethical work *Pele' Yo'ets* (Constantinople 1825; Bucharest 1860).

On occasion, Mirsky engages with Rav Kook's *halakhah*. Addressing another work from this period, *Li-Nevukhei ha-Dor*, Mirsky speculates that Rav Kook has adopted the position of the medieval Provençal authority Rabbenu Menaḥem ha-Me'iri (p. 291). This stands to reason, as later, in a letter datelined "21 Menaḥem-Av, 5664," to his disciple Moshe Seidel, Rav Kook will write: "The main opinion is that of the Me'iri, that all the peoples who are bound by proper mores between man and man are already considered '*gerim toshavim*' ['resident aliens'] with all the human obligations."[7] By the same token, in his role of *posek*, or halakhic decisor, Rav Kook would later adopt the position that "Ishmaelites," or Muslims, inasmuch as they are monotheists, qualify as "*gerim toshavim*." (Given that perspective, the prohibition of "*Lo taḥanem*" would not apply to them. This became the basis for his "*heter mekhirah*" in regard to *Shemitah*.)

As the biographer of Rav Kook's fellow Lithuanian kabbalist, Rabbi Pinḥas Hakohen Lintop, I must point out that, contrary to what is written on page 282, Rabbi Lintop never set foot in *Erets Yisrael*. He died in Birzh, Lithuania, in 1924, before he had the opportunity to avail himself of the certificate Rav Kook procured for his *'aliyah*.

Though stories abound of Rav Kook's youthful longing for and love of *Erets Yisrael*, Professor Mirsky finds the thought category of *Erets Yisrael* to be lacking from the writings of this period. It might strike the reader as ironic that for the first four decades of his life, Rav Kook, whose name later becomes synonymous with the Land, was not thinking—or at least not writing—in such terms. One is left wondering whether the identification with *Erets Yisrael* was born of necessity or was the result of a mystical conversion, such as described by Rabbi Abraham Azulai: "When one merits to enter *Erets Yisrael*, there comes to one a new soul of *Yetsirah* and is garbed in one's old soul; and the first night that one sleeps in *Erets Yisrael*, the two souls depart [from the body] and rise above, and [upon waking] only the new soul returns [to the body]."[8]

Eight Letters from Rabbi Zvi Yehuda Kook about Historiosophy, Philosophy, Theology and Zionism* (Hebrew and German). *Edited by Ḥagay Shtamler.

Jerusalem: Carmel, 2021. 282 pp.

> *"A person does not understand the opinion of his teacher until [after] forty years."* (*Talmud Bavli*)

As this Purim marks the fortieth *Yahrzeit* of Rav Zvi Yehuda Kook (14 Adar, 5742—14 Adar, 5782), it is only appropriate that on this occasion his students (and students' students) grapple with the legacy of this elusive teacher.

BIOGRAPHY

Zvi Yehuda was born to Reiza Rivka (Rabinowitz-Te'omim) and Rav Avraham Yitzḥak Hakohen Kook in Zeimel (Zeimelis), Lithuania, on the eve of Passover 1891. Later, the family relocated to Boisk (Bauska), Latvia. Shortly before *Shavu'ot* of 1904, Zvi Yehuda and his family arrived in Jaffa, where his father would serve as Rav of "Jaffa and the Settlements" for the next decade. Zvi Yehuda's formal *yeshivah* education was acquired at Torat Ḥayyim in Jerusalem under the tutelage of Rabbi Zeraḥ Epstein. Before World War One, Zvi Yehuda gravitated to Halberstadt, Germany, to round out his largely autodidactic secular education and perfect his knowledge of European languages (French and German). The war years were spent in Switzerland. (There was a year that he and his father were together in St. Gallen, before the elder Kook assumed the rabbinate of Maḥzikei Hadat in London's East End.) With war's end, father and son returned to the Holy Land. There, Rav Avraham Yitzḥak Kook would serve as Rav of Jerusalem and Ashkenazic Chief Rabbi of Erets Yisrael until his death in 1935.

For the next seventeen years, Rav Zvi Yehuda was hidden from the public view, devoting himself to editing and publishing his father's voluminous manuscripts in *Halakhah* and *Aggadah*, Jewish Law and Jewish Thought. Only in 1952, with the passing of Rav Ya'akov Moshe Ḥarlap, his father's premier disciple, did Rav Zvi Yehuda take the helm of Merkaz Harav, the *yeshivah* founded by his father in 1923. He served in this capacity of *Rosh Yeshivah* until his passing in 1982.

In those thirty years, Rav Zvi Yehuda raised a generation of disciples who imbibed his "*Torat Erets Yisrael*," a distinct ideology that combined rabbinic learning with religious Zionism. In the aftermath of the Six-Day War in June of 1967, Rav Zvi Yehuda rose to national prominence, as his students spearheaded the settlement movement known as Gush Emunim (the Bloc of the Faithful). From his humble abode at 30 Ovadiah Street in the Ge'ulah section of Jerusalem, came the inspiration that translated into monumental deed. This frail, unassuming scholar of diminutive physical stature, proved a spiritual powerhouse.

Never one to remain an abstract ideologist, the elderly rabbi, in poor health, trekked to the incipient settlements of Kiryat Arba (adjacent to Ḥebron) and Elon Moreh (adjacent to Shechem) in solidarity with the settler movement.

EIGHT LETTERS

We come now to Ḥagay Shtamler's recent book, *Shemoneh Iggerot*, which may or may not throw a curve into the hagiography that has grown up around Rav Zvi Yehuda Kook. It certainly will add contours to an otherwise two-dimensional portrait.

Shtamler's first book concerning Rav Zvi Yehuda, *'Ayin be-'Ayin*, based on his doctoral dissertation at Bar-Ilan University, was withdrawn from circulation by the publisher at the request of Rav Zvi Thau because it was found insufficiently reverential. The book has since been re-issued by another publisher in, it is assumed, an expurgated, less controversial version.

Shtamler is by profession both a communal rabbi and an academician, a delicate balancing act. Growing up, he was mentored by close students of Rav Zvi Yehuda. (He mentions by name Rabbi Avraham Yehoshua Zuckerman. The eight manuscript letters were provided by Rabbi Eliezer Waldman, founding *Rosh Yeshivah* of Nir Kiryat Arba, who passed away recently.) His intellectual horizon has broadened so that today he is eminently conversant with the writings of German Jewish thinkers such as Hermann Cohen and Franz Rosenzweig. So, from a strict vantage point of "*Torat Erets Yisrael*," this book, like its predecessor, may very well arouse the ire of certain individuals.

HELENA BAER

Zvi Yehuda's letters were written for the most part in German to Helena Baer (1891-1981) of Halberstadt. Helena came from a distinguished family. Her father, a wealthy businessman, was the leader of the Jewish community. Her older brother, Yitzḥak (Fritz) Baer, would go on to become a famous Jewish historian. She would marry Yehuda (Leo) Barth, the son of Rabbi Dr. Jacob Barth, a student and son-in-law of Rabbi Azriel Hildesheimer, and a member of the faculty of the Hildesheimer Seminary in Berlin. Leo's brother, Aaron Barth, was a prominent Israeli banker and the author of a popular work of Jewish Thought.

Helena sounds like a complex individual in her own right, navigating between Agudah and Mizrachi, the Diaspora and the Land. After her *'aliyah*, Helena served as director of the Mizrachi women teachers' seminary in Jerusalem, where she left a lasting impression upon a young Zelda Schneurson. In later years, the by now famous poet, known simply as "Zelda," would refer to her erstwhile teacher as a "queen." According to Shtamler, Helena Barth's individualistic style of teaching ran afoul of Rabbi Meir Berlin (Bar-Ilan) and she was dismissed from the directorship.

CHRISTIANITY AND "THE PROGRAM OF THE ANTI-PROGRAM"

Of the eight letters, it is undoubtedly the first and longest which will evoke the most interest. In a sprawling historiosophy, Zvi Yehuda views Christianity as a "historic mistake," "the program of the anti-program."

I had occasion to translate the letter (from its Hebrew version) to English in my collection, *When God Becomes History: Historical Essays of Rabbi Abraham Isaac Hakohen Kook* (Orot, 2003; Kodesh, 2016). What I could not have known at that time, was the identity of the recipient, Helena Baer Barth. (As Shtamler points out, in *Zemaḥ Zvi: Letters of Rav Zvi Yehuda Hakohen Kook* [1991], where the letter first appeared, the gender was changed from feminine to masculine, thus *"tisleḥi"* became *"tislaḥ,"* etc.) I conjectured, wrongly, that it was written to Zvi Yehuda's recent acquaintance, David Cohen (later, in Jerusalem, referred to as the "Nazir"). Also, the placement of the letter in that collection, threw me off as to the date. Since it was sandwiched between letters written in 1918, I assumed, mistakenly, that it too was from that year. In truth, it was written earlier, in 1915.

In the letter to Baer, Zvi Yehuda references his father's recent essay, *"Le-Mahalakh ha-Ide'ot be-Yisrael"* ("To the Process of Ideas in Israel"), which had been edited by Zvi Yehuda and published in Rabbi Meir Berlin's journal *Ha-'Ivri* in 1912. Indeed, I found similarities between the son's historiosophy and that of his father. But where it seemed to me that the father subscribed to the famous position of Maimonides at the conclusion of *Mishneh Torah* (in uncensored versions) that Jesus and Muḥammad had been part of a divine plan to pave the way for the righteous Messiah, by exposing the peoples of the world to Biblical teachings (albeit in a distorted fashion)—Zvi Yehuda clearly objected to this reading of history. As I stated in *When God Becomes History*, this was not the lone opinion of Maimonides. It was endorsed later by Naḥmanides in his sermon, *Torat Hashem Temimah*, and conveyed earlier by Rabbi Yehuda Halevi in his *Kuzari* (IV, 23). (In his edition of the *Kuzari*, Rabbi Kafaḥ rejects the notion that Maimonides borrowed this idea from Halevi, whom he never mentions. Rabbi Kafaḥ assumes, instead, that the idea circulated among the "sages of Israel," and that both Halevi and Maimonides absorbed it from the "Jewish Diaspora.")

In a reading that betrays Nietzschean influence (Nietzsche's name appears in the letter alongside his term "*Sklavenmoral*," or "slave morality"), the original divine plan was for the pagan peoples to come under direct Judaic influence, without the vitiating and psychologically damaging effect brought on by Christianity's dualism of soul and body. Judaism, with its non-dualistic approach to spirituality, would have been a better teacher to the evolving nations. Viewed from this perspective, Christianity threw a monkey wrench into the divine scheme. The secularization of Europe comes to correct this distortion.

Shtamler tries to reconcile the seemingly disparate views of father and son. Let the reader judge whether his solution is satisfactory.

HERMANN COHEN— A CONTRAPUNTAL READING

Shtamler believes that the unnamed nemesis of Zvi Yehuda in this letter is none other than Hermann Cohen (1842-1918), founder of the Marburg School of neo-Kantianism, and the regnant German Jewish philosopher of the day. Cohen's vision of Judaism would reach full expression in his posthumous work, *Religion der Vernunft aus den Quellen des Judentums* (*Religion of Reason out of the Sources of Judaism*) (1919). For Cohen, Judaism is essentially an ethical, prophetic, Messianic idea. Hermann Cohen's Judaism is disembodied and *dépaysé* (Cohen despised the Zionist movement), whereas Zvi Yehuda Kook's Judaism is full-bodied and landed: "Israel's influence upon human civilization, consists not of sermons by Jewish leaders or their exemplary lifestyle, neither in 'humanism,' nor in an abstract, illusionary 'Judaism,' but only in an indivisible Jews-and-Judaism, in the existence of the *nation itself*, through which the light of God is manifested in the world."

Shtamler includes a lengthy appendix entitled, "The Polemic Regarding the Destiny of the People of Israel," designed to demonstrate how Zvi Yehuda refutes Hermann Cohen point by point. (And with all that, he remained a great admirer of Cohen, as attested to by Rav Zvi Yehuda's letters and lectures.)

RAV KOOK AND NIETZSCHE

Since Shtamler has summoned my experience with Rav Zvi Yehuda regarding Nietzsche (*Eight Letters*, pp. 79-80, n. 331), I should like to disclose more details concerning that memorable meeting in the month of Tevet (January) 1978. I was newlywed and newly arrived in Jerusalem. I came to the meeting with Rav Zvi Yehuda—whom I had never met before—equipped with an analysis of *Orot ha-Teshuvah* (*Lights of Return*), a work that Rav Zvi Yehuda had compiled from his father's writings in 1924. I had submitted this Hebrew essay as a term paper to Professor Arthur Hyman for his course in Modern Jewish Philosophy at Yeshiva University's Bernard Revel Graduate School. (Hyman graded it "A.") Rav Zvi Yehuda read through it, commenting here and there. He liked it. (Understatement.) When he came to the part comparing Rav Kook's philosophy of *Teshuvah* to that of the Ḥasidic master, Rabbi Zadok Hakohen of Lublin, he commented that his father remarked on the similarities between their two outlooks: "Rabbi Zadok and I are saying the same thing except that he expresses it in a more radical fashion." When Rav Zvi Yehuda came to the section on Nietzsche, he asked that I delete it, saying that it is unbefitting to situate his father, "a man who wore *tefillin* all day," together with Nietzsche. I honored his request, and later, when I published the essay, "*Zedonot na'asot ke-zakhuyot be-mishnato shel Harav Kuk,*" in the journal *Sinai*, I deleted the section on Nietzsche.

But there is more to this story. When I was seated at Rav Zvi Yehuda's table, my opening line was: "How much your father loved the Jewish People!" Rav Zvi Yehuda reacted with hearty laughter. *"Ahavat Yisrael?"* "Love of Israel?" "My father loved the whole world, even *zome'aḥ* (the vegetable kingdom), even *domem* (the mineral kingdom)!"

The two halves of the story, the exclusionary and the inclusionary, are mutually complementary and integral to Rav Zvi Yehuda's *Weltanschauung*. They are as the systole and diastole of the heart.

*

So, how do we reconcile the writer of the *Eight Letters* with the later leader? Was this a fleeting European phase? Did the universalism persist into old age? Is nationalism evident even in the youthful letters?

These are the questions that await resolution on the fortieth *Yahrzeit* of Rav Zvi Yehuda Hakohen Kook, of blessed memory.

Endnotes

Foreword

[1] My English translation was first brought out by Jason Aronson (Northvale, NJ, 1993). It was later re-issued by Maggid, a subdivision of Koren (Jerusalem, 2015). At that time, it appeared in both an English-only softcover version and a bilingual hardcover version.

The date on the title page of the first edition of *Orot* reads "5680." Yet, in his introduction to the second edition of *Orot*, penned on "15 Av, 5709" (i.e., 1949), the editor, Rabbi Tsevi Yehudah Hakohen Kook, wrote that *Orot* first appeared in the year 5681. This was also the recollection of Rabbi Tsevi Yehudah's brother-in-law, Rabbi Yehoshua Hutner, in his "blessing" of the Beit El 2004 edition of *Orot*, penned on *Lag ba-'Omer* of that year. Finally, in the historical backdrop appended to that edition ("*Le-Toledot ha-'Orot*"), we read on page 374: "The publication of the book *Orot* was effectively delayed until the beginning of the year 5681, though on the title of the book there remained printed '5680.'"

Frankly, I am at a loss to understand how this "historic revisionism" came about. There is no clearer proof that the book was already in circulation in the year 5680 than Rabbi Ya'akov Moshe Ḥarlap's defense of the work, *Tovim Me'orot*. The title page of *Tovim Me'orot* (*Good Are the Lights*, a pun on *Orot*, or *Lights*) provides not only the year but the month as well: "Elul, 5680." The contents are a 14-page letter to Rabbi Eizik Ben-Tovim, datelined "Jerusalem, 2 Elul 5680," defending Rav

Kook's newly issued work, *Orot*, especially the much maligned chapter 34 that sings the praises of young Jewish athletes. See my introduction to *Orot* (2015), pp. 26-27.

2 In his introduction to that second edition of *Orot*, Rabbi Tsevi Yehudah acknowledged that these later additions were made at the suggestion of his brother-in-law, Rabbi Yehoshua Hutner. See also Rabbi Hutner's blessing to the 2004 edition, p. 11.

3 See *When God Becomes History: Historical Essays of Rabbi Abraham Isaac Hakohen Kook*, ed. Bezalel Naor (New York, NY: Kodesh Press, 5777/2016), pp. 89-112.

4 As I was putting the finishing touches on this book, there came my way a new study by Menachem Lorberbaum, *Lifnei Heyot ha-Ḥasidut* (Before Ḥasidism) (Jerusalem: Bialik Institute, 2022). In a lengthy footnote, the author attempts to situate the aticle *"Ha-Neshamot shel 'Olam ha-Tohu"* within the kabbalistic tradition, sorting out aspects of Rav Kook's thought that are indebted to Beshtian Ḥasidism, as opposed to others influenced by Luzzatto. From the Ba'al Shem Tov (whose system Lorberbaum believes to be a response to the preceding Kabbalah of Nathan of Gaza), Rav Kook garnered the notion of the *tsaddik* (righteous individual) mending souls. From Rabbi Moshe Ḥayyim Luzzatto, on the other hand, Rav Kook received the indispensable vehicle of historical process. See ibid. p. 256, n. 43, and earlier p. 251, n. 33.

5 See, e.g., *Iggerot ha-RAYaH*, vol. 2 (Jerusalem: Mossad Harav Kook, 1961), pp. 201-202 (Letter 562). In the letter, Rav Kook requests that his son, Tsevi Yehudah, bring to Reḥovot various books and manuscripts. The books include *Ḥoshen Mishpat* with *Be'ur ha-GRA*, and works of Lurianic Kabbalah: *Adam Yashar* and *Arba Me'ot Shekel Kesef*. The manuscripts are Rav Kook's supercommentary to the *Be'ur ha-GRA* (i.e., *Be'er Eliyahu*) and a journal of Rav Kook's *pensées* (*"kovets...rishmei ra'ayonot"*). Light summer reading!

In *Orot ha-RAYaH* (Jerusalem: Mossad Harav Kook, 1969), a collection of poems, the editor, Rav Tsevi Yehudah Hakohen Kook, specified that the later poems written in Erets Yisrael, were written either in Jaffa or Rehovot. See also Yehoshua B.

Be'ery, *Ohev Yisrael bi-Kedushah*, vol. 4 (Tel-Aviv, 1989), pp. 300 (facsimile), 302; and Rabbi Ya'akov Moshe Ḥarlap, *Mei Marom*, vol. 20 (*Iggerot Kodesh*) (Jerusalem, 2021), Letter 27 (p. 42).

6 See Amihud Naḥmani, *Pirkei Reḥovot* (New York, 1962), a collection of articles that appeared in *HaDo'ar*. Naḥmani's psychic experiences are recorded in Aharon Zeitlin's study of parapsychology, *Ha-Metsi'ut ha-Aḥeret* (The Other Reality) (Tel-Aviv: Yavneh, 1967). In our many conversations in Naḥmani's apartment in the Washington Heights section of Manhattan, he regaled me with these extraordinary encounters: the clouds over the skies of Erets Yisrael auguring World War One; the deceased Yiddish poet Yehoash appearing to both Naḥmani and his wife, requesting burial in Erets Yisrael; and the Hebrew version of the Flying Dutchman.

7 Rabbi Ya'akov Moshe Ḥarlap, who accompanied his master Rav Kook on his visit to the irreligious kibbutzim of the Galilee, witnessed first-hand Rav Kook's effect upon these settlers. In a eulogy for Rav Kook three years after his passing, he observed:

> In such encompassing souls (*neshamot kolelot*) there is revealed a peculiar quality, a magnetism. Many hearts are drawn to them. To such world-class *tsaddikim* (righteous ones), many souls gravitate, without themselves knowing why.
> (*Mei Marom*, vol. 17 [Jerusalem, 2010], *Shi'ur Komah*, *ma'amar* 18 [p. 107])

And see ibid. pp. 80-81.

8 *Pinkesei ha-RAYaH*, vol. 7 (Jerusalem: Makhon RZYH Kook, 5782/2021), *Kovets mi-Tekufat Yaffo-Schweiz*, par. 73 (p. 168). This entry was brought to my attention by Rabbi Nachman Schneider.

According to Rabbi David Cohen ("the Nazir"), the magnum opus that he edited, *Orot ha-Kodesh*, was conceived precisely to remedy the seemingly inchoate state of Rav Kook's thought. See the introduction to *Orot ha-Kodesh*, vol. 1 (Jerusalem: Mossad Harav Kook, 1985), p. 18; and the discussion in Shaḥar Raḥmani, *Li-Nevukhei ha-Dor* (Tel-Aviv: Yedioth Ahronoth, 2014), pp. 285-290.

One aspect of Rav Kook's system has received special attention. See *Orot ha-Kodesh*, ibid. pp. 20-21 (*"Hit'alut ha-'Olam"*), and vol. 2, pp. 529-534; Yosef Ben Shlomo, *"Shelemut ve-Hishtalmut be-Torat ha-Elohut shel Ha-Rav Kook," Iyyun*, vol. 33 (Tevet-Nissan 5744/1984), pp. 289-309; and Rabbi Matithyahu Kahn, *"Ha-Ein Sof ve-ha-Gevul, ve-ha-Sheleimut ve-ha-Hishtalmut."* I thank Rabbi Kahn for sharing with me his unpublished manuscript, in which he explores the relation of Rav Kook to the *Questions* of the medieval Kabbalist, Rabbi Azriel of Gerona. (Rabbi David Cohen recorded a conversation with Rav Kook, whereby the Rav pointed to Rabbi Azriel of Gerona as a source for his thoughts on spiritual evolution. The quote from Rabbi Azriel reads: "The *Ein Sof* is perfection without lack; and if you say that it has unlimited power but does not have limited power, then its perfection is lacking.") As I wrote to Rabbi Kahn, Rav Kook would certainly have been familiar with Rabbi Azriel's famous statement from Rabbi Meir ibn Gabbai's *'Avodat ha-Kodesh* I, beginning chapter 8; in turn, quoted by Rabbi Menaḥem Mendel Schneersohn of Lubavitch, *Derekh Mitsvotekha* (Poltava, 1911), *"Hallel," Shenat* 5611, 153a. Although there is no reason to assume that Rav Kook did not read Rabbi Meir ibn Gabbai's less popular work, *Derekh Emunah*. Rav Kook's teacher in Kabbalah, Rabbi Shelomo Eliashov, quotes the statement from *Derekh Emunah*, chap. 3. See *Mikhtevei Ba'al ha-Leshem*, in the preface to Rabbi Immanuel Ḥai Ricchi, *Mishnat Ḥasidim*, with commentary *Kesef Mishneh* by Rabbi Naftali Herz Halevi of Jaffa, ed. Shmuel Ya'akov Feffer (New York: Makhon ha-GRA, 2006), p. 57.

The manuscript of *Derekh Mitsvotekha* was lent to Rav Kook by his neighbor, Shneur Zalman Slonim, Rabbi of the ḤaBaD community of Jaffa. See *Iggerot la-RAYaH*, ed. Rabbi Benzion Shapira (Jerusalem: Makhon RZYH Kook, 1990), Letter 206 (pp. 313-314), in which Rabbi Slonim reminds Rav Kook that on one occasion he borrowed from him the manuscript of *"Sefer ha-Mitsvot le-ADMOR Ts[emaḥ] Ts[edek]."*

I see now that Rav Kook refers to Ibn Gabbai's *Derekh Emunah* (and Rabbi Azriel) in *Pinkesei ha-RAYaH*, vol. 3, *pinkas* 15, chap. 33 (p. 77).

Introduction

1 Born in Zeimel, Lithuania, in 1891, Tsevi Yehudah was all of twenty-two at this time.

2 See *Orot, Zer'onim*, chap. 3 (pp. 121-123).

3 Rabbi Ya'akov Moshe Ḥarlap's portrayal of the way in which "*neshamot she-ba-'olam ha-tohu*" ("souls that are in the World of Chaos") manifest in contemporary "*posh'ei Yisrael*" ("sinners of Israel") appears as a marked departure from his master Rav Kook's collective psychoanalysis:

> At the End of Days, it occurs that the inner desire for performance of all the commandments, surpasses every limit, and they cannot be satisfied with but a portion of the commandments. This is the source of all the spiritual destruction "that appears as a plague within the house" [cf. Leviticus 14:35] .... If they do not know how to "sweeten" the desire—it may on occasion cause us to act against our better judgment and that of our Maker, rendering us "drunk but not from wine" [cf. Isaiah 51:21]. And those are the sinners of Israel (*posh'ei Yisrael*) of our time.

The statement occurs in a letter penned by Rabbi Ḥarlap in 5706 (i.e., 1946) supporting the re-institution of the *mitsvah* of *Hakhel* (Assembly) at the conclusion of the sabbatical year (*shemitah*). (While yet in Lithuania, before assuming his position as Assistant Rabbi of Jerusalem, Rabbi Elijah David Rabinowitz-Te'omim [ADeReT], Rav Kook's father-in-law, advocated a commemorative *Hakhel* ceremony. See Rabbi Tsevi Yehudah Hakohen Kook, *Li-Netivot Yisrael*, vol. 1 [Beit El, 2002], "*Hakhel et ha-'Am,*" p. 70.) From a kabbalistic perspective, Rabbi Ḥarlap proposed that adoption of the commandment of *Hakhel* might indirectly help to cure the malady of the generation. His letter was published at the very end of volume 5 of *Mei Marom, Nimmukei ha-Mikra'ot*, 2nd edition (Jerusalem, 1981).

Perhaps even more perplexing, and certainly more provocative, is Rabbi Ḥarlap's assertion that the martyrs of the Holocaust were "*neshamot me-'olam ha-tohu*" ("souls of the World of Chaos"):

> All those who ascended on the pyre, were killed and stoned, strangled and burnt ... their souls from the World of Chaos are so great that the entire world could not contain them; their souls rose above and they are on such a level that the seraphim above cannot be with them in their division.

The passage occurs in a letter to Rabbi Baruch Duvdevani, a student of Rabbi Ḥarlap at Merkaz Harav, who acted as an emissary to the survivors of the Holocaust in displaced persons camps in Italy. The letter is datelined, "Jerusalem, 8 Tishri, 5707 [1946]." See *Iggerot Marom*, ed. Ya'ir Ḥarlap (Beit El, 2020), pp. 230-231.

4 Statement of Rabbi Abahu in *Genesis Rabbah* 3:7; 9:2. See Rabbi Menaḥem Recanati, Commentary to Torah (Venice, 1523), *Vayyishlaḥ*, s.v. *Ve-Eleh ha-melakhim* (Genesis 36:31); Rabbi Menaḥem Tsiyoni, Commentary to Torah (Cremona, 1560), *Vayyishlaḥ*, 25c-d, *Hagahah* (excerpted from Recanati) (for "'*olam she-neherag*," read "'*olam she-neḥerav*"); Rabbi Baḥya ben Asher ibn Ḥalawa, Commentary to Torah, ed. Chavel (Jerusalem: Mossad Harav Kook, 1971), vol. 1, Genesis 36:39 (pp. 301-302); Rabbi Zadok Hakohen of Lublin, *Peri Tsaddik*, vol. 1 (Lublin, 1901), *Vayyishlaḥ*, 53a.

Linguistically, I find fascinating the words of the anonymous author of *Sefer ha-Ḥinnukh* (commandment 87): "It is in His hand to return all of them [i.e., the creatures] with the rest of the world to *Tohu va-Vohu* (Chaos) by setting His desire on nullification (*be-hanaḥat ḥeftso be-bittul*), just as He created them by setting His desire on creation (*be-hanaḥat ḥeftso bi-beri'ah*)." This is definitely not idiomatic Hebrew.

Perhaps it reads better in Catalan. (The author was a Levite of Barcelona.)

5 See Rabbi Dov Baer of Lubavitch, *Torat Ḥayyim*, *Bereshit* (Brooklyn, NY: Kehot, 1993), *Bereshit*, 9a; *Vayyishlaḥ*, 187a, 191a; Rabbi Aharon Halevi Horowitz of Staroshelye, *'Avodat Halevi* (Lemberg, 1861; photo offset Jerusalem, 1972), *Vayyishlaḥ* 42c-d.

An alternate wording is: "In the World of *Tikkun*, the lights are few and the vessels numerous (*'orot mu'atin ve-kelim merubin*), and in [the World of] *Tohu*, the lights are numerous and the vessels few (*'orot merubim ve-kelim mu'atim*)" (Rabbi Isaac Dov Baer Schneerson of Lyady, *Siddur 'im Peirush MaHaRID* [Berdichev, 1913; photo offset Kefar Ḥabad, 1991], vol. 1, 45a, s.v. *gadol adoneinu*).

*

The intent of Rabbi Isaac Luria (ARI) was to interpret the myth of the Death of the Kings (*sod mitat ha-melakhim*) contained in the *Idra*, a work within the *Zohar*. However, left to its own resources, the tragedy of the *Idra* is the lopsidedness of the masculine force, and its *tikkun*, if you would have it, consists in the opposition of the feminine force to the masculine force, and the subsequent *mitkala*, or balance, of those two opposing dimensions. The concept of overwhelming light or energy does not occur in this myth (though it does occur elsewhere in the *Zohar*) and represents an innovation on the part of Rabbi Isaac Luria. See Yehuda Liebes, *Studies in the Zohar* (Albany: State University of New York Press, 1993), p. 125.

6 *Be'ur ha-GRA* on *Sifra di-Tseni'uta*, ed. Samuel Luria (Vilna, 1882), 2b, s.v. *lo havu mashgiḥin apin be-apin*. (In the *editio princeps* published by the Gaon's grandson, Rabbi Jacob Moses of Slonim [Vilna and Horadna, 1820], the passage occurs on 3b.) And see the almost identical language in *Be'ur ha-GRA* to *Tikkunim mi-Zohar Ḥadash* (Vilna, 1867), 27b, s.v. *ve-da memalel*. Finally, in the Gaon's commentary to the *Heikhalot* (*Heikhal* 6), the Gaon reiterates that which he wrote to *Tikkunei Zohar Ḥadash*; see *Yahel 'Or*, ed. Naftali Herz Halevi (Weidenbaum) (Vilna, 1882), *Pekudei*, 254b,

s.v. *zarik li-telat me'ah ve-'esrin 'eivar u-varir pesolet mi-go maḥshavah ve-'itbarir.*

[7] *b. Ḥagigah* 13b.

[8] Rabbi Shelomo Eliashov was perplexed by the Gaon's equation of the nine hundred and seventy-four generations with the *'Erev Rav* (Mixed Multitude). See his *Leshem, Shevo ve-Aḥlamah: Sefer ha-Kelalim*, Part One (Mishor Adumim: Barzani, 2010), *Kelalei Hitpashtut ve-Histalkut* 18:8 (p. 249, col. b).

The *Leshem* is emphatic that the nine hundred and seventy-four generations will eventually be corrected (*tikkun*) by the Holy One, blessed be He: "They are constantly reincarnating, reincarnation after reincarnation (*gilgul aḥar gilgul*), until they are corrected" (ibid.). According to the colophon, *Sefer ha-Kelalim* was completed by the author in Homel in 1921. It was first published in Jerusalem in 1926. In *Sefer ha-Kelalim*, the author references his earlier work, *Sefer ha-De'ah* (*Derushei 'Olam ha-Tohu*) (Piotrków, 1912), Part One, *Ma'amar Kelali*, par. 3 (2a-d); and Part Two, 4:17 (69d-73a).

It is highly conceivable that Rav Kook heard such ideas—at least in a seminal state—from Rabbi Eliashov when they studied together back in 1889. At that time, Rav Kook received permission from his community of Zeimel to spend a month studying Kabbalah with the master Rabbi Eliashov at his residence in Shavel. See Rabbi Moshe Tsevi Neriyah, *Siḥot ha-RAYaH* (Tel-Aviv, 1979), pp. 152, 159; and Yehudah Mirsky, *Towards the Mystical Experience of Modernity: The Making of Rav Kook, 1865-1904* (Boston: Academic Studies Press, 2021), p. 89.

(Although this is pure conjecture on my part, the title of our essay might have been inspired by the title of Rabbi Eliashov's work, *Derushei 'Olam ha-Tohu*, published the previous year. See Rav Kook's oblique reference to that work by "the greatest of the Kabbalists of the generation," in *Iggerot ha-RAYaH*, vol. 2, p. 114 [Letter 473, datelined "Jaffa, 17 Kislev, 5673"]. Receipt of Rabbi Eliashov's previous work, *Hakdamot u-She'arim* [Piotrków, 1908], was acknowledged in a letter to the author, datelined "Jaffa, 24 Tevet, 5669." See *Iggerot ha-RAYaH*, vol. 1

(2nd edition, Jerusalem: Mossad Harav Kook, 1962), pp. 236-237 [Letter 181]. In that letter, Rav Kook expresses his desire to see the as yet unpublished manuscripts of Rabbi Eliashov, and alludes to the deep spiritual bond that connects them, quoting Genesis 30:8.)

In his notes to the Gaon's commentary to *Sifra di-Tseni'uta* (15b, s.v. *u-ve-shem Yisrael yekhaneh*), Rabbi Elijah Ragoler of Kalisz backs up the prediction that the nine hundred and seventy-four generations will eventually return to holiness, with a *gematria*: "*u-ve-shem Yisrael yekhaneh*" ("and nickname himself by the name of Israel") (Isaiah 44:5) has the numerical value of 974. (These notes were published as an appendix to Samuel Luria's Vilna 1882 edition of *Sifra di-Tseni'uta*, 40b.)

In Rabbi Naftali Bacharach's *'Emek ha-Melekh*, several chapters were devoted to the topic of the rehabilitation of the nine hundred and seventy-four generations. See *'Emek ha-Melekh* (Amsterdam, 1648), *Sha'ar 'Olam ha-Tohu*, chaps. 30, 31, 35.

Earlier, Rabbi Moses Cordovero devoted a section to the rehabilitation of the nine hundred and seventy-four generations through reincarnation and purgatory; see Cordovero, *Shi'ur Komah* (Warsaw, 1883), chap. 60 ("*Boneh 'olamot u-maḥarivan*"), 66d-67b.

*

In a letter to RIDBaZ (a.k.a. Rabbi Ya'akov David Wilovsky), penned in 1913, Rav Kook predicted that eventually, the *'Erev Rav* (Mixed Multitude) too will be raised up, in fulfillment of Moses' aspiration. See *Iggerot ha-RAYaH*, vol. 2, p. 188.

For an earlier statement of Rav Kook concerning the "*'Erev Rav* (Mixed Multitude) who have been aroused in our days, the days of *'Ikva Meshiḥa* (the footsteps of Messiah)," see the letter to the ḤaBaD Ḥasid, Rabbi Eliezer Hakohen Bichovsky, in *Iggerot ha-RAYaH*, vol. 1, p. 161 (Letter 132). Rabbi Tsevi Yehudah Kook sources the statement in the *Be'ur ha-GRA* to *Tikkunim mi-Zohar Ḥadash*, 27b, s.v. *ve-da memalel.* See the additional notes at the end of volume 2 of *Iggerot ha-RAYaH*, p. 342.

[9] *b. Ḥagigah* 14a. According to this statement of Rabbi Simon the Pious, the original divine intention was that the Torah be given at the end of one thousand generations, as it says, "the word He commanded to a thousand generations" (Psalms 105:8), but seeing that the world could not last that long without Torah, the original plan was aborted and the Torah was given at the end of twenty-six generations (from Adam to Moses). The remaining nine hundred and seventy-four generations were then destined to be implanted in every generation. They are distinguished by their brazen character. See Rashi *ad loc.* And see Rashi, *Shabbat* 88b, s.v. *tesha' me'ot ve-shiv'im ve-arba'ah dorot.*

[10] Printed in *Zohar* III, 125b.

On the topic of despicable leaders, Rabbi Isaac of Komarno recorded a vision of the Ba'al Shem Tov that distressed him immensely:

> Our holy master... Rabbi Israel Ba'al Shem Tov, at the time of the afternoon prayer on the way, one time banged his head and plucked his hair, and said after, that he saw with his divine spirit (*ru'aḥ ha-kodesh*) that close to the Days of Messiah, there will be *rebbes* [as numerous] as poppy seeds (*yak mak*, Polish *jak mak*).
>
> (*Heikhal ha-Berakhah* [Lemberg, 1869], *Pekudei*, 318a)

The Komarner's illustration of improper *rebbes* are those who do not adhere to the prescribed times for prayer, reciting *shaḥarit* in the afternoon and *minḥah* at night!

A defense of this practice (of delaying the time of prayer), instituted by the *Yehudi ha-Kadosh* (i.e., Rabbi Jacob Isaac of Pshysucha, spelled in Polish, Przysucha), is found in Rabbi Mordechai Yosef Leiner of Izhbitsa (Polish, Izbica), *Mei ha-Shilo'aḥ*, vol. 2 (Lublin, 1922), *Beha'alotekha*, s.v. *'al pi Hashem yaḥanu* (29a).

The prime pupil of the Vilna Gaon, Rabbi Ḥayyim of Volozhin, derided the well-intentioned delay of prayer (and other commandments, as well). See *Nefesh ha-Ḥayyim*, ed. Yissachar Dov Rubin (B'nei Berak, 1989), chapters between Gates III-IV, chap. 4 (pp. 194-197).

[11] In addition to the aforementioned *Be'ur ha-GRA*, Rabbi Tsevi Yehudah drew attention to Rabbi Yitzḥak Eizik Ḥaver (Wildman)'s *Pitḥei She'arim* (Warsaw, 1888; photo offset Tel-Aviv, 1964), Part One, *Netiv Shevirat ha-Kelim*, chap. 17; and *Netiv 'Olam ha-Tikkun*, chap. 5 ("*nefashot shel 'Olam ha-Tohu*"). Rabbi Eizik Ḥaver is sometimes referred to as "the third mouth to the Vilna Gaon" ("*peh shelishi la-GRA*"), having studied under Rabbi Menaḥem Mendel of Shklov, a direct disciple of the Gaon.

Recently, Yosef Avivi has pointed out that the exact phraseology of Rav Kook, "*Neshamot shel 'Olam ha-Tohu*," occurs in Naftali Bacharach's *'Emek ha-Melekh* (Amsterdam, 1648), Author's Introduction, Second Introduction, chap. 2 (7a). See Yosef Avivi, *Kabbalat ha-RAYaH* (Jerusalem: Yad Yitzḥak Ben-Zvi, 2018), vol. 2, p. 604.

However, the context is the superiority of Lurianic Kabbalah over the earlier Cordoveran Kabbalah. Rabbi Moses Cordovero's teaching was designed for the "souls of the World of Chaos"; Rabbi Isaac Luria's teaching spoke to "the souls of the World of Establishment" ("*nishmot 'Olam ha-Tikkun*"). See further *'Emek ha-Melekh*, *Sha'ar 'Olam ha-Tohu*, chaps. 55-56 (32d-34a).

In an earlier statement of the superiority of Lurianic over Cordoveran Kabbalah, Rabbi Menaḥem Azariah of Fano wrote that the author of *Pardes Rimonim* taught of the *'Olam ha-Belimah* (of *Sefer Yetsirah*), while Rabbi Isaac Luria taught the fundamentals of the *Idra* and *Sifra di-Tseni'uta*, which are occupied with the *Mitkala* (Balance). See the Author's Introduction to *Pelaḥ ha-Rimon* (Venice, 1600), f. 4. *Pelaḥ ha-Rimon* is da Fano's commentary to Cordovero's *Pardes Rimonim*.

See too Meir Benayahu, *Toledot ha-ARI* (Jerusalem: Makhon Ben-Zvi, 1967), p. 100, n. 1; p. 158, adjacent to note 10.

Whatever the wording, the import of the statement is the superiority of the new Lurianic Kabbalah which provided for holographic *partsufim*, while the older Cordoveran Kabbalah was restricted to linear *sefirot*. See Rabbi David Cohen (the Nazir), *Kol ha-Nevu'ah*, (Jerusalem: Mossad Harav Kook, 1979), p. 209, n. 199.

However, the Nazir qualifies that though Cordovero's magnum opus, *Pardes Rimonim*, is restricted to *sefirot*, his later work, *Elimah*, does deal with *partsufim*. See *Kol ha-Nevu'ah*, pp. 209-210, and earlier p. 199, n. 174. Scholem, too, wrote that in *Elimah*, Cordovero has five "*temunot*"; see Gershom G. Scholem, *Major Trends in Jewish Mysticism* (New York: Schocken, 1971), p. 412, n. 78. (See our Appendix E concerning the *gematria* [numerical equivalence] "*partsuf Adam = temunah.*")

The entirety of Cordovero's voluminous commentary to *Zohar*, *'Or Yakar*, was unavailable to the Nazir. In his day, only the first three volumes, on *Parashat Bereshit*, were published from a manuscript. See *Kol ha-Nevu'ah*, p. 191, n. 146. Since then, besides *Elimah*, one can find in vol. 9, p. 136 of *'Or Yakar* (to *Zohar* II, 278b) reference to three (as opposed to Luria's five) *partsufim*: *Arikh Anpin*, *Ze'ir Anpin* and *Nukva*. (Omitted are *Abba* and *Imma*.) See Esther Liebes, "*Cordovero ve-ha-ARI—Beḥinah meḥudeshet shel mythos mitat malkhei Edom*," in *Ma'ayan 'Eyn Ya'akov le-Rabbi Moshe Cordovero* (*Ha-Ma'ayan ha-Revi'i mi-Sefer Elimah*), ed. Bracha Sack (Beer Sheva: Ben Gurion University Press, 2009), pp. 47, 60.

For historical details of da Fano's conversion from a Cordoveran Kabbalist to a Lurianic Kabbalist after the impactful encounter with the peripatetic and enigmatic figure, Rabbi Israel Sarug, see Robert Bonfil, "New Information on Rabbi Menaḥem Azariah da Fano and his Age" (Hebrew) in *Studies in the History of Jewish Society in the Middle Ages and in the Modern Period* (Jacob Katz *Festschrift*) (Jerusalem: Magnes, 1980), pp. 113-115.

12 Rabbi Tsevi Yehudah referenced *Torat Ḥayyim*, *Vayyishlaḥ*, s.v. *Vayyishlaḥ*, par. 9. He misattributed the work to Rabbi Shneur Zalman of Lyady (a common error), when in fact, the work is that of Rabbi Shneur Zalman's son, Rabbi Dov Baer

of Lubavitch (referred to as the "*Mitteler Rebbe*," or "Middle Rabbi"), compiled from transcripts of *ḥasidim*.

That portion of *Torat Ḥayyim* was first published in Warsaw in 1866. See A.M. Habermann, "*Sha'arei ḤaBaD*," in *'Alei 'Ayin* (Salman Schocken Jubilee Volume) (Jerusalem, 1948-1952), pp. 361-362, no. 291.

See now Rabbi Dov Baer [Shneuri], *Torat Ḥayyim, Bereshit* (Brooklyn, NY: Kehot, 1993), 184d-185a.

*

The figures of Esau and Jacob (which is to say, *Tohu* and *Tikkun*) were read back into the mythos of *Bereshit*. The Talmud (*b. Shabbat* 77b) records an exchange between Rabbi Zeira and Rav Yehudah (who was in a mirthful mood), whereby Rabbi Zeira asked why in a flock the goats walk ahead, followed by the sheep. To which, Rav Yehudah responded that they imitate the pattern of the creation of the world (*ki-beriyato shel 'olam*), when there was first darkness followed by light. (Rashi explains that generally the goats are black in color and the sheep are white.) Rabbi Dov Baer explains that the goat is symbolic of Esau, "Se'ir" (cf. Naḥmanides, Leviticus 16:8), and the sheep, symbolic of Jacob or Israel (Ezekiel 36:37-38). (In the latter regard, see also Ezekiel 34:17, 31.) See *Torat Ḥayyim, Vayyishlaḥ*, 185a; 189a-b.

Cf. Rabbi Yitzḥak Eizik Ḥaver, *Afikei Yam* (Jerusalem, 1994), *Shabbat* 77b, and idem, *Berit Yitzḥak*, ed. Samuel Luria (Warsaw, 1888), *Idra de-Mishpatim*, 5c-d.

13 Without entering into all the intricacies of Rav Kook's genealogical chart, suffice it to say that Rav Kook was the product of a "mixed marriage." His father's people were students of the famed Volozhin Yeshivah, founded by Rabbi Ḥayyim of Volozhin, the illustrious disciple of the Vilna Gaon; his mother's people were ḤaBaD Ḥasidim, whose particular allegiance was to the Kopyster branch of the movement, founded by Rabbi Judah Leib Schneerson of Kopyst, a son of Rabbi Menaḥem Mendel of Lubavitch (author of the responsa *Tsemaḥ Tsedek*).

In a letter to his fellow Lithuanian Kabbalist, Rabbi Pinḥas Hakohen Lintop of Birzh, Rav Kook expressed his fervent desire that by bridging the gap, a synthesis of the various schools would arise: "In the last generation, we regard as very lovely all the conversation of the disciples of the Gaon Rabbi Elijah together with the disciples of the Ba'al Shem Tov—who back in the day, were so opposed to one another" (*Iggerot ha-RAYaH*, vol. 1, Letter 266 [pp. 304-305]). The letter is datelined "Jaffa, 11 Shevat 5670 [i.e., 1910]."

The context of the letter is a clarification of Rav Kook's essay *"Derekh ha-Teḥiyah,"* which was recently published in the journal *Ha-Nir*. In that context, the Ḥasidism of the Ba'al Shem Tov represents the charismatic, pneumatic tradition of Judaism, while the Vilna Gaon represents the textual tradition or book-learning. An English translation of the essay, "The Way of Renascence," is available in *When God Becomes History: Historical Essays of Rabbi Abraham Isaac Hakohen Kook*, ed. Bezalel Naor (New York, NY: Kodesh Press, 2016), pp. 63-77.

In my edition of Rav Kook's commentary to *The Legends of Rabbah bar Bar Ḥannah* (New York: Orot/Kodesh, 2019), I discussed the eclectic nature of Rav Kook's Kabbalah. In this respect, he was "on the same page" as his friend Rabbi Pinḥas Hakohen Lintop of Birzh, Lithuania, who recommended a triangulation of RaMḤaL, the Vilna Gaon and ḤaBaD. See ibid. pp. 10, 19-20. Thus, Rav Kook stands out in opposition to Rabbi Shelomo Eliashov (author of *Leshem, Shevo ve-Aḥlamah*), who definitely was opposed to ḤaBaD (but also eschewed RaMḤaL), seeing himself as continuing the line of the Vilna Gaon and his disciple, Rabbi Ḥayyim of Volozhin.

Though there are those who, for whatever reason, engage in a form of historic revisionism, whereby they distance Rav Kook from the ḤaBaD tradition, the truth is that he was a "hybrid." Someone as impartial (and as caustic) as Rabbi Judah Leib Hakohen Maimon (Fishman) recounted this detail from his visit to Jaffa in 1908, at which time, he attended a public assembly celebrating the writing of a *Sefer Torah*:

All the rabbis of Jaffa, headed by Rav Kook, were gathered there. When I arrived, the celebration began. Rav Kook delivered a long speech in the Hebrew language. The contents of his speech were deep thoughts in the teaching of Ḥ aBaD (one of his specialties), without any relevance to the event of the day.

(*Igrot Harav Maimon*, vol. 1 [5656-5680/1896-1920], ed. Bick, Yosifon, Frankel and Reich [Jerusalem: Mossad Harav Kook, 1979], Letter 89 [datelined "Lag ba-'Omer 5668, Jerusalem"], p. 110)

[14] In common with Rabbi Moshe Ḥayyim Luzzatto, the heirs of the Vilna Gaon shared a temporal, as opposed to a spatial, approach to Kabbalah. Regarding the temporality of Luzzatto's Kabbalah, see Rabbi David Cohen, *Kol ha-Nevu'ah*, p. 306. And see Raphael B. Shuchat, "The Historiosophy of the Vilna Gaon and the Influence of Luzzatto on Him and His Disciples" (Hebrew), *Da'at* 40 (1998), pp. 125-152.

[15] *b. Sanhedrin* 97a; *'Avodah Zarah* 9a.

[16] See Rabbi Zadok Hakohen of Lublin, *Peri Tsaddik*, beginning *Vayyishlaḥ*.

[17] *Be'ur ha-GRA* on *Sifra di-Tseni'uta*, ed. Samuel Luria (Vilna, 1882), 2b; Rabbi Yitzḥak Eizik Ḥaver, *Pitḥei She'arim*, *Netiv Shevirat ha-Kelim*, chap. 17; and *Netiv 'Olam ha-Tikkun*, chap. 5. In *Be'ur ha-GRA* to *Tikkunim mi-Zohar Ḥadash*, 27b, s.v. *ve-da memalel*, there occurs the brief, barbed statement, "and now is the *Tohu*" ("*ve-akhshav hu ha-Tohu*").

[18] "The physical Esau is the prince of bloodshed ('By your sword shall you live') and harsh rigors (*gevurot kashot*), Edom—however, his root above is mighty, strong lights (*'orot takifim ve-ḥazakim*) of *Tohu* that precedes *Tikkun*" (*Torat Ḥayyim*, *Vayyishlaḥ*, 189a). See also 195b: "Esau represents the supernal rigors (*gevurot 'elyonot*) of *Tohu*."

Rabbi Naftali Herz Halevi (Weidenbaum), who preceded Rav Kook as Rabbi of Jaffa, wrote that the souls of the gentiles are from the World of Chaos (*'Olam ha-Tohu*) and the souls of Israel are from the World of Establishment (*'Olam ha-Tikkun*).

See Halevi's *Siddur ha-GRA* (Jerusalem, 1896-1898; photo offset Jerusalem, 1971), Part One, *Imrei Shefer*, 15a.

19 See Nathan of Gaza, *Sefer ha-Beri'ah*, ed. Leor Holzer (Jerusalem, 2019), pp. 336-338. Nathan juxtaposes this to the "mystery of the death of the Kings" (*"sod mitat ha-melakhim"*) (ibid. p. 337).

Nathan believed himself to be the reincarnation of Rabbi Isaac Luria, in fulfillment of Luria's promise before his death to come back and reveal further mysteries; see Benayahu, *Toledot ha-ARI*, p. 122, n. 4.

Rabbi Moshe Ḥayyim Luzzatto viewed the kabbalistic teachings of Nathan of Gaza the way that Rabbi Meir viewed the teachings of Elisha ben Avuyah (a.k.a. Aḥer, "the Other"): "Rabbi Meir found a pomegranate; its inside he ate, its peel, he threw away" (*b. Ḥagigah* 15b). See Simon Ginzburg, *Rabbi Moshe Ḥayyim Luzzatto u-v'nei doro* (collection of letters and documents) (Tel-Aviv: Dvir, 1937), vol. 1, p. 152. Quoted in Isaiah Tishby, *Paths of Faith and Heresy: Essays in Kabbalah and Sabbateanism* (Hebrew) (Jerusalem: Magnes, 1994), p. 171. The manuscripts of Nathan's works, *Sefer ha-Beri'ah* and *Zemir 'Aritsim*, were made available to Luzzatto by his teacher, Rabbi Isaiah Bassani of Padua. Ibid., pp. 170-172. Bassani's father-in-law, Rabbi Benjamin Cohen Vitale (RaBaKh) of Reggio, was a Sabbatian believer, or what I term a "crypto-Sabbatian." It should be stressed that in terms of observance, RaBaKh was strictly halakhic. His hidden belief in the Messiahhood of Shabbetai Tsevi did not express itself in antinomian behavior. In this respect—strict observance of Halakhah—the Italian school of Sabbatian Kabbalists differed from some other branches of the movement. See Bezalel Naor, *Post-Sabbatian Sabbatianism* (Spring Valley, NY: Orot, 1999), pp. 49-52, 175-177.

Unaware of Nathan's Kabbalah, Rav Kook arrived independently at the notion that *Tohu* represents the dark, destructive side of existence and of human personality, while *Tikkun* represents the radiant, constructive aspect. See further *Shemonah Kevatsim* 1:172, 173.

[20] *b. Yoma* 78b; Rabbi Yitzḥak Eizik Halevi Epstein of Homel, *Ḥannah Ariel* (Israel: Kehot, 2019), vol. 1, *Noaḥ*, pp. 43-44. Rabbi Eizik equates *'Olam ha-Tohu* and *Nekudim* with *Katnut*.

My presentation of the passage in *Ḥannah Ariel* is a simplification. For the complexity and convolution of the author's thought, one would do well to consult the passage directly.

[21] Genesis 17:1.

[22] *b. Hagigah* 12a.

[23] Rabbi Gershon Ḥanokh Leiner of Radzyn, *Sod Yesharim*: *Rosh Hashanah* (Warsaw, 1902), par. 54 (31c). See earlier par. 48 (28b), and par. 67 (38d) where "the worlds that were destroyed" are opposed to the *'Olam ha-Tikkun*.

(In the Cyrilic, the title reads, "*Tiferes Hagershuni.*" Perhaps this was the original title of the work, which was subsequently changed to "*Sod Yesharim.*" Rabbi Gershon Ḥanokh's commentary on the *Zohar* is entitled "*Tif'eret ha-Ḥanokhi.*")

Cf. *Pinkesei ha-RAYaH*, vol. 1 (Jerusalem: Makhon RZYH Kook, 2008), *Pinkas* 7, chap. 60 (p. 430).

[24] Rabbi Joseph Isaac Schneersohn, *Sefer ha-Siḥot 5701* (Brooklyn, NY: Kehot, 1964), p. 97. For the sake of clarification, Rabbi Joseph Isaac Schneersohn (1880-1950) was quoting his great-grandfather, Rabbi Menaḥem Mendel Schneersohn of Lubavitch (1789-1866), known after the title of his work of halakhic responsa as "*Tsemaḥ Tsedek.*" The latter was referring to the spiritual transformation wrought by *his* grandfather, Rabbi Shneur Zalman of Lyady, referred to in Lubavitch as the "*Alter Rebbe*" ("Old Rabbi") (1745-1812).

Rabbi Mikhel Opotzker (after his birthplace Opotzk) is described in the *siḥah* as an outstanding Torah scholar who, at an advanced age, became a *ḥasid* of the *Alter Rebbe*. See ibid. pp. 96-97. It is difficult, therefore, to glean in what sense Rabbi Mikhel Opotzker was transformed by the *Alter Rebbe* from a "*tohu'diker*" to a "*tikkun'nik.*" Evidently, in popular Ḥasidic sociology, the term "chaotic soul" carried a different nuance than that ascribed to it by Rav Kook.

An excerpt from a *ma'amar* of the great ḤaBaD thinker, Rabbi Eizik of Homel, will put things into proper perspective:

> Sometimes there come into this world souls from the World of *Tohu*. Without any knowledge or study, his soul burns with ardor for the LORD, and he throws away all worldly matters, paying no attention to his honor and the honor of his ancestors, and the laws of etiquette (*nimmusei derekh 'erets*). And this is really the "mighty lights" (*'orot takifin*) of *Tohu*, untouched by the hands of "Adam" of *Tikkun*. [This soul] was brought to this world to be corrected precisely with intellect and character traits; and thought, speech and action, arranged according to wisdom and divine reason and the *nomoi* of Torah, and preceded by the laws of etiquette (*hilkhot derekh 'erets*). Before this soul is corrected in this world, it is possible that he will do things that are irrational, but they all "proceed from a holy place" [Ecclesiastes 8:10]. However, this is so only when he is still beyond reason, but if his "mighty lights" have already been mitigated by reason, then he is obligated to contain his words and ways judiciously, and if not, he will damage his holiness, God forbid. Likewise, while he is still in a state beyond reason, [it is his obligation] that all his ways be extensions of the holiness of his godly soul, i.e., no infraction of the three hundred and sixty-five negative commandments must come about through him, for the negative commandments damage every soul of Israel.
>
> (Rabbi Yitzḥak Eizik Halevi Epstein of Homel, *Ḥannah Ariel* [Israel: Kehot, 2019], vol. 2, *Ḥukkat*, p. 720)

Rabbi Eizik of Homel's portrayal of a "soul from the World of Chaos" is of a law-abiding Jew, whose unbridled passion for God is likely to take him beyond the pale of civilized behavior. His "*tikkun ha-neshamah*" ("correction of the soul") consists in tempering the primitive passion with reason and the trappings of civilization.

[25] See Yehoshua B. Be'ery, *Ohev Yisrael bi-Kedushah*, vol. 4, chap. 25 ("*Ha-RAYaH Kook ve-ha-Sofer Sh.Y. Agnon*"), pp. 139-156; Jeffrey Saks, "A Portrait of Two Artists at the Crossroads: Between Rav Kook and S.Y. Agnon," *Tradition* 49:2 (2016), pp. 32-52.

[26] The term occurs toward the end of Agnon's story, "*'Agunot*" (Jaffa, 1908). "*'Olam ha-Tohu*" was translated into English by Baruch Hochman as "world of confusion." See *A Book That Was Lost and Other Stories by S.Y. Agnon*, ed. Alan Mintz and Anne Golomb Hoffman (New York: Schocken, 1995), p. 47.

Rabbi Jeffrey Saks informs me that Agnon used the phrase "*'Olam ha-Tohu*" in later works as well, including *Ve-Hayah he-'akov le-mishor* (Jaffa, 1912), which Rav Kook read in manuscript.

[27] See Elḥanan Shilo, *Ha-Kabbalah bi-Yetsirat S.Y. Agnon* (Ramat Gan: Bar-Ilan University, 2011).

[28] See Rabbi Abraham Isaac Hakohen Kook, *Shemonah Kevatsim* (*Eight Journals*), 2nd edition, vol. 1 (Jerusalem, 2004), 1:265, 297, 135, 243.

[29] See *Shemonah Kevatsim* 1:243.

[30] This work, suppressed for well over a century, formed the basis for Shaḥar Raḥmani's doctoral dissertation under Dov Schwartz at Bar-Ilan University. The manuscript was an untitled work that had been referred to in the past as "The New Guide of the Perplexed" ("*Moreh Nevukhim he-Ḥadash*"). Raḥmani gave it the title *Li-Nevukhei ha-Dor* (*For the Perplexed of the Generation*). It was brought out in Tel-Aviv in 2014 by Yedi'ot Aḥaronot. For the fascinating history of the work, see Raḥmani's introduction. He dates it to Rav Kook's last year or so in Boisk (Bauska). That would be 1903-1904. See Shaḥar Raḥmani, *Li-Nevukhei ha-Dor*, Introduction, p. 18; Yosef Avivi, *Kabbalat ha-RAYaH*, vol. 2, p. 598; Yehudah Mirsky, *Towards the Mystical Experience of Modernity: The Making of Rav Kook, 1865-1904*, p. 287.

[31] Hebrew, "*mussar 'avadim*." The allusion to Nietzsche is transparent. (See Avivi, vol. 2, pp. 599-600.) In the original German, Nietzsche's term was "*Sklavenmoral*."

The German vintage *"Sklavenmoral"* has been preserved in a letter of Rabbi Tsevi Yehudah Kook datelined "St. Gallen [Switzerland], 27 Kislev [1915]," published in his collected letters, *Tsemaḥ Tsevi*, vol. 1 (5667-5679) (Jerusalem, 1991), p. 181. (For the provenance and background of this particular letter, see in this volume my review of Ḥagay Shtamler's *Eight Letters.*) For my own experience confronting Rabbi Tsevi Yehudah with the Nietzschean elements in his father's *oeuvre*, see my introduction to *Orot* (bilingual edition, Orot/Maggid, 2015), pp. 61-62.

32 Hebrew, *ha-shiga'on ha-ge'oni*, literally "madness of genius." There was a common saying that there is a fine line between *ga'on* (genius) and *shiga'on* (madness). Undoubtedly, Rav Kook was referring to Nietzsche's madness. Indeed, Mirsky (p. 295) translates, "mad genius." I prefer to translate the coinage as "megalomania."

33 Literally, "shells" or "husks." A kabbalistic term for the realm of evil.

34 Hebrew, *Ḥokhmat Yisrael.* Unlike its usage in the literature of the Haskalah movement, where it serves as a Hebrew rendition of *Wissenschaft des Judentums*, Rav Kook intends it here as a synonym for Kabbalah.

35 *Li-Nevukhei ha-Dor*, p. 152.

36 The common denominator of antinomianism and a break from conventional morality, is what, in Rav Kook's mind, links Shabbetai Tsevi and Nietzsche: "Shabbetai Tsevi, may the name of the wicked rot, was the analog to Nietzsche as Judaism relates to general humanity; and just as this one [i.e., Nietzsche] went mad, this one [i.e., Shabbetai Tsevi] went away from his religion. One *kelipah* attributable to the 'footsteps of Messiah'" (*Pinkas Aḥaron be-Boisk*, par. 40, in *Kevatsim mi-Ketav Yad Kodsho*, ed. Boaz Ofen, vol. 1 [Jerusalem, 2006], p. 56). And see Rav Kook's remarks concerning the moral depravity of the Sabbatians in his response to Rabbi Samuel Alexandrov; in *Iggerot ha-RAYaH*, vol. 1, p. 174 (Letter 140).

37 The loanword *psychit* occurs in the Hebrew.

38 *Li-Nevukhei ha-Dor*, p. 152.

Avivi assumes that either directly or indirectly, Rav Kook was responding to the Hebraic Nietzscheanism of Micha Yosef Berdichevsky. See Avivi, vol. 2, pp. 600-603.

According to Rabbi Tsevi Yehudah, his father encountered Berdichevsky in their student days in the Volozhin Yeshivah. Berdichevsky confessed to Avraham Yitzḥak Kook that his disenchantment with traditional Judaism went back to a bizarre scene he witnessed, when Berdichevsky's grandfather, an elderly erudite rabbi, was spoken to in a less than deferential manner by his adolescent Ḥasidic *rebbe* known as the "*Yenuka*" ("Infant"). The *Yenuka* inquired: "*Nu, bist eppes a yerei shomayim?*" "Are you a bit God-fearing?" This anecdote was told to me by Rabbi Tsevi Yehudah. The wording recorded by Lifshitz differs slightly. For more details of the meeting between A.Y. Kook and M.Y. Berdichevsky, see my edition of *Orot*, p. 533, n. 395; and Ḥayyim Lifshitz, *Shivḥei ha-RAYaH* (Jerusalem: Nezer David, 1995), pp. 46-47. (See also Abraham Jacob Brawer, in Yehoshua B. Be'ery, *Ohev Yisrael bi-Kedushah*, vol. 5, p. 67.)

I long assumed that the unnamed *Yenuka* was the Rebbe of Stolin, Rabbi Yisrael Perlov. Lately, I tend to think that it may have been Rabbi Menaḥem Naḥum Twersky, the Rebbe of Talne-Tulchin. Geographically, that makes more sense. Berdichevsky was from Dubova (near Uman), which is in the region of Podolia, as is Talne (pronounced by the Jews of the region as "Tolna"). In 1882, Berdichevsky, newlywed, went to live with his in-laws in Teplyk, another town in that vicinity. Stolin, on the other hand, is nowhere near Podolia, rather in Belarus in the vicinity of Pinsk-Karlin. Upon the passing of his famed grandfather, Rabbi David Twersky of Talne (author of *Magen David*) in 1882, Menaḥem Naḥum, aged thirteen (celebrating his *bar mitsvah*) was named his successor as Talner Rebbe.

Chronologically, there is no significant difference between the *Yenuka* of Stolin and the *Yenuka* of Talne. The Stoliner was a few months older than the Talner. The Stoliner too was formally installed as Rebbe upon his *bar mitsvah*, at the end of 1881. Berdichevsky (the same age as Rav Kook), was born in 1865.

[39] The verse in Daniel 11:14 begins: "And the children of the rebels of your people shall lift themselves up…" (*"U-v'nei paritsei 'amkha yinnass'u…"*).

For an intimate portrait of Berdichevsky, see Chaim Tchernowitz (Rav Tza'ir), *Masekhet Zikhronot: Partsufim ve-Ha'arakhot* (*Book of Memoirs: Portraits and Appraisals*) (New York, 1945), pp. 217-229. On page 219, there is a bibliography of Berdichevsky's rabbinic articles that appeared in *HaMisdaronah* (edited by Rabbi Ḥayyim Hirschensohn of Jerusalem) in the year 1888.

[40] Genesis 36:31.

[41] Ibid. verses 32-39.

Rav Kook alludes to the mystery of the Death of the Kings found in the *Idra* (and *en passant* in *Sifra di-Tseni'uta*). At the conclusion of *Parashat Vayyishlaḥ*, there is a roster of eight kings of Edom who reigned before the establishment of the kingdom in Israel. In regard to the first seven, it is written "and he died." Only in regard to the eighth king, Hadar, is this tone of finality not sounded. The seven kings who die symbolize the *'Olam ha-Tohu* (World of Chaos), which is unstable and doomed to destruction. The eighth king, Hadar, symbolizes the new world order of *Tikkun* (Establishment). The secret of the stability of *Tikkun* is its balance (*mitkala*), symbolized by the fact that in regard to Hadar—and only Hadar—is there mention of a wife: "And the name of his wife [was] Meheitavel…." For the *Idra*, balance (*mitkala*) is achieved by the psychodynamic of male and female, husband and wife. See *Idra Rabba* in *Zohar* III, 135, 142a; *Idra Zuta* in *Zohar* III, (290a), 292. Also *Zohar* I, 223b.

Rabbi Isaac Hutner interpreted Psalms 149:6-9 as reflective of the Zoharic myth of the Death of the Kings and the unique role of Hadar. See *Be'ur Sifra di-Tseni'uta mi-Ba'al Paḥad Yitzḥak*, ed. Rabbis Shelomo Carlebach and Aharon Y. Cohen, p. 70. See earlier RSZ of Lyady, *Siddur 'im DAḤ*, 69c-d, s.v.

La'asot bahem mishpat katuv; and *Siddur MaHaRID*, vol. 1, 58b-59a, s.v. *La'asot bahem mishpat katuv.*

The great Baghdadi Kabbalist, Rabbi Yosef Ḥayyim (*"Ben Ish Ḥai"*) lumps together the narratives of "the sister of Lotan, Timna" (Genesis 36:23), "Timna was the concubine of Eliphaz" (Genesis 36:12), and "These are the kings who reigned in the Land of Edom" (Genesis 36:31), as examples of stories of the Torah which seem superfluous, and which King Menasseh made light of (*b. Sanhedrin* 99b). See Rabbi Yosef Ḥayyim, *Benayahu*, vol. 3, ed. Yeshu'ah Salem (Jerusalem, 1990), *y. Rosh Hashanah* 3:5 (213b), s.v. *Haytah ka-'oniyot soḥer.* To set the record straight, Menasseh mocked only the first two verses. It seems that the *"Ben Ish Ḥai"* wrote under the influence of Maimonides' *Guide* 3:50, where the last verse concerning the Kings of Edom is juxtaposed to Menasseh's mockery. Needless to say, when Maimonides refers (ibid., beginning chapter 50) to these stories as *"Sitrei Torah"* ("Secrets of the Torah") he does not allude to the mysteries of the *Idra.*

En passant, a legend that lends itself to Lurianic interpretation, is that concerning the establishment of the *Mishkan*, or Tabernacle, in the Wilderness. Every day throughout the Seven Days of Installation (*Shiv'at Yemei ha-Millu'im*), Moses would put the Tabernacle up, only to take it down. It was not until the eighth day that this process of assembly and disassembly, construction and deconstruction ceased, leaving a permanent structure. As the *Mishkan* is famously a microcosm of the universe, its assembly and disassembly is a transparent trope for "building worlds and destroying them." See *Sifra*, end *Mekhilta de-Millu'im*; *y. Yoma* 1:1; *Numbers Rabbah* 12:9; Rashi, Numbers 7:1; Rabbi Ḥayyim Vital, *Likkutei Torah* (Vilna, 1880), *Shemini*, 74a; and *Sefer ha-Likkutim* (Jerusalem, 1913), end *Vayyakhel*; Rabbi Yitzhak Eizik Ḥaver (Wildman), *Pitḥei She'arim* (Warsaw, 1888; photo offset Tel-Aviv, 1964), Part One, *Netiv Shevirat ha-Kelim*, chap. 29, n. 26 (f. 63); *Netiv 'Olam ha-Tikkun*, chap. 16 (72b).

In this regard, one notes with interest the commentary of the great Kabbalist, Rabbi Isaac Safrin of Komarno, to

Torat Kohanim (i.e., *Sifra*), *'Assirit ha-'Eifah* (Lemberg, 1849), *Tsav*, 61b, par. 36. Invoking the myth of "*shevirat ha-kelim*" (the shattering of the vessels), the Komarner explains the dissenting opinion of Rabbi Yosé ben Rabbi Judah that Moses disassembled the *Mishkan* on the eighth day as well, by having recourse to the verse in 1 Chronicles 1:51 where the eighth king (Hadad for Hadar) too dies.

For further thoughts of the Komarner concerning the death of Hadar (i.e., Hadad) in Chronicles, see *Heikhal ha-Berakhah* (Lemberg, 1869), *Tsav*, 52a.

Rabbi Meir Leibush Wisser (Malbim) offered a simple solution to the discrepancy between Genesis 36:39 and 1 Chronicles 1:51. When Moses wrote the Torah, Hadar yet lived; by the time that Ezra the Scribe wrote Chronicles, Hadar or Hadad had already died. See Malbim's commentary to Chronicles, *Yemei Kedem*; and Rabbi Zadok Hakohen, *Peri Tsaddik*, vol. 1 (Lublin, 1901), *Vayyishlaḥ*, 53a. Also, Rabbi Yitzḥak Eizik Ḥaver, *Netiv 'Olam ha-Tikkun*, chap. 26, *Beit Netivot*, note 30 (79a).

42 *Li-Nevukhei ha-Dor*, p. 154.

43 By Rav Kook's own estimation, he was gifted with the ability to intuit the latent good tucked away in the souls of some sinners of Israel (*posh'ei Yisrael*). When accused by his contemporary, RIDBaZ, the Rabbi of Safed, of embracing sinners, Rav Kook (then Rabbi of Jaffa) responded in a well-known letter that he is selective as to which sinners he attracts: "The LORD knows that I do not attract all the sinners—only those I feel a great peculiar power (*ko'aḥ seguli*) lies in their interior. And there are many ways by which this knowledge comes about..." (*Iggerot ha-RAYaH*, vol. 2, p. 188 [Letter 555]).

44 See *Shemonah Kevatsim* 1:74 (= *Orot ha-Kodesh*, vol. 3, p. 129); 3:336 (= *Orot ha-Kodesh*, vol. 4, pp. 516-517); 6:144 (= *Orot ha-Kodesh*, vol. 4, p. 517). And see the discussion in Benjamin Ish-Shalom, *Rabbi Abraham Isaac Kook—Between Rationalism and Mysticism* (Hebrew) (Tel Aviv: Am Oved, 1990), pp. 150-151, 259-260.

45 *Li-Nevukhei ha-Dor*, p. 158.

[46] Hosea 14:10. See *b. Nazir* 23a; *Horayot* 10b.

[47] Specifically in regard to Abraham, see *b. Yoma* 28b and *Kiddushin* 82a. For a broader discussion, inclusive of Isaac and Jacob, see the rabbinic sources cited in Rabbi Judah Löw (MaHaRaL) of Prague, *Tif'eret Yisrael*, chap. 19.

This call to emulate the level of observance of the Patriarchs before the giving of the Torah on Mount Sinai should sound the alarm in the mind of a Talmudist. The principle clearly enunciated by Rabbi Ḥanina states: "One who is commanded and does, is greater than one who is not commanded and does" (*b. Kiddushin* 31a; *Bava Kamma* 38a; 87a; *'Avodah Zarah* 3a).

Fortunately, we have statements attributed to Rav Kook that may clear things up.

First, his disciple Rabbi Ḥayyim Zevulun Ḥarlap (son of Rabbi Ya'akov Moshe Ḥarlap) quotes Rav Kook as saying: "The 'not commanded' (*eino metsuveh*) of the Patriarchs is more beautiful than our 'commanded' (*metsuveh*)." See Rabbi Ḥayyim Zevulun Ḥarlap, *Be'er Ḥayyim* (n.p., 1995), p. 99. This passage occurs in a letter (datelined "Jerusalem, *Tu bi-Shevat* 5681," i.e., 1921) to his older brother Rabbi Yeḥiel Mikhel Ḥarlap in New York. The sprawling letter is an attempt to interpret the intriguing saying of the Rabbis: "The conversation of the servant of the Patriarchs is more beautiful than the Torah of the children" (*Genesis Rabbah* 60:8). Rav Kook's delphic pronouncement is thrown in for support. See ibid. pp. 98-101. (By the way, though innumerable interpretations have been offered for the rabbinic maxim, Rabbi Joshua ibn Shu'aib understood it simply as a tribute to the wisdom and exalted stature of Eliezer, servant of Abraham. See *Derashot Rabbi Joshua Ibn Shu'aib*, ed. Rabbi Ze'ev Metzger [Jerusalem, 1992], *Ḥayyei Sarah*, p. 45.)

The identical statement was uttered by Rav Kook at a Third Meal discourse, *Parashat Lekh Lekha*, 5690 (i.e., 1929), as recorded by his student Rabbi Kalman Eliezer Frankel. See Frankel's *Shemu'ot RAYaH*, Part One: *Bereshit* (Jerusalem, 1939), p. 26: "The aspect of the Patriarchs was a greater, higher aspect than 'commanded and does' (*metsuveh ve-'oseh*)."

Independently of his master Rav Kook, Rabbi Ya'akov Moshe Ḥarlap wrote that the Torah and Israel are essentially one, and therefore, in truth no *kabbalah*, or formal acceptance of the Torah, was required of Israel at Mount Sinai. That formality actually represents a spiritual demotion. By definition, *kabbalah* (acceptance) implies that the two entities (Torah and Israel) are capable of existing apart from one another. See Rabbi Ya'akov Moshe Ḥarlap, *Mei Marom*, vol. 8 (*Bereshit*) (Jerusalem, 1994), *Noaḥ*, *ma'amar* 8 (pp. 28-29); and *ma'amar* 10 (p. 35). In this way, the thoughts of the son, Ḥayyim Zevulun Ḥarlap, and the father, Ya'akov Moshe Ḥarlap, dovetail. Furthermore, the latter asserts (highly reminiscent of Rav Kook) that the generation's removal from the formal command stems from its aspiration to emulate the Patriarchs who kept the Torah before its giving at Mount Sinai. See Rabbi Ya'akov Moshe Ḥarlap, *Mei Marom: Razi Li* (vol. 18 of the *Mei Marom* series) (Jerusalem: Beit Zevul, 2012), s.v. *Nefilat ha-Dorot*, pp. 88-89.

48 *Li-Nevukhei ha-Dor*, p. 158.

49 Statement of Rav Yosef in *Niddah* 61b; *Iggerot ha-RAYaH*, vol. 1, p. 51 (Letter 44). Cf. *Li-Nevukhei ha-Dor*, p. 55.

This discussion of "*mitsvot beteilot le-'atid lavo*" is one aspect of the extensive correspondence between Rav Kook and Rabbi Samuel Alexandrov of Bobruisk. See further *Iggerot ha-RAYaH*, vol. 1, pp. 173-177 (Letter 140). And see Rabbi Judah Löw, *Tif'eret Yisrael*, chaps. 52-53. In vol. 2 of *Iggerot ha-RAYaH*, pp. 250-251 (Letter 630), there is a different, lengthy discussion of "*mitsvot beteilot le-'atid lavo.*"

In *Li-Nevukhei ha-Dor*, beginning chapter 51 (p. 249), as proof that the future goal of Israel and humanity is to achieve autonomous—as opposed to heteronomous—morality, Rav Kook quotes two verses: " … I shall place My Torah in their midst and write it upon the tablet of their heart … " (Jeremiah 31:32); "And no longer shall a man teach his friend, and a man his brother, saying, 'Know the LORD,' for all of them shall know Me, from their small to their great" (Ibid. verse 33).

50 Statement of Rabbi Yannai son of Rabbi Shim'on in *Song of Songs Rabbah* 1:3, s.v. *Le-rei'aḥ shemanekha tovim.*

See now *Metsi'ot Katan*, par. 240 (in *Pinkesei ha-RAYaH*, vol. 7, pp. 95-100 [especially p. 98, n. 32]; in Beit El edition of 2018, pp. 379-381, especially p. 381).

51 *Shemu'ot RAYaH*: *Sefer Bereshit*, ed. Rabbi Kalman Eliezer Frankel, *Toledot* 5690 [i.e., 1929], pp. 49-50, 53.

52 In a letter to Rabbi Samuel Alexandrov of Bobruisk, datelined "Jaffa, 13 Kislev 5667 (i.e., 1906)," Rav Kook sounded a harsh rejoinder: "Not to Kant shall we return, but to the Reed Sea, to Sinai, to Jerusalem, to Abraham, to Moses, to David, to Rabbi Akiva and to Rabbi Shim'on ben Yoḥai, and to all our beloved, who are our life and the joy of our heart for ever and ever" (*Iggerot ha-RAYaH*, vol. 1, p. 48 [Letter 44]).

An English translation of this fascinating and lengthy letter is available in Tzvi Feldman, *Rav A.Y. Kook: Selected Letters* (Ma'aleh Adumim, 1986), pp. 80-107. The quote occurs there on pp. 94-95.

For the classic medieval discussion of the advantage of autonomous morality over heteronomous morality, see the sixth of Maimonides' *Eight Chapters* (Maimonides' introduction to Tractate *Avot*).

For critiques of Kant's epistemology by disciples of Rav Kook, see Rabbi Ya'akov Moshe Ḥarlap, *Mei Marom*: *Razi Li*, p. 202; and Rabbi David Cohen, *Kol ha-Nevu'ah*: *Ha-Higayon ha-'Ivri ha-Shim'i* (Jerusalem: Mossad Harav Kook, Jerusalem, 1979), pp. 113-114.

53 Earlier, in 1906, just a couple of years after his arrival in Jaffa, Rav Kook published a collection of essays entitled *'Ikvei ha-Tson* (*The Footsteps of the Flock*). The title was taken from the verse in Song of Songs 1:8: "If you do not know, fairest among women, go forth in the footsteps of the flock, and tend your kids by the shelters of the shepherds." The motto of the book reads, "*Go forth in the footsteps of the flock*—This teaches that the Holy One, blessed be He, showed Moses all the leaders of Israel until the last generation, until the heel (*'ekev*)."

The Midrash is not found in *Song of Songs Rabbah*, but in *Yalkut Shim'oni*, Song of Songs, par. 982. Rav Kook's wording differs slightly from that of the *Yalkut*: "*Go forth in the footsteps of the flock*—This teaches that the Holy One, blessed be He, showed Moses all the pastors and leaders of Israel until the heel (*'ekev*), until the end of all generations."

[54] The reference is to Rav Kook's defining sentence in the first of the chapters of *Zer'onim*, "Thirst for a Living God": "Our resting place is only in God." Reprinted in the 1950 edition of *Orot*, p. 119.

[55] Ibid. This coinage of Rav Kook, *"ha-teiruf ha-kal'i,"* conjures the kabbalistic imagery of the *"kaf ha-kela',"* or "slingshot," the drivenness, the psychic torture that awaits errant souls. See *Zohar* III, 25a: "Woe to those wicked ones whose soul does not merit this world, all the more so the world to come. Regarding them, it is written, 'the soul of your enemies will be shot in a sling' [1 Samuel 25:29], for they go wandering in the world and find no place of rest to connect to."

[56] Hebrew, *"Yissurim Memarkim."* This is the fifth chapter of *Zer'onim*, since 1950 appended to *Orot*. See there, pp. 124-129.

[57] Yosef Ḥayyim Brenner in *Ha-Aḥdut*, 1914, no. 9; quoted in Ish-Shalom, p. 39.

[58] Earlier, in 1906, Tsevi Yehudah Kook sent a copy of his father's recently published work, *'Ikvei ha-Tson*, to Brenner, then residing in London, requesting that he review it in his literary journal, *Ha-Me'orer*. In the cover letter, Tsevi Yehudah (aged fifteen) described the author:

> My father, the author, is an Orthodox rabbi. Besides his genius in "Torah," he also merited a reputation as a "*Tsaddik*." And with that, he is a free philosopher in the full sense of the word. There is no block before him. He investigated in depth the theories of the philosophers of the nations, and penetrated the foundations of our Torah, even arriving at the chambers of Kabbalah.
>
> With a torn and burning heart, he beheld the brokenness of his beloved people, torn as it is to pieces. He recognized the source of all the evils in

the ignorance of brothers, in their distance from, and unfamiliarity with, one another. There is lacking a clear, truthful recognition of each other's [spiritual] wealth and aspirations.

For example: At one extreme, Judaism has become synonymous with hatred of life, unworldliness, et cetera, and [at the other extreme] secular education and living aspirations have become synonymous—in the eyes of the old—with disbelief, heresy and "revulsion for the sacred"... and the rift that has resulted from this has expanded, until our present condition, which is unprecedented. Never was there such a condition!

Three years ago, he came to Erets Yisrael, and saw the full ugliness of this rift. He directed his efforts to ascending the public platform and to work for the good of his people with all his strength. With a literary pen, he publishes his thoughts in various forms and various venues, and with learned language, he speaks with whomever he deems worthy. He speaks and writes relentlessly. And despite his many detractors—mostly from the older generation—he has already accomplished much, relatively speaking.

For example: Here in Jaffa, in the "Talmud Torah" that he took under his wing, he established a workshop to teach the youngsters a trade. One who dwells in the Land and sees the situation, knows how great a step this is.

Individuals among the young have responded to his voice—even in the Diaspora. His influence on the new generation, who recognize his uniqueness, is very great. He stands as the central pillar between the two sides, planting the good in each, while attempting to bring them close and introduce them to one another. And his vantage point: Understanding the essence of Judaism and its particulars, together with its commentators and elucidators.

> And for this purpose, he composed... the book sent to you. I divide this book into two sections: The first, addressed to the older generation... to allow them to understand that even in our militant youngsters there is a good portion, as it were... and the second section, addressed to the younger generation... to make comprehensible to them and to familiarize them with the old Judaism.

Tsevi Yehudah adds that the final two chapters of the book—"Knowledge of God" and "Service of God"—have their basis in a lecture of Professor Hermann Cohen that was published—in Hebrew translation—in *Ha-Shilo'aḥ* 13:4 (Nissan 1904). For details of Cohen's lecture, see Ish-Shalom, p. 266, n. 11.

The letter to Brenner is the first in Rabbi Tsevi Yehudah Kook's collected letters. See *Tsemaḥ Tsevi*, vol. 1 (1906-1919), pp. 1-2. A facsimile of the handwritten letter is available in Yehoshua B. Be'ery, *Ohev Yisrael bi-Kedushah*, vol. 5, pp. 19-25.

In 1925, the Warsaw journalist (and mystic) Hillel Zeitlin interviewed Rav Kook (and his opposite number, Rabbi Yosef Ḥayyim Sonnenfeld) in Jerusalem. When Zeitlin challenged Rav Kook's romanticization of the secular *ḥalutsim*, Rav Kook responded: "I read your eulogy for Brenner." Zeitlin failed to follow Rav Kook's response. "You praised Brenner though he attacked religious Judaism." When Zeitlin parried that Brenner was different, Rav Kook shot back: "In 'Ein Ḥarod, there are many Brenners, great and small." See Hillel Zeitlin, *"Bein Shnei Harim Gedolim,"* in idem, *Sifran shel Yeḥidim* (Jerusalem: Mossad Harav Kook, 1979), p. 239.

Zeitlin's eulogy of Brenner (to which Rav Kook alluded) was first published in *HaTekufah* (Tel-Aviv) 12 (Tammuz-Elul 5681/1921), pp. 383-384. (It appears in chapter 16 of Zeitlin's *"Tefillot,"* or "Prayers.") For the events leading up to the eulogy and relations between Zeitlin and Brenner, see Aharon Zeitlin, *Bein Emunah la-'Omanut*, vol. 1 (Tel-Aviv: Yavneh, 1980), pp. 191-193. (It should be noted that in transcribing his father's eulogy for Brenner, Aharon Zeitlin deleted a word. Where

Hillel Zeitlin wrote, "In Your words (*bi-devarekha*) there is no more dressing for my wounds," the son left out the word *bi-devarekha*. Ibid., p. 192.)

Apropos to Brenner's remarks concerning the displacement of light by darkness, Aharon Zeitlin (ibid., p. 197) quotes the finale of Brenner's play, *"Shivrei Maḥazot,"* subtitle of *Me-'Ever li-Gevulin* (London, 1907). The character Yoḥanan experiences before his end "an exalted moment, an infinite moment, an infinite light (*'or ein sofi*)." But then the play concludes on this somber note: "The small tongue of fire sputters in a dark, black cave."

En passant, Rabbi Tsevi Yehudah Kook held Hillel Zeitlin in the highest regard. When I questioned Rabbi Tsevi Yehudah as to the difference between his father's theology and that of ḤaBaD, he quoted to me Hillel Zeitlin's pronouncement: "There are three schools of Kabbalah. The Kabbalah of the ARI (i.e., Rabbi Isaac Luria) is the Kabbalah of the Cosmos. The Ba'al Shem Tov, and especially ḤaBaD, bequeathed the Kabbalah of Man. Finally, Rav Kook treats us to the Kabbalah of the Nation." See Hillel Zeitlin, *"Ha-Kav ha-Yesodi ba-Kabbalah shel Harav Kook,"* in idem, *Sifran shel Yeḥidim*, pp. 235-237. It looks as if the article, which first appeared in *HaTzofeh*, *Erev Rosh Hashanah* 5699 [i.e., 1938] has been abridged. See Rabbi Moshe Tsevi Neriyah, *Ḥayyei ha-RAYaH* (Tel-Aviv, 1983), p. 171, for more of the article.

See further Jonatan Meir, "Longing of Souls for the Shekhina: Relations between Rabbi Kook, Zeitlin and Brenner" (Hebrew), in *The Path of the Spirit*: *Eliezer Schweid Jubilee Volume* (*Jerusalem Studies in Jewish Thought*, vol. 19, 2005, 2), pp. 771-818; Ehud Nahir, *"Ha-Ḥut ha-meshullash*: *Ma'arekhet ha-yaḥasim ha-mitpataḥat bein Brenner, ha-RAYaH Kook ve-ha-RZYH Kook," Oreshet* 9 (2020), pp. 107-144.

Noteworthy is Rabbi Avraham Eliyahu Kaplan's review of Brenner's last work, *Shekhol ve-Kishalon*. Kaplan, a product of the Slabodka Yeshivah, was the rector of the Hildesheimer Rabbinical Seminary in Berlin. Kaplan concludes his review with wishful thinking: "Who knows? Perhaps if Yosef Ḥayyim had lived longer, he might still have returned to us." See A.E. Kaplan, *Be-'Ikvot ha-Yir'ah* (Jerusalem: Mossad Harav Kook, 1960).

English Translation

1 Cf. Rabbi Shelomo Eliashov's differentiation between the good and evil elements in the "nine hundred and seventy-four generations." See *Leshem, Shevo ve-Aḥlamah: Sefer ha-Kelalim*, Part One, *Kelalei Hitpashtut ve-Histalkut* 18:8 (p. 249).

2 See at great length, Rabbi Dov Baer Shneuri, *Torat Ḥayyim*, *Vayyishlaḥ*, regarding the roots of the souls of Esau and Jacob.

3 The imagery is that of the *Idra Zuta*; printed in *Zohar* III, 292b. See further Rabbi Ḥayyim Vital, *'Ets Ḥayyim*, *Sha'ar* 8 (*Derushei Nekudot*), chap. 6; *hagahot* to *Be'ur ha-GRA* on *Sifra di-Tseni'uta* (Vilna, 1882), 3a, n. 4; Rabbi Yitzḥak Eizik Ḥaver, *Pitḥei She'arim*, *Netiv Shevirat ha-Kelim*, chaps. 11-12 (53a-b).

4 Hebrew, *"ha-middah."* This may likely be a reference to the kabbalistic term *"kav ha-middah."* See *Ma'amar Kav ha-Middah* in *Zohar Ḥadash*, *Va-Etḥannan*. (The source of the term *"kav ha-middah,"* or "the measuring line," is Jeremiah 31:38.) That, in turn, becomes synonymous with the *"mitkala"* ("balance") sorely lacking in the realm of *Tohu*. See Rabbi Dov Baer Shneuri, *Torat Ḥayyim*, *Vayyishlaḥ*, s.v. *Vayyikaḥ min ha-ba' ve-yado minḥah le-'Esav 'aḥiv*, paragraphs 2, 4-5 (189c, 191a and c).

5 To be precise, the imagery is taken from the wine industry, upon which the early agricultural settlements in Erets Yisrael, funded by Baron Edmond de Rothschild of Paris, were heavily dependent. In that context, *"tesisah"* is "fermentation," and *"shoketet"* refers to the settling of the dregs at the bottom of the cask. Cf. *Orot*, *Orot ha-Teḥiyah*, chap. 45 (and end chap. 20).

6 *b. Ḥagigah* 14a; *Be'ur ha-GRA* to *Sifra di-Tseni'uta* (Vilna, 1882), 2b, s.v. *lo havu mashgiḥin apin be-apin.*

7 *Halakhah* distinguishes between the *mumar le-hakh'is* (transgressor to anger) and the *mumar le-tei'avon* (transgressor for appetite), dealing more severely with the blatant, willful

transgressor than with the transgressor motivated by desire. See *b. Gittin* 46b-47a; *Ḥullin* 4a-b; Maimonides, *MT*, *Hil. Teshuvah* 3:9; *Hil. Sheḥitah* 4:14 and commentaries; RAYH Kook, *Zivḥei RAYaH*, *Ḥullin* 4a, s.v. *'ella peshita mumar la-'areilut*.

8 The Hebrew, *"ha-'olam mitashtesh,"* would seem to be a translation of the *Zohar*'s Aramaic, *"mitashtesh(a) 'alma."* See *Zohar* II, 173b; III, 170b.

9 Cf. *m. Sotah* 9:15: "In the footsteps of Messiah, *ḥutspah* (impudence) will wax."

10 Cf. Isaiah 25:7: "And he will destroy in this mountain the face of the covering (*p'nei ha-lot*) that is cast over all the peoples, and the mask (*ha-masekhah*) that is spread over all the nations."

11 Cf. Isaiah 2:6.

12 Cf. Isaiah 23:9: "to desecrate all glorious beauty" (*"le-ḥallel ge'on kol tsevi"*).

13 Hebrew, *"ve-ha-ḥalashim she-ba-'olam ha-banui."* The original in *Shemonah Kevatsim* 1:243 has: *"ve-ha-'olam ha-banui, ve-khol yoshevav ha-meyushavim"* ("and the constructed world, and all of its settled inhabitants").

14 Isaiah 33:14.

15 Hebrew, *"gibborei ko'aḥ."* See Psalms 103:20. The sense is spiritual strength.

16 The final words, "man and the world" (*ha-adam ve-ha-'olam*), are not found in *Shemonah Kevatsim* 1:243.

17 In *Torat Ḥayyim*, *Vayyishlaḥ*, 191b, the point is made that the *'orot de-Tohu*, the lights of Chaos (of Esau) must reside in the *kelim de-Tikkun*, vessels of Establishment (of Jacob).

18 Hebrew, *"'amitat ha-tikkun ve-ha-binyan."* This may be wild speculation on my part, but the thought occurs to this writer that Rav Kook is playing on the term *"'ammat ha-binyan"* (a builder's level). The instrument is used to determine that the building is balanced and not off-kilter. See *b. Shabbat* 31a: "[Shammai] pushed him away with the builder's level (*'ammat ha-binyan*) that was in his [i.e., Shammai's] hand." See our remarks above (note 4) concerning the *"kav ha-middah."*

Parenthetically, the Ḥasidic master, Rabbi Ḥayyim Tyrer of Chernovits, equates Shammai's *'ammat ha-binyan* with the *kav ha-middah*. See Rabbi Ḥayyim Tyrer, *Sha'ar ha-Tefillah* (Warsaw, 1874), Gate III ("*Na'akah*"), 31d.

The hallmark of the *'Olam ha-Tikkun* is its scale (*mitkala*), its balance and proportion. *Sifra di-Tseni'uta* (The Book of Concealment) introduces itself as "*sifra de-shakil be-mitkala*" ("the book that weighs on the scale") and proceeds to lament the various calamities that occurred in the previous state of *Tohu*, "whilst yet there was no scale" (*"'ad de-lo havah mitkala").*

Despite commentaries to the contrary, a better vocalization might be "*safra de-shakil be-mitkala*" ("the counter/scribe that weighs on the scale"), an allusion to Isaiah 33:18: "Where is one who counts? Where is one who weighs?" ("*Ayeh sofer? Ayeh shokel?*") And see the wordplay in *b. Kiddushin* 30a: "The early sages were called '*soferim*' ('scribes') because they would count (*soferim*) all the letters of the Torah."

Without resorting to wordplay, "*'amitat ha-tikkun*" conjures up the image of Jacob, synonymous with "*'emet*," or truth (Micah 7:20), and the *sefirah* of *Tif'eret*, which balances the two extremes of *Ḥesed* and *Gevurah*, and thus effects *Tikkun*. See *Torat Ḥayyim*, *Vayyishlaḥ*, s.v. *Vayyikaḥ min ha-ba ve-yado minḥah le-'Esav 'aḥiv*, par. 7 (194a-d).

19 Rav Kook runs down the traditional trichotomy of intellect (*sekhel*), emotion (*regesh*) and action (*ma'aseh*). These translate into the *sefirot* of *ḤaBaD* (*Ḥokhmah, Binah, Da'at*), *Vav Kestavot* (*Ḥesed, Gevurah, Tif'eret, Netsaḥ, Hod, Yesod*), and *Malkhut*.

(Continued on page 193.)

20 Isaiah 29:18.

Appendix A

1 As opposed to the integrative configuration of three *kavin* (lines)—the two extremes and the middle arbitrating between them—characteristic of *tikkun*, the "seven kings" appeared as detached units one atop the other. The former arrangement is

called *"reshut ha-yaḥid"* (the private domain, or literally, "the domain of the one"); the latter arrangement, *"reshut ha-rabbim"* (the public domain, or literally, "the domain of the many"). See *'Ets Ḥayyim, Sha'ar* 9 (*Sha'ar Shevirat ha-Kelim*), beginning chap. 3 and beginning chap. 8; *KaLaḤ Pitḥei Ḥokhmah*, ed. Yosef Spinner (Jerusalem, 1987), *petaḥ* 52, pp. 186-187, s.v. *ve-'az hayu nikra'im reshut ha-rabbim.*

The *Idra* begins with Rabbi Shim'on's plaint to the companions: "How long shall we dwell in the existence of one pillar (*ḥad samkha*)?" (*Zohar* III, 127b). Rabbi Ḥayyim Yosef David Azulai explains: "Until now they were involved with the *'Olam ha-Tohu*, which consisted of one pillar, one atop the other, and Rabbi Shim'on ben Yoḥai wanted to inform them of [*'Olam*] *ha-Tikkun*, which consists of three lines" (*Nitsutsei Orot* ad loc.). See earlier *'Ets Hayyim* 9:3; Rabbi Ya'akov Tsemaḥ, *Kol be-Ramah* (Commentary to *Idra Rabba*), ed. Rabbi Eliyahu Attiah (Jerusalem: Makhon B'nei Yissachar, 2001), pp. 5-6; quoted by Rabbi Tsevi Elimelech Spira of Dynów in his glosses to Rabbi Tsevi Hirsch Eichenstein of Zydaczów, *Sur me-Ra' va-'Aseh Tov: Hakdamah ve-Derekh le-'Ets ha-Ḥayyim* (Jerusalem: Munkatch, 1997), pp. 10-11, note 14.

2 See *Iggerot ha-RAYaH*, vol. 1, Letter 266 to Rabbi Pinḥas Hakohen Lintop (datelined "Jaffa, 11 Shevat, 5670 [i.e., 1910]"), p. 303. In characterizing *Tohu*, Rav Kook conflates two Biblical verses: 1 Kings 1:5 (*"Ani emlokh"*) and Isaiah 47:8 (*"Ani ve-'afsi 'od"*).

It is necessary to clarify here an issue which, unfortunately, has been obfuscated. Reading the later kabbalistic literature of various persuasions (Ḥasidic and Mitnagdic), one receives the mistaken impression that in the *Idra*'s myth of the Death of the Kings (*mitat ha-melakhim*), there was contained this element that each king (anticipating Adoniyahu ben Ḥagith's ambitious statement in 1 Kings 1:5) boasted saying, "I shall reign." See, e.g., Rabbi Menaḥem Mendel Schneersohn of Lubavitch (*"Tsemaḥ Tsedek"*), *Derekh Mitsvotekha* (Poltava, 1911; photo offset Kefar Ḥabad: Kehot, 1973), *Be'ur Ve-Shavtah 5562*, chap. 2 (170b).

The truth be known, this motif does not occur in the *Idra*, not even in Lurianic reconstructions thereof. Perhaps the earliest appearance of *"Ani emlokh"* (or in the Aramaic Targum to Kings, *"Ana emlokh"*) in this connection, is in Rabbi Moses Zacuto's commentary to *Zohar*. See *Peirush ha-RaMaZ la-Zohar*, ed. Rabbi Yitzḥak Naḥum (Jerusalem, 1998-2005), *Vayyeshev*, p. 210; and *Pinḥas*, p. 396. (I am indebted to Rabbi Moshe Zuriel for providing the latter references.) Zacuto, the doyen of Italian Kabbalists, lived from circa 1625 to 1697.

As stated above, this motif of *"Ani emlokh"* or *"Ana emlokh"* shows up in both Ḥasidic and Mitnagdic sources. On the one hand, see, e.g., Rabbi Dov Baer of Mezritch, *Maggid Devarav le-Ya'akov* (Brooklyn: Kehot, 1986), *Likkutei Amarim*, par. 102 (22b) and *'Or Torah, Mikkets*, s.v. *ve-hayah ha-okhel le-pikadon*, par. 54 (19b); Rabbi Aharon Halevi Hurwitz of Staroshelye, *'Avodat Halevi* (Lemberg, 1861; photo offset Jerusalem, 1972), *Vayyishlaḥ* 42c; and Rabbi Yitzḥak Eizik Halevi Epstein of Homel, *Ḥannah Ariel*, vol. 1, *Mikkets*, s.v. *Vayyikkats Shelomo*, p. 194; vol. 2, *Behar–Beḥukkotai*, s.v. *ve-safarta lekha*, p. 594. On the other hand, see e.g. Rabbi Abraham Simḥah of Mstislav, *"Ma'amar be-'Inyan Shevirah ve-Tikkun,"* in *Mi-Ginzei ha-GRA u-Veit Midrasho*, ed. Kalman Redisch (Lakewood, 1999), pp. 315-316; Rabbi Yitzḥak Eizik Ḥaver, *Afikei Yam*, *Sotah* 5a, s.v. *Amar Rabbi Aleksandri, kol adam she-yesh bo gasut ru'aḥ* (p. 255).

3 See Rabbi Ḥayyim Vital, *Sha'ar ha-Kelalim* (printed in beginning of *'Ets Ḥayyim*), chaps. 1-2; *'Ets Ḥayyim, Sha'ar* 11 (*Sha'ar ha-Melakhim*), chap. 7; Rabbi Immanuel Ḥai Ricchi, *Mishnat Ḥasidim, Masekhet 'Orot ha-Nekudim* 2:7; *Masekhet Yetsi'at MaH he-Ḥadash* 2:2; Rabbi Barukh of Kosov, *'Amud ha-'Avodah* (Chernovits, 1863), *Kuntresim le-Ḥokhmat ha-'Emet*, 97a (in the new Monsey 2007 edition of *Yesod ha-'Emunah*, ed. Rabbi Yaakov Ilowitch, f. 367, par. 76); Rabbi Yitzḥak Eizik Ḥaver, *Pitḥei She'arim, Netiv Shevirat ha-Kelim*, chap. 13; *Netiv 'Olam ha-Tikkun*, chaps. 8, 14; *Iggerot ha-RAYaH*, vol. 1, Letter 184, p. 239, n. 1.

[4] See Rabbi Menaḥem Mendel Schneersohn of Lubavitch (*Tsemaḥ Tsedek*), *Be'ur Ve-Shavtah 5562* [i.e., 1802], in idem, *Derekh Mitsvotekha*, chap. 2 (170b).

[5] See Rabbi Yitzḥak Eizik Ḥaver, *Pitḥei She'arim*, *Netiv 'Olam ha-Tikkun*, chap. 4 (f. 65) and chap. 11 (69b).

[6] Ibid. chap. 5 (65b-66a).

[7] See *b. Megillah* 31b; *Nedarim* 40a: "The building of children is tearing down and the tearing down of elders is building" (*binyan yeladim setirah u-setirat zekenim binyan*).

[8] Exodus 16:7. See the conclusion of *Sefer ha-Beri'ah*, p. 499; and Rabbi Yitzḥak Eizik Epstein of Homel, *Ḥannah Ariel*, vol. 2, *Behar–Beḥukkotai*, s.v. *ve-safarta lekha*, p. 594.

See also the note (thought to be by Rabbi Yitzḥak Eizik Ḥaver) to Rabbi Abraham Simḥah of Mstislav's *"Ma'amar be-'Inyan Shevirah ve-Tikkun,"* in *Mi-Ginzei ha-GRA u-Veit Midrasho*, ed. Kalman Redisch, p. 316: "...*Tohu* and *Tikkun*; arrogance and humility. Arrogance (*gasut ru'aḥ*) is the mystery of *Tohu*, [the name] *SaG* (or *gas*); humility is the name *MaH*, as it is said ... *"Ve-naḥnu mah?"*

Rabbi Samuel Teich (of Pshemishel/ Przemyśl) wrote that "the *tikkun* of *'Ana emlokh'* is *'Ve-naḥnu mah,'* the name *MaH* that corrects all the kings" (*Otsar Emet 'al Mo'adei ha-Shanah*: *Purim* [Brooklyn, 1979], p. 34).

An epistemological explanation of the name *MaH* is found in Rabbi Gershon Ḥanokh Leiner of Radzyn, *Tif'eret ha-Ḥanokhi* (Warsaw, 1900; photo offset New York, 1974), *Vayyera*, 11a (to *Zohar* I, 97b).

[9] *b. Tamid* 32a.

[10] 1 Kings 1:5.

[11] The word occurs in the Hebrew: *obyektiviyut*.

[12] A term from Zoharic literature. In *Iggerot ha-RAYaH*, vol. 1, p. 143 (Letter 112), Rav Kook quotes the full sentence: "The souls of the wicked are the damagers of the world." See *Zohar* II, 118a; III, 25a, 70a; *Zohar Ḥadash*, *Bereshit*, *Midrash ha-Ne'elam* 11a. (See the additional notes provided by the editor Rabbi Tsevi Yehudah Kook at the conclusion of volume 2 of *Iggerot ha-RAYaH*, p. 342.)

[13] Cf. Psalms 92:10. See also *Iggerot ha-RAYaH*, vol. 1, p. 369 (Letter 332); and *Orot Yisrael* 4:6 (in *Orot*, p. 149) = *Pinkesei ha-RAYaH*, vol. 7, *Kovets mi-Tekufat Yaffo-Schweiz*, par. 184 (p. 217). See Rabbi Yitzḥak Eizik Ḥaver, *Pitḥei She'arim*, *Netiv 'Olam ha-Tikkun*, chap. 8 (67a), whereby this verse of Psalms (*"yitpardu kol po'alei 'aven")* is associated with *Nekudim* (or *nekudot*), a state of disconnection and dissociation.

[14] *Iggerot ha-RAYaH*, vol. 1, p. 303 (Letter 266).

[15] Rav Kook alludes to the first discourse in Rabbi Ḥayyim Vital's magnum opus, *'Ets Ḥayyim*, *Derush 'Iggulim ve-Yosher*. The subject of that discourse is the reconciliation of two different models or schemes of the *sefirot*: concentric circles (*'Iggulim*) versus the human form (*Yosher*, or Straightness). It is explained there that *'Iggulim* (which corresponds to the lower level of the soul, *nefesh*) precedes *Yosher* (which corresponds to the higher level of the soul, *ru'aḥ*). (See Rabbi Shelomo Eliashov, *Ḥelek ha-Be'urim*, Part One [Jerusalem, 1935], 22c-d.) Later, this opposition is reiterated in the different arrangements of *Tohu* and *Tikkun*. In the *'Olam ha-Tohu* (World of Chaos), the *sefirot* manifest as *nekudot* (dots or points), one atop the other. Subsequently, the *sefirot* are re-arranged as "*kavim*" (lines), which is to say, they are presented in three columns. At the same time, they evolve from the more primitive stage of *nefesh* (symbolized by the divine name *BaN*) to the more developed stage of *ru'aḥ* (symbolized by the new divine name of *MaH*).

For the sake of consistency with kabbalistic teaching, I have slightly emended the text of the passage in *Shemonah Kevatsim* 4:118. See below Appendix C, note 2.

[16] Psalms 46:3.

[17] A line from the *piyyut* (religious poetry), "*Ve-Khol Ma'aminim*," recited in the Ashkenazic liturgy for *Mussaf* of Rosh Hashanah and Yom Kippur.

[18] Psalms 139:16.

[19] Rav Kook alludes to the *sefirah* of *Tif'eret*—symbolic of harmony, inclusivity and synthesis—being synonymous with Torah. See the commentary of Rabbi Ya'akov Margi, *Emet le-Ya'akov*, to the *Idra* (*Zohar* III, 128a), s.v. *ve-tanna*,

salik bi-re'uteh le-mivrei 'oraita, for the equation of the new name *MaH* with the Written Torah, code for *Ze'ir Anpin* (i.e., *Tif'eret*) and *ru'aḥ*. (In the *Ahavat Shalom* edition of *Emet le-Ya'akov* [Jerusalem, 2021], this comment is found on p. 77.) So too in the commentary to the *Idra* of Rabbi David de Medina, *Ru'aḥ David* (Saloniki, 1747), ibid.

[20] *m. Avot* 3:16; *Shemonah Kevatsim* 4:118.

Appendix B

[1] Genesis 31:10.

[2] See Rabbi Ḥayyim Vital, *'Ets Ḥayyim*, *Sha'ar* 6 (*Sha'ar 'Akudim*), chap. 1; and Rabbi David Cohen ("the Nazir"), *Kol ha-Nevu'ah*, pp. 297-298, note 431.

As the Nazir points out, this *derush* is not found in the *Zohar* but originates with Rabbi Isaac Luria (ARI). The thought occurs to this writer (BN) that it was inspired by the initials of *'Akudim, Nekudim, Berudim*: *'Enav*, or grape. In *Sifra di-Tseni'uta*, we find the simile, "hanging like grapes in a cluster" ("*talyan ka-'anavim be-'etkala*"). Though the context is by no means clear, it might have suggested itself to Luria as an image of the descent or downward evolution of the *sefirot*. See *Zohar* II, 179a.

[3] In *Sha'ar 'Akudim* (loc. cit.) the linguistics are supported by referencing Genesis 22:9: "[Abraham] bound Isaac his son." Cf. Rabbi David Kimḥi (RaDaK) to Genesis 30:35 and 2 Kings 10:12; and Rabbi Abraham, son of the Vilna Gaon, *Tirgem Avraham*, ed. Elijah Landau (Jerusalem, 1896), Genesis 30:35. Also, *Peirushei Rabbeinu Sa'adyah Gaon 'al ha-Torah*, ed. Rabbi Yosef Kafaḥ (Jerusalem: Mossad Harav Kook, 1963), Gen. 30:35.

[4] See the explanation of Rabbi Gershon Ḥanokh Leiner of Radzyn, quoting his father Rabbi Ya'akov Leiner of Izbica and Radzyn, in *Tif'eret ha-Ḥanokhi*, *Lekh Lekha*, 10c (on *Zohar* I, 85b, s.v. *ve-kad nishmatin nafkin*).

[5] Rabbi Samuel Teich (of Pshemishel/ Przemyśl) drew a picture of the future *'Olam ha-'Akudim*; see his *Otsar Emet 'al Mo'adei*

ha-Shanah: Purim (Brookyn, 1979), *Kuntres ha-Derushim, Tu bi-Shevat*, chap. 3 (p. 108).

6 There are four different ways to spell out the Tetragrammaton, *YHVH*, referred to as: *'AB* (72), *SaG* (63), *MaH* (45), *BaN* (52), after their numerical values. They correspond to the four kabbalistic worlds of *Atsilut, Beri'ah, Yetsirah, 'Asiyah*.

'AB is arrived at by spelling out the divine name using the letter *yod* (*millui yodin*); in *MaH*, the name is filled with the letter *alef* (*millui alfin*); in *BaN*, with the letter *hé* (*millui hehin*). (*SaG* is a mixture of *yodin* and *alef*.)

An obvious question arises: Why is the number 52 expressed as *BaN*, a reversal of the normal expression of *NaB*? A simple solution is that it is expressed this way so as to avoid confusion with *'AB* (72). See *Kelalei Hatḥalat ha-Ḥokhmah*, ed. Rabbi Aharon Meir Altschuler (Warsaw, 1893), chap. 3, par. 69 (9b).

However, there is a lengthy explanation attributed to Rabbi Samson of Ostropolia (d. 1648). In an exchange with his fellow Kabbalist, Rabbi Kalonymos Kalman of Chaus (Belarus, *Chavusy*), the Vilna Gaon challenged Rabbi Samson's solution and Rabbi Kalonymos Kalman defended it. This was conveyed to Rabbi Altschuler in a letter from Rabbi Shelomo Eliashov. (In a manuscript in the possession of Rabbi Altschuler, his grandfather Rabbi Kalonymos Kalman's position was worded in a slightly different manner.) See ibid. footnote.

Inter alia, Rabbi Eliashov was descended from Rabbi Samson of Ostropolia; see the introduction to Rabbi Eliashov's *Hakdamot u-She'arim* (Piotrków, 1908). One speculates that for this reason, Rabbi Eliashov entitled his series *Leshem, Shevo ve-Aḥlamah*. *Leshem* (amethyst) was the stone on the breastplate of the high priest that represented the tribe of Dan. Rabbi Samson of Ostropolia, who identified with Dan, entitled his work *Dan Yadin*.

Rav Kook offered his own original explanation as to why it is *BaN* and not *NaB*. See *Metsi'ot Katan*, par. 217 (in *Pinkesei ha-RAYaH*, vol. 7, pp. 21-23; in Beit El edition of 2018, pp. 349-350).

[7] Rabbi Ḥayyim Vital, *'Ets Ḥayyim, Sha'ar* 10 (*Sha'ar ha-Tikkun*), chaps. 2-3.

As discussed above, the new world order of *Tikkun* is symbolized by the eighth, enduring king, Hadar. The key to his survival (when his seven predecessors, symbolic of *Tohu*, succumbed) is the fact that unlike the first seven kings, who were single, Hadar is wedded to Meheitavel. See *Idra Rabba* in *Zohar* III, 135b. In Lurianic Kabbalah, her name, Meheitavel, is pregnant with meaning. Numerically, it bespeaks the interaction of *MaH*, the clarifier (*mevarer*), and *BaN*, the clarified (*mitbasem* or *mitbarer*), for the name breaks down into two components: *MaH* and YTBEL (which has the numerical value of *BaN*, or 52). See *'Ets Ḥayyim, Sha'ar* 10 (*Sha'ar ha-Tikkun*), chap. 3. (And see *Sha'ar* 9 [*Sha'ar Shevirat ha-Kelim*], chap. 8.)

And beyond that, *BaN* has the numerical value of *Behemah*, or beast (52), while *MaH* has the numerical value of *Adam*, or man (ibid.). In this regard, the Kabbalists often invoke the verse in Psalms 36:7: "Man and beast, You preserve, O LORD." See, e.g., Rabbi Yitzḥak Eizik Ḥaver, *Pitḥei She'arim, Netiv 'Olam ha-Tikkun*, chap. 2 (64a), chap. 16 (72b); and the *Likkutim* (Collectanea) published at the conclusion of Samuel Luria's edition of *Be'ur ha-GRA le-Sifra di-Tseni'uta* 37b, s.v. *'Inyan ha-birurin*. And see Rabbi Naftali Herz Halevi's ingenious interpretation of the line from the morning prayer, *"ki rov ma'aseihem Tohu... u-motar ha-adam min ha-behemah 'ayin,"* in *Siddur ha-GRA*, 15a.

An aside: According to the Vilna Gaon, the Tetragrammaton filled with *Alfin* (*MaH*) is the *Shem ha-Meforash* (Ineffable Name). See the commentary of the Gaon to *Sefer Yetsirah* (Warsaw, 1884), 1:1, *ofan* 3 (3a); cited in Rabbi Aryeh Leib Lipkin, *Kelalei Hatḥalat ha-Ḥokhmah* (Warsaw, 1893), chap. 3, par. 10 (9b). What results is that the Ineffable Name has the numerical value of Adam. Perhaps this kabbalistic insight inspired the title of Abraham Joshua Heschel's collection of Yiddish poems, *Der Shem ha-Meforash: Mensch* (Warsaw:

Insel, 1933). It has since been translated into English as *The Ineffable Name of God: Man* (New York: Continuum, 2004).

*

Though one is tempted to interpret the *metsaḥ*, or forehead, as symbolic of the cerebral, in kabbalistic tradition it is equated with *ratson*, or will.

(Yet, Rabbi Reuven Margaliyot has quoted in this context Rabbi Solomon ibn Gabirol's *Tikkun Middot ha-Nefesh*: "The will is by power of the thoughts that are in the forehead [*ba-metsaḥ*]." See *Nitsutsei Zohar* to *Idra* in *Zohar* III, 129a, note 9. Margaliyot relied on the printed edition of Ibn Gabirol's work. However, see the critical edition of Ḥayyim Pollak based on manuscripts [Pressburg, 1896], p. 16. For *ba-metsaḥ*, read *ba-mo'aḥ* [in the brain].)

See Rabbi Joseph Gikatilla, *Sha'arei Tsedek* (Riva di Trento, 1561), 26c (*"metsaḥ ha-ratson"*); *Idra Rabba* in *Zohar* III, 129a (*"ha-hu mitsḥa de-ikrei 'ratson'"*); *Idra Zuta* in *Zohar* III, 288b (*"Mitsḥa de-itgalei ba-'Atika Kadisha, 'ratson' itkerei"*); Rabbi Ḥayyim Vital, *'Ets Ḥayyim*, *Sha'ar* 10 (*Sha'ar ha-Tikkun*), chap. 2; *Sha'ar* 13 (*Sha'ar Arikh Anpin*), chaps. 6, 13; Rabbi Yitzḥak Eizik Ḥaver, *Pitḥei She'arim*, Part One, *Netiv 'Olam ha-Tikkun*, chap. 1 (63b), 8 (67a), 9 (68a); Israel Shabtai Ratner, *Le-'Or ha-Kabbalah* (Kefar Ḥabad: Abraham Zioni, 1961), p. 111.

In the *Idra* (*Zohar* III, 129a), the forehead has been linked to will, based on the verse in Exodus 28:38 (concerning the *tsits*, or gold plate, on the forehead of Aaron the High Priest): "It shall be always upon his forehead (*mitsḥo*) for acceptance (*le-ratson*)."

For Rabbi Abraham Simḥah of Mstislav, the will of the *metsaḥ*, is that expressed in the Torah. See his "*Ma'amar be-'Inyan Shevirah ve-Tikkun*," in *Mi-Ginzei ha-GRA u-Veit Midrasho*, ed. Kalman Redisch, pp. 315-318. Rabbi Abraham Simḥah studied Kabbalah under his paternal uncle, Rabbi Ḥayyim of Volozhin. In this brief *ma'amar*, which first appeared as an appendix to *Megillat Ruth 'im Peirush ha-GRA* (Jerusalem, 1896), the author treats us to a unique reading of the Lurianic tropes of *Tohu* and *Tikkun*. There are two ways in which man can come to a realization of divine providence (*hashgaḥah*): by studying the world, and by studying Torah. The first way, observation of the creation, is subject to corruption and misinterpretation. (The nations concluded that God has abandoned the world.) This is symbolized by the fact that the "*shevirah*" (break) occurred in the eye. The repair of the break comes about through the subsequent revelation of *ratson*, the divine will, in the Torah. Cf. Rabbi David Cohen, *Kol ha-Nevu'ah*, pp. 225-226; Rabbi Tsevi Elimelekh of Dynów, *Igra de-Pirka* (Lemberg, 1858), chap. 297; Rabbi David Yitzḥak Eizik Rabinowitz of Skolya, *Mekor ha-Berakhah* (*'al ha-Mitsvot*), vol. 1 (Brooklyn, 1967), Introduction, 4a, 11a-b.

In this vein too, Rabbi Abraham Simḥah understands *Nekudim* as hierarchical, "tunnel" vision, as opposed to a global vision of the world which allows for divine intervention in worldly affairs.

*

In *Likkutei MOHaRaN Tinyana*, chap. 4 ("*Ve-'Et ha-'Orevim Tsiviti Lekhalkelekha*"), par. 7, Rabbi Naḥman of Breslov would link all the wills of the world to the root of will (*shoresh ha-ratson*), *metsaḥ ha-ratson*, namely God's free will in creating the world from complete absence (*he'eder gamur*), in opposition to the opinion of the scientists ("*ḥakhmei ha-teva'*"), for whom the origin of the world is necessity (*ḥiyyuv ha-teva'*). (By the way, today the scientific consensus has swung to the opposite opinion, as it now endorses the Big Bang theory.) Earlier in that chapter (par. 6), Rabbi Naḥman discusses how the naturalistic view disposes of miracles. (Cf. Maimonides, *Guide of the Perplexed* II, 25, who writes that the theory of the eternity of the world is incompatible with belief in miracles. I have demonstrated elsewhere that though Rabbi Naḥman was opposed to the study of the *Guide*, it is obvious that he was quite familiar with the work and engaged with it in the formulation of his own thought. See Bezalel Naor, "Rabbi Naḥman's *Shir Na'im* as a Reply to Maimonides," in idem, *Navigating Worlds* [New York, NY: Kodesh, 2021], pp. 237-246.)

The idea that all the wills in the world are subservient to the supernal will (*ratson ha-ʿelyon*) is found earlier in *KaLaḤ Pitḥei Ḥokhmah* (Koretz, 1785), *petaḥ* 1, a work of which Rabbi Naḥman might have availed himself.

In *ʿArpilei Tohar* (Jerusalem, 1914), Rav Kook has much to say about the opposition of *ratson* (volition) versus *hekhraḥ* (necessity) in regard to the divinity. See *ʿArpilei Tohar*, ed. Rabbi Yitzḥak Shilat (Greenspan) (Jerusalem: Makhon RZYH Kook, 1983), pp. 30, 44-45, 129, 135. These passages are found today in *Shemonah Kevatsim* 2:72, 118, 340, 356.

*

The *mitsḥa* (Aramaic, forehead) figures prominently in Rabbi Isaac Luria's hymn for the Third Meal of the Sabbath (associated in Kabbalah with *Zeʿir Anpin*). There, too, it is equated with *ratson* (will). See Rabbi Ḥayyim Tyrer of Chernovits, *Sidduro shel Shabbat* (Warsaw, 1876; photo offset Jerusalem, 1955), Part Two, *Derush ha-Rishon*, 72a; and Yehuda Liebes, "*Zemirot li-Seʿudot Shabbat she-Yisad ha-ARI ha-Kadosh*," *Molad* 4 (1972), pp. 540-555. And see Rabbi Abraham ben Naḥman Halevi Ḥazan of Tulchin, *Beʾur ha-Likkutim* (Jerusalem, 1989), *Hashmatot*, s.v. *Hamshakhat ha-Ratson* (f. 329, column a), remarking on the forehead (Yiddish, *Stern*) of Rabbi Nathan Sternharz. (By the way, according to Breslov tradition, Rabbi Abraham ben Naḥman visited Rav Kook in Jaffa and was his mentor in Breslov Ḥasidism.)

Unprecedented, the Lithuanian Kabbalist, Rabbi Pinḥas Hakohen Lintop, ascribed to the *metsaḥ* associated with the divine name *MaH* and *ʿOlam ha-Tikkun*, the sense of "*ʿazut di-kedushah*" ("holy brazenness," a popular Ḥasidic expression found in *Likkutei MOHaRaN* and other works). See *Kanaʾuteh de-Pinḥas*, ed. Bezalel Naor (Spring Valley, NY: Orot, 2013), Letter to Rav Kook, p. 43, and 140, n. 193. In this connection, see the discussion in Rabbi Yaʿakov Margi, *Peirush ʿal ha-Idra Zuta Kadisha* (Vienna, 1887), 7a, s.v. *mitsḥa de-ʾitgelei be-A"K ʿratsonʾ ʾitkerei*. And see ibid. 29b.

It seems that the way Rabbi Lintop arrived at the equation of the forehead with "holy brazenness," was by taking note of the *Idra*'s statement: "At the hour when below there is revealed the forehead (*mitsḥa*), there is found *ḥutspah*, as it says [Jeremiah 3:3], 'and you had the forehead (*metsaḥ*) of a harlot; you refused to be ashamed'" (*Zohar* III, 129a). Evidently, Rabbi Lintop reasoned that the *Idra* was setting up an exact opposition. "God made one opposite the other" (Ecclesiastes 7:14). For the forehead of holiness to be diametrically opposed to the "forehead of the harlot," it too must represent *ḥutspah*, holy *ḥutspah*, or *'azut di-kedushah*.

8 See *'Ets Ḥayyim*, *Sha'ar* 10 (*Sha'ar ha-Tikkun*), end chap. 3 (and commentary of Rabbi Menaḥem Menkhin Heilperin, *Hagahot u-Be'urim*, ad loc.). And see Rabbi Menaḥem Mendel Schneersohn of Lubavitch ("*Tsemaḥ Tsedek*"), *Derekh Mitsvotekha, Be'ur Ve-Shavtah 5562*, chap. 2 (170b-171a); Rabbi Isaac Safrin of Komarno, *Heikhal ha-Berakhah* (Lemberg, 1869), *Tsav*, 52b; and Rabbi Gershon Ḥanokh Leiner of Radzyn, *Tif'eret ha-Ḥanokhi*, *Bereshit*, 2c, last paragraph. (Correct the text to read "*ve-shem MaH she-mevarer shem BaN.*")

Rabbi Yitzḥak Eizik Ḥaver understands that in the future, the divine name *BaN* shall be transformed to the name *SaG* (which is another way of saying that *Malkhut* ascends to *Binah*). In this regard, he quotes the conclusion of the *Sifra di-Tseni'uta*: "*Keren be-yovela it'atar, 'asira'ah be-'imma*" ("The horn is crowned in the Jubilee, the tenth in Mother"). See the Gaon's commentary thereto (Samuel Luria edition, 36b), which refers to the seventh millennium. See *Pitḥei She'arim*, *Netiv 'Orot de-Nekudim*, chap. 10 (42a); *Netiv Shevirat ha-Kelim*, chap. 21 (60a); *Netiv 'Olam ha-Tikkun*, chap. 2, note 27 (*Beit Netivot*), chaps. 9-10 (68b-69a), chap. 15 (f. 72), chap. 18 (74a), chap. 22 (76b), chap. 25 (77b). In his supercommentary to the Vilna Gaon's commentary to the Pentateuch, *Aderet Eliyahu*, Rabbi Eizik Ḥaver explains the reversion of *BaN* to *SaG* in terms of the tripartite division of the soul: *nefesh*, *ru'aḥ*, and *neshamah*. Beyond the *'Olam ha-Tohu* of the wicked (*BaN* or *nefesh*), and the *'Olam ha-Tikkun* of the righteous (the interaction of *MaH* and *BaN*; *ru'aḥ* and *nefesh*), in the future there will emerge the highest level of the soul, *neshamah* (*SaG*). See Rabbi Elijah Gaon, *Aderet Eliyahu*, with commentary of Rabbi Yitzḥak Eizik Ḥaver, *Be'er Yitzḥak*, ed. Samuel Luria (Warsaw, 1887), *Balak* (*mahadura ḥamisha'ah*), s.v. *'ad mah Ashur tishbeka* [Numbers 24:22] (p. 297).

This was also the understanding of the Moroccan Kabbalist, Rabbi Ya'akov Margi (1640-circa 1710), that in the Jubilee, the name *BaN* will revert back to its original name, *SaG*. See his commentary to the *Idra* (in *Zohar* III, 136a), s.v. *ḥamishin shenin de-Yovela*, and the earlier comment (128a), s.v. *bi-shemahan ikrun ve-lo itkayymu*. See *Sefer ha-Zohar 'im Peirush Emet le-Ya'akov* (Jerusalem: Ahavat Shalom, 2021), pp. 76, 200. (There is remarkable overlap between Margi's commentary to that passage of the *Idra* [ibid. pp. 76-77] and the later commentary of de Medina. See Rabbi David de Medina, *Ru'aḥ David ve-Nishmat David* [Saloniki, 1747], 4d-5a. One speculates that de Medina, during his years in Safed and Jerusalem, came into possession of the commentary of the seventeenth-century Moroccan Kabbalist. That would not have been difficult. Margi's commentary enjoyed wide popularity, as witnessed by the some 25 manuscripts recorded by the National Library of Israel.)

The reversion of the name *BaN* back to its original name of *SaG* in the eschatological future (and on a small scale every Sabbath) is also stated in Rabbi Shneur Zalman of Lyady, *Torah 'Or, Megillat Esther*, 97c. And see *Siddur MaHaRID*, vol. 1, 59a, s.v. *La'asot bahem mishpat katuv*; 66b, s.v. *be-har naḥalatkha*; 67b, s.v. *Ve-hayah Hashem le-melekh 'al kol ha-'arets*.

Inter alia, Rav Kook once speculated that the 63 elements (of his day) correspond to the name *SaG*. See *Mussar Avikha* (Jerusalem: Mossad Harav Kook, 1985), chap. 3, par. 2 (39a). In 1869, Russian chemist Dmitri Mendeleev arranged 63 elements into an early periodic table. In the recently published *Metsi'ot Katan*, Rav Kook grapples with the discrepancy between the four *yesodot* (elements) of the Kabbalah (fire, air, water, earth) and the more numerous elements of modern science. See *Metsi'ot Katan*, ed. Harel Cohen (Jerusalem: Maggid,

2018), chap. 63 (p. 83), chap 147 (p. 240), and chap. 176 (p. 278). It should be noted that the attempt to correlate between Kabbalah and Science runs throughout the works of the Mitnagdic Kabbalist who preceded Rav Kook as Rabbi of Jaffa—Naftali Herz Halevi Weidenbaum.

9 Rabbi Shneur Zalman's opponent, the Vilna Gaon, writes that during the seventh millennium, the souls of the preceding six millennia will be clarified from the *"kelipot"* ("shells" or "husks," i.e., forces of impurity) and will be renewed as they were in the beginning. See *Be'ur ha-GRA* to *Sifra di-Tseni'uta*, ed. Samuel Luria (Vilna, 1882), chap. 1 (11b), s.v. *teleisar yakim lon be-raḥamei u-mitḥadshan ke-kadmita.*

10 Rabbi Shneur Zalman of Lyady, *Torah 'Or*, *Bereshit*, 3c.

11 See *Siddur 'im Peirush MaHaRID* (Berdichev, 1913; photo offset Kefar Ḥabad, 1991), vol. 1, 29a, s.v. *Hashem melekh*; 54b, s.v. *Halleluyah shiru la-Hashem shir ḥadash ("Le-ma'alah mi-Tohu ve-Tikkun,"* however in the *Alter Rebbe's Siddur 'im DAḤ* [67c] the wording is *"Le-ma'alah mi-beḥinat ha-shevirah ve-ha-tikkun");* 55a (*"le-ma'alah me-ha-shevirah de-Tohu ve-Tikkun"*; cf. *Torah 'Or*, *Bereshit*, 3c); 59a, s.v. *La'asot bahem mishpat katuv*; 62b, s.v. *u-ve-yadkha legaddel u-leḥazek la-kol.*

12 *Peirush MaHaRID* is a composite work, a multilayered compilation of esoteric teachings representing several generations within the Schneerson dynasty, most notably the founder, Rabbi Shneur Zalman of Lyady, and his daughter's son, Rabbi Menaḥem Mendel of Lubavitch (author of the halakhic responsa *Tsemaḥ Tsedek*), down to and including the author, Rabbi Isaac Dov Baer Schneerson (MaHaRID) of Lyady. MaHaRID was a grandson of the *Tsemaḥ Tsedek*, through his son Rabbi Ḥayyim Shneur Zalman of Lyady (circa 1814-1879).

Unavailable for close to eighty years, the *Siddur 'im Peirush MaHaRID* was brought back into print in Kefar Ḥabad in 1991, in a two-volume photo offset edition. It was provided with an introduction by the indefatigable researcher Yehoshua Mondshine. On pages 8-9 of the introduction, there appear facsimiles of four letters handwritten by Rabbi Isaac Dov Baer

Schneerson to the illustrious halakhic authority, Rabbi Moshe Naḥum Jerusalimski of Kielce (1855-1916). Jerusalimski's wife (by a second marriage) was a Schneerson descendant. One assumes that the originals of the letters are to be found in the Schocken Institute in Jerusalem, which houses the extensive Moshe Naḥum Jerusalimski collection.

From a scholarly perspective, a long overdue desideratum is a properly annotated edition which, by careful cross-comparative analysis, utilizing both the printed and manuscript recensions of Ḥ aBaD literature, would identify the various layers within the *Peirush MaHaRID* and their authors.

Rabbi Moshe Dov Baer Rivkin (1893-1977), a ḤaBaD Ḥasid, who penned the chronicle of the final days of his master, Rabbi Shalom Dov Baer Schneersohn (RaShaB of Lubavitch) in Rostov-on-Don, *Ashkavta de-Rabbi*, came from a family of Ladier Ḥasidim. Later, in the United States, Rabbi Rivkin became a prominent *rosh yeshivah* at Yeshivah Torah vo-Da'ath in Brooklyn. His *shi'urim*, or Talmudic lectures, were collected in a volume, *Tif'eret Zion* (New York, 1975). In telephone conversation, the author's son, Rabbi Shalom Rivkin of Saint Louis, Missouri, revealed to the writer (BN) that the family was in possession of *bikhelakh* of Ladier *Ḥasidut*. This phone conversation took place circa 1990.

[13] *KaLaḤ Pitḥei Ḥokhmah*, ed. Yosef Spinner (Jerusalem, 1987), *petaḥ* 49 (p. 174).

[14] *b. Sanhedrin* 92b.

[15] *Kelalim Rishonim*, chap. 9, in *Sefer ha-Kelalim*, appended to *Da'at Tevunot*, ed. Rabbi Ḥayyim Friedlander, 2nd edition (B'nei Berak, 1975), pp. 253-255. See the discussion in Rabbi Yisrael Eliyahu Weintraub, *Nefesh Eliyahu: Hakdamot ve-Shi'urim* (Israel, 2012), *Ma'amar be-Pitḥei She'arim*, p. 21, n. 50.

[16] See *Berit ha-Menuḥah*, ed. 'Oded Porat (Jerusalem: Magnes, 2016), Author's Introduction, pp. 151-152. In his letter, Luzzatto sings the praise of Rabbi Ḥayyim Vital for having rejected the theory of some medieval Kabbalists whereby

there are seven *shemitot*, each lasting seven millennia (for a total of forty-nine thousand years).

Concerning the medieval controversy regarding the doctrine of *Shemitot*, see Yehuda Liebes, *Studies in the Zohar*, pp. 123-125. For one, Rabbi Moses de Leon rejected the doctrine. See Rabbi Moses de Leon, *Ha-Nefesh ha-Ḥakhamah* (Basel, 1608), chap. 6, "*Seder Teḥiyat ha-Metim*"; cited by Liebes, p. 216, n. 222.

17 *Iggerot Pitḥei Ḥokhmah va-Da'at*, chap. 23, in *Sha'arei RaMḤaL*, ed. Rabbi Ḥayyim Friedlander (B'nei Berak, 1989), pp. 380-381.

I am indebted to my esteemed friend, Rabbi Mordechai Chriqui, for bringing to my attention these sources in the writings of Rabbi Moshe Ḥayyim Luzzatto (RaMḤaL).

18 Statement of Rav Katina in *b. Sanhedrin* 97a.

19 Both printed editions of the *Be'ur ha-GRA*—the grandson Jacob Moses of Slonim's edition of Vilna and Horadna 1820 (55d), and Samuel Luria's edition of Vilna 1882 (34c)—have in parentheses the word, "*ba-hakdamah*," "in the introduction." However in the Library of Congress manuscript written in Vilna 1818, the word is missing. See *Be'ur ha-GRA le-Sifra di-Tseni'uta mi-tokh ketav yad*, ed. Bezalel Naor (Jerusalem, 1998), f. 124, n. 36.

20 *Be'ur ha-GRA* to *Sifra di-Tseni'uta*, ed. Samuel Luria (Vilna, 1882), chap. 5, s.v. *yod bilḥodoi kad itgalya bi-ze'ira itmashakh be-'eser alfin shanin* (34c); quoted in Rabbi Yitzḥak Eizik Ḥaver, *Pitḥei She'arim*, Part One, *Netiv Shevirat ha-Kelim*, chap. 17 (57b). Thus, according to the Vilna Gaon, the seven millennia correspond to the seven *sefirot* of *Ḥesed* through *Malkhut* (*zayin taḥtonot*), while the next three millennia correspond to *Binah*, *Ḥokhmah*, and finally, *Keter* (*gimmel rishonot*). See *Tikkunei Zohar Ḥadash* (89c), quoted in *Be'ur ha-GRA* to *Sifra di-Tseni'uta*, chap. 1, s.v. *shita alfei shanin talyan be-shita kadma'ei* (9b); *Be'ur ha-GRA* to *Tikkunim mi-Zohar Ḥadash* (Vilna, 1867), f. 49; and Rabbi Yisrael Eliyahu Weintraub, *Nefesh Eliyahu*, loc. cit. Rabbi Weintraub makes

the point that the Vilna Gaon's eschatology differs from that of Luzzatto.

See also Rabbi Abraham Simḥah of Mstislav, "*Ma'amar be-'Inyan Shevirah ve-Tikkun*," in *Mi-Ginzei ha-GRA u-Veit Midrasho*, ed. Kalman Redisch, p. 317.

21 See *Berit ha-Menuḥah*, p. 152, lines 154-155.

22 Rabbi Shelomo Eliashov, *Hakdamot u-She'arim*, 7:7:3 (57d).

In the last of his works to be published, *Ḥelek ha-Be'urim* (Jerusalem, 1935), Rabbi Eliashov adopts a more radical position. At the end of the tenth millennium, existence "will depart from all limits and measures, and the *Tsimtsum* (Contraction) will be nullified, and [existence] will return to the *Ein Sof* (Infinite) as before. And that is the ultimate intention (*ha-kavvanah ha-takhlitit*) of the sanctity of all existence, that after it be purified and sanctified, it then depart from the limited to the unlimited, and return to its First Cause" (*Ḥelek ha-Be'urim*, Part One, 22d). For more of Rabbi Eliashov's eschatology, teleology and theodicy, see Appendix G, "The *Leshem* and Luzzatto."

Appendix C

1 See *Likkutei ha-GRA*, appended to *Be'ur ha-GRA* to *Sifra di-Tseni'uta*, ed. Samuel Luria (Vilna, 1882), 38c-d: "... the *Tsimtsum* is *Nukva* (feminine)... and the *Kav* is *Vav Kestavot* (masculine)."

2 For the equation of *nekudot* with *'Iggulim* (*nefesh* and the name *BaN*), on the one hand, and on the other hand, the alignment of Hadar (*Yesod*) with *Yosher*, *ru'aḥ* and the name *MaH*, see Rabbi Ḥayyim Vital, *'Ets Ḥayyim*, *Sha'ar* 9 (*Sha'ar Shevirat ha-Kelim*), chap. 8, and the glosses of Rabbi Jacob Tsemaḥ; and Rabbi Gershon Ḥanokh Leiner of Radzyn, *Tif'eret ha-Ḥanokhi*, *Naso*, 62c-d (to *Zohar* III, 127b, s.v. *Tanei Rabbi Shim'on*).

See also Rabbi Abraham Simḥah of Mstislav, "*Ma'amar be-'Inyan Shevirah ve-Tikkun*," in *Mi-Ginzei ha-GRA u-Veit Midrasho*, ed. Kalman Redisch, p. 318: "And so they said, *Tohu* is the mystery of *'Iggulim* and *Tikkun* is the mystery of *Yosher*."

In *Pithei She'arim, Netiv 'Olam ha-Tikkun*, chap. 12 (70b-71a), Rabbi Yitzḥak Eizik Ḥaver sets up successive binaries: *Kav—Reshimu*; *Yosher—'Iggulim*; *Tikkun* (*MaH*)—*Tohu*/*Nekudot* (*BaN*).

In light of the equation of *nekudot* with *'Iggulim*, the text of *Shemonah Kevatsim* 4:118 may be in need of emendation. Presently it reads: "… the rind must precede the fruit; *nekudot* [must precede] the *'Iggulim* and lines of *Yosher*." ("*… tserikhah kelipah li-heyot kedumah la-peri; nekudot la-'Iggulim ve-kavim shel Yosher.*") I suggest that the text should read: "… the rind must precede the fruit; *nekudot* and *'Iggulim* [must precede] lines of *Yosher*." ("*… tserikhah kelipah li-heyot kedumah la-peri; nekudot ve-'Iggulim le-kavim shel Yosher.*")

3 *'Ets Ḥayyim, Sha'ar* 9 (*Sha'ar Shevirat ha-Kelim*), end chap. 6.

4 In fine, the divine name *MaH* clarifies the divine name *BaN*. For Rabbi Yitzḥak Eizik Ḥaver, this ongoing process is synonymous with the passage of time. To illustrate the point, we are told that the word *zeman* (time) has the numerical value (97) of the two names *MaH* (45) and *BaN* (52) combined. See *Pithei She'arim, Netiv 'Olam ha-Tikkun*, chap. 10 (69a), chap. 18 (74a); *Netiv Partsuf Arikh Anpin*, chap. 18 (99b).

This *gematria* (numerical value) is found earlier in the writings of Rabbi Moshe Ḥayyim Luzzatto. See his *Peirush Ma'amar Areimat Yedai*, in *Adir ba-Marom*, Part Two, ed. Rabbi Yosef Spinner (Jerusalem, 1988), p. 91. In the recent edition of *Adir ba-Marom* edited by Rabbi Mordekhai Chriqui (Jerusalem: Makhon Ramhal, 2018), the passage is found on p. 671. (Rabbi Baruch Klein pointed out to me the passage in Luzzatto. Rabbi Klein is readying for publication a new edition of *Adir ba-Marom*.) We know for a fact that the manuscript of *Adir ba-Marom* was in the possession of the circle of the Vilna Gaon; see Bezalel Naor, "*Gilgulei ketav-yad 'Adir ba-Marom' le-RaMḤaL she-hayah be-ba'alut mishpaḥat ha-GRA*," *Sinai*, *Tishrei-Ḥeshvan* 5759 [1998], pp. 53-62. It seems inescapable to conclude that the *gematria* found its way from RaMḤaL to Rabbi Yitzḥak Eizik Ḥaver.

By a stretch, Rabbi Naḥman of Breslov might have alluded to this kabbalistic insight when he told of the ongoing sharing of time that takes place between the Heart (*Lev*) and the Spring (*Ma'ayan*). See *Rabbi Nachman's Stories* (*Sippurey Ma'asioth*), ed. Rabbi Aryeh Kaplan (n.p.: Breslov Research Institute, 1983), "The Seven Beggars," The Third Day, pp. 385-390. In Rabbi Naḥman of Tcherin's *Rimzei ha-Ma'asiyot* (printed at the end of standard editions of *Sippurei Ma'asiyot*), it is explained that the "*tikkun ha-'olamot*" ("correction of the worlds") depends upon the connection of the Heart to the Spring (a symbol of *Ḥokhmah*, or Wisdom). Thereby, "the *Shevirah* (the Shattering of the Vessels) is corrected, which is the correction of all." (Rabbi Kaplan offers that the Heart is *Binah*, or Understanding; op. cit. p. 386, note s.v. *heart*.) If Rabbi Naḥman's symbols allow for my interpretation, then the Spring would correspond to the name *MaH*, and the Heart would correspond to *BaN*.

According to Rabbi Yitzḥak Eizik Ḥaver, the *birurim* (clarifications) are necessary for the benefit of the souls (*neshamot*), "but the worlds (*'olamot*) themselves have already been clarified and corrected (*nivreru ve-nitkenu*)" (*Pitḥei She'arim*, *Netiv 'Olam ha-Tikkun*, chap. 15 [72a]).

Cf. Rabbi Ḥayyim Vital, *Sha'arei Kedushah* (Israel: Mishor, 2005), 3:2 (pp. 242-243), gloss of Rabbi Shalom Shar'abi thereto, and footnote 29 of Rabbi Ze'ev Wolf Ashkenazi, quoting Rabbi Ḥayyim De la Rosa, *Torat Ḥakham* (Salonika, 1848), 73a and 158b. (Rabbi De la Rosa was the pupil of Rabbi Shar'abi.) *Torat Ḥakham* is quoted also by Rabbi Yosef Ḥayyim of Baghdad, *She'elot u-Teshuvot Rav Pe'alim*, Part One (*Oraḥ Ḥayyim*) (Jerusalem, 1901), no. 2 (3c-d). And see *Rav Pe'alim*, Part Two (Jerusalem, 1903), *Kuntres Sod Yesharim*, no. 5 (125c). However, in the sources cited, the opposition is not between *'olamot* and *neshamot*, but between "*Maḥtsav ha-Sefirot*" (the "Quarry of *Sefirot*") and "*Maḥtsav ha-Neshamot*" (the "Quarry of Souls").

5 Cf. Rabbi Zadok Hakohen of Lublin, *Likkutei Ma'amarim*, chap. 9, in *Divrei Soferim* (Lublin, 1913), 56d-57a, 57d.

[6] See *b. Bava Batra* 74b, "Everything that the Holy One, blessed be He, created in His world, was created male and female," and the cosmic expansion on the theme by Rabbi Yitzḥak Eizik Ḥaver, *Pitḥei She'arim*, *Netiv 'Olam ha-Tikkun*, beginning chap. 11 (69b).

Appendix D

[1] See Rabbi Israel Lipkin of Salant, *'Or Yisrael*, ed. Rabbi Isaac Blaser of Petersburg (Vilna, 1900), *Iggeret ha-Mussar*, 53a-b. See also ibid. *Sha'arei 'Or*, 6c; and *'Or Yisrael*, chap. 30 (42d ff.), quoting from Baḥya ibn Paquda, *Duties of the Heart*, *Sha'ar 'Avodat Elohim*, the dialog between reason and soul. And see Yochanan Silman, "Psychology in the Teachings of Rabbi Israel Lipkin (Salanter)" (Hebrew), *Bar-Ilan* XI (1973), pp. 291-292.

[2] See the commentary of Rabbi Samuel Ashkenazi Yaffe to *Bereshit Rabbah*, *Yefeh To'ar* (Venice, 1597-1606), *Genesis Rabbah* 34:12 (in Vilna ed. 34:10), s.v. *'aluv hu ha-se'or* (214b).

[3] *b. Bava Batra* 15a.

[4] See Maimonides, *Guide of the Perplexed* III, 22 (Schwarz ed., pp. 496-497); Naḥmanides, *Commentary to Job*, ed. Rabbi Judah Leib Friedman (Israel, Feldheim, 2018), Introduction, pp. 24-30.

Rabbi Moshe Maimon has pointed out to me an important passage in the writings of Abraham Maimonides where the author equates *yetser ha-tov* with intellect and *yetser ha-ra'* with corporeal desires. See Rabbeinu Avraham ben ha-RaMBaM, *Ma'amar 'al ha-Derashot ve-'al ha-Aggadot*, ed. Rabbi Moshe Maimon (Monsey, NY, 2020), pp. 49-50.

Abulafia, founder of the so-called school of Prophetic Kabbalah, equated the *yetser ha-tov* with the *mal'akh tov* (good angel), and *yetser ha-ra'* with the *mal'akh ra'* (bad angel). See Abraham Abulafia, *Imrei Shefer*, ed. Amnon Gross (Jerusalem, 1999), p. 26. Recently, an anonymous fragment, identified by Idel as Abulafian, connects the two *yetsarim* to the two angels Metatron and Sandalfon. See Moshe Idel, "Multilingual Gematriot in Abraham Abulafia and Their Significance: From the

Bible to Text to Language" (Hebrew), in *Nit'e Ilan: Studies in Hebrew and Related Fields Presented to Ilan Eldar* (Jerusalem: Carmel, 2014), p. 201.

It seems that the author of the alleged commentary of Rashi to Tractate *Horayot*, understood the *yetser ha-ra'* in a mystical light, for he identified it with a "*sar*" or "prince." See Pseudo-Rashi, *Horayot* 13a, s.v. *amar lahem, mi-p'nei she-suran ra'.* For this etymology, cf. *b. Berakhot* 51a, "Suriel, *Sar ha-Panim*," and Rashi ad loc.

[5] *'Ets Ḥayyim, Sha'ar* 26 (*Sha'ar ha-Tselem*), chap. 1.

However, in *Sha'arei Kedushah* 3:2 (p. 240), after equating the *yetser ha-tov* with the "light of the angels" and the *yetser ha-ra'* with the "light of the *kelipot*," Rabbi Ḥayyim Vital then goes on to explain why the soul is attracted to the *yetser ha-tov*, and the body to the *yetser ha-ra'.*

[6] See *Tanya* I, 9 (13b).

[7] *Alfei Menashe*, Part Two, ed. Rabbi Yitzḥak Spalter (Vilna, 1905), par. 139 (55a). And see *Alfei Menashe*, Part One (Vilna, 1822), par. 93 (32b): "Desire and imagination are the emissaries of the *yetser ha-ra'.*"

[8] *Pitḥei She'arim*, Part One, *Netiv Shevirat ha-Kelim*, chap. 1 (48a).

[9] Ibid. *Netiv 'Olam ha-Tikkun*, chap. 16 (72b). Rabbi Yitzḥak Eizik Ḥaver equates the *yetser ha-ra'* with the name *BaN* and Torah with the name *MaH*. See ibid. chap. 25 (77b) and the quote from *b. Kiddushin* 30b: "The Holy One, blessed be He, said to Israel: 'My children, I created the *yetser ha-ra'* and I created Torah as its antidote.'" And see above (Appendix A, note 19) the commentaries of Margi and de Medina to the *Idra* regarding the equation of the Written Torah with the name *MaH*.

[10] Genesis 8:21.

[11] See *Shemonah Kevatsim* 1:172, 173.

The precise definition of the rabbinic term "*yetser ha-ra'*" continues to exercise scholars to this day. See Ishay Rosen-Zvi, "Two Rabbinic Inclinations? Rethinking a Scholarly Dogma," *Journal for the Study of Judaism* 39 (2008), pp. 1-27;

idem, *Demonic Desires: "Yetzer Hara" and the Problem of Evil in Late Antiquity* (Philadelphia: University of Pennsylvania Press, 2011).

Appendix E

1 So that there be no misunderstanding, I should clarify that in works of Jewish Thought the term "*tsurat ha-adam*" (the form of man) refers to the non-physical entity, as opposed to Halakhah, where the reference is to the physical body of man. See e.g. *m. Kereitot* 1:3 and *Niddah* 3:2 (concerning miscarriages). Or Maimonides, *MT*, *Hil. 'Avodah Zarah* 3:10-11 (concerning the prohibition of representing the human body in relief).

In medieval Jewish philosophy, which subscribed to the Aristotelian dichotomy of form and matter, the prevalent terms are *tsurah* (form) and *ḥomer* (matter). See Maimonides, *Moreh Nevukhim*, transl. Michael Schwarz (Jerusalem: Tel-Aviv University Press, 2002), vol. 1, p. 251, n. 19. For an example of "*tsurat adam*" yet embedded in this Aristotelian matrix, see Rabbi Joseph Gikatilla's commentary to Maimonides' *Guide*, appended to Don Isaac Abravanel, *She'elot le-he-Ḥakham Rabbi Shaul Hakohen* (Venice, 1574), chap. 14 (31c).

MaHaRaL's thought is permeated with this terminology, though as we shall see below, MaHaRaL transports the term "*tsurat ha-adam*" to destinations far removed from Aristotelian (and Maimonidean) philosophy. Certainly, by the time we come to the Ḥasidic thought of Radzyn, "*tsurat ha-adam*" has taken on new nuances of meaning.

2 See Bezalel Naor, "Ascent and Descent in the Yom Kippur Rite (From the Ḥasidic Thought of Izbica-Radzyn)," in idem, *From a Kabbalist's Diary*: *Collected Essays* (Spring Valley, NY: Orot, 5765/2005), p. 102, n. 16.

See Rabbi Gershon Ḥanokh Leiner, *Tif'eret ha-Ḥanokhi*, *Vayyera*, 11a (to *Zohar* I, 97b), "*tsurat adam*"; 13a (to *Zohar* I, 102a), "*mi-sitra de-tsurat adam*" (the reference is to his father's *Beit Ya'akov*, *Vayyera*, par. 16 [72a-b]).

These are examples of "*tsurat ha-adam*" in the works of MaHaRaL: *Be'er ha-Golah*, *be'er* 5 (f. 98, col. b); *Derekh Ḥayyim* on *Avot* 3:14 (f. 143, col. a, and f. 146, col. a); *Gevurot Hashem*, chaps. 41 (f. 155), 64 (f. 295, col. a), and 67 (f. 311, col. b); *Ner Mitsvah* (B'nei Berak, 1972), f. 10; *Netivot 'Olam*, *Netiv Ahavat Rei'a*, chap. 1 (f. 53, col. b); *Netsaḥ Yisrael*, chap. 11 (f. 73, col. b); *Tif'eret Yisrael*, chap. 4 (f. 16, col. a, and f. 17, col. b).

It appears to me that MaHaRaL, in turn, borrowed the antiquated Aristotelian term, "*tsurat ha-adam*"—from Maimonides. In his *Sefer ha-Madda'* (Book of Knowledge), Maimonides gave definition to the Biblical "*tselem*":

> And the extra knowledge found in the soul of man is the form of the man (*tsurat ha-adam*) who is whole in his knowledge. And concerning this form, it is said in the Torah: "Let us make man in our image (*be-tsalmenu*), in our likeness" [Genesis 1:26]. (Maimonides, *MT*, *Hil. Yesodei ha-Torah* 4:8)

Later, in his *Guide of the Perplexed* (I, 1), Maimonides would expand upon this theme and further clarify his position, whereby the *tselem*, the essence of man, resides in his intellect. (The late Rabbi Isadore Twersky once felicitously likened *Mishneh Torah* to *Mishnah* and the *Guide* to *Gemara.*) See Rabbi Kafaḥ's note to his edition of *Moreh ha-Nevukhim* (Jerusalem: Mossad Harav Kook, 1977), p. 18, n. 15. In both *Mishneh Torah* and the *Guide*, Maimonides differentiates between the Hebrew terms *tselem* and *to'ar*. (The former refers to the essence, while the latter is restricted to the outer physical appearance.)

MaHaRaL categorically rejected Maimonides' equation of "*tselem Elohim*" (*imago Dei*) with intellect. For MaHaRaL, the "*tselem*" surpasses intellect. See MaHaRaL, *Derekh Ḥayyim* 3:14 (f. 142, col. a); and Benjamin Gross, *Yehi 'Or* (on MaHaRaL, *Ner Mitsvah*) (Jerusalem: Rubin Mass, 1995), p. 66, n. 10. Yet, at the same time, MaHaRaL co-opted Maimonides' term "*tsurat ha-adam*," turning it into a *terminus technicus* to be repurposed in ways Maimonides never dreamt possible (e.g., as the exclusive domain of Israel over and against the nations).

I don't think it logical to assume that Rabbi Gershon Ḥanokh of Radzyn derived the term "*tsurat ha-adam*" directly from Maimonides, bypassing MaHaRaL. True, Rabbi Gershon Ḥanokh went to great lengths to defend Maimonides' philosophy, even going so far as to justify various passages in the *Guide* based on kabbalistic tradition! See his introduction to his father's *Beit Ya'akov: Bereshit* (Warsaw, 1890; photo offset Jerusalem, 1998), 5b-7c. Also published separately under the title, *Ha-Hakdamah ve-ha-Petiḥah.*

(For example, Rabbi Gershon Ḥanokh seized on the fact that Maimonides threw up his hands in defeat when seeking a reason for the table [*shulḥan*] and showbread [*leḥem ha-panim*] to "prove" Maimonides' familiarity with Kabbalah. See *Beit Ya'akov*, 6a, and *Guide* III, 45 [Schwarz ed. p. 604]. In this regard, see Rabbi Asher ben David, end of *Sefer ha-Yiḥud*, in Daniel Abrams, *R. Asher ben David: His Complete Works and Studies in His Kabbalistic Thought* [Hebrew] [Los Angeles: Cherub Press, 1996], pp. 142-144. Rabbi Samuel ben Jacob of Troyes, thought to be a descendant of Rashi, explained that the table and showbread in the Temple were designed to disabuse the nation of any anthropomorphic notions. The fact that at week's end the bread remained uneaten, demonstrated that the deity has no need of bread. And by the same token, the less obvious vessels could not be imputed to any shortcomings of the deity. The incense altar could not be suspected of stimulating the deity's olfactory sense, nor could the *menorah*, the candelabrum, be assumed to provide light for the deity's visual needs.)

Yet, other than that isolated instance in *Mishneh Torah*, one would be hard pressed to find another occurrence of "*tsurat ha-adam*" in Maimonides' lexicon. ("*Tsurat adam*" in the Hebrew translations of the very first chapter of the *Guide* refers to the physical entity rather than to the essence of man, which is how MaHaRaL and later the Radzyner use it.) So I remain convinced that the conduit to the Radzyner was MaHaRaL.

(I must admit that Rabbi Meir ibn Gabbai, who preceded MaHaRaL by a generation, uses the term "*tsurat ha-adam*"; see *'Avodat ha-Kodesh* I, 17; III, 25. In another context relating to the *sefirot*, MaHaRaL quotes from ibn Gabbai's *'Avodat ha-Kodesh* [I, 2] in *Derekh Ḥayyim*, MaHaRaL's commentary to *Avot* 5:6 [234 col. b]. So MaHaRaL was definitely familiar with the work and might have taken the term *"tsurat ha-Adam"* from there. Recently, Joshua Golding has suggested that MaHaRaL's psychology is indebted to ibn Gabbai. See Joshua L. Golding, "Maharal's Conception of the Human Being," *Faith and Philosophy* 14, 4 [October 1997], p. 452. Yet, as Golding writes earlier [p. 451], for MaHaRaL, the *"tselem"* or *"tsurah"* is not reckoned as one of three parts of the human being but its essence [a fourth dimension, if you would have it]. In Ibn Gabbai, on the other hand, *"tsurat ha-adam"* is simply the sum of the three parts, not an added dimension. This is an important distinction.)

Mutatis mutandis, before Maimonides, the Andalusian Neoplatonist, Batalyawsi (d. 1127), had to come to terms with the problem of *imago dei* and *"tsurat adam"* when confronted with a *ḥadith* which read: *"Allah khalaqa adam 'ala suratihi"* (God created man in his/His form). See Ayala Eliyahu, "From *Kitab al-hada'iq* to *Kitab al-dawa'ir*: Reconsidering Ibn al-Sid al-Batalyawsi's Philosophical Treatise," *Al-Qantara* 36:1 (January-June 2015), p. 185. (Eliyahu informs us that the Biblical idea, "and God created man in His image" [Genesis 1:27], does not appear in the *Qur'an*. Ibid. n. 79.)

In Shamma Friedman's article, *"Tselem, Demut ve-Tavnit," "Qur'an"* on page 110 is a typographical error and should read "Qumran." See S.Y. Friedman, *"Tselem, Demut ve-Tavnit," Sidra* 22 (2007), pp. 89-152.

*

In a definitive chapter, Rabbi Ḥayyim Vital breaks man down into three levels: *tsurah* or form (i.e., the soul) and *ḥomer* (i.e., the body), and an intervening level which he calls *"tselem."* The division into form and matter is Aristotelian (and abounds in the works of Vital's contemporary, MaHaRaL.) What is new, is the intermediate level of *tselem*. Note too, that in contradistinction to Maimonides, who equated the Biblical *"tselem"* with *tsurah*, Vital differentiates between them. See *'Ets Ḥayyim, Sha'ar* 26 (*Sha'ar ha-Tselem*), chap. 1.

3 Bezalel Safran found that earlier, Rabbi Menaḥem Mendel of Vitebsk (known in ḤaBaD circles as "Reb Mendel Horodoker") was influenced by MaHaRaL. See Bezalel Safran, "Maharal and Early Ḥasidism," in *Ḥasidism: Continuity or Innovation?*, ed. Bezalel Safran (Cambridge, Massachusetts: Harvard University Press, 1988), pp. 47-144.

I might add that besides Rabbi Menaḥem Mendel of Vitebsk, at least one other disciple of Rabbi Dov Baer, the Maggid of Mezritch, references MaHaRaL. See Rabbi Jacob Joseph ben Judah, the Maggid of Ostroh, *Rav Yeivi* (Ostroh, 5568; Brody, 5634), *Ḥiddushim*, 123b, citing MaHaRaL, *Netivot 'Olam, Netiv ha-Teshuvah*.

As for the Mezritcher Maggid himself, while not explicit, the *terminus technicus "tsurat ha-adam"* is implicit in his play on the words *"shtei ḥatsotserot"*—*"shtei ḥatsi tsurot"* ("two trumpets"—"two half forms") followed immediately by the reference to the verse in Ezekiel 1:26. Whether the Maggid was beholden to MaHaRaL for this terminology, requires further study. See Rabbi Dov Baer ben Abraham of Mezritch, *'Or Torah* (Koretz, 1804), *Beha'alotekha*, s.v. *'Aseh lekha shtei ḥatsotserot kesef* [Numbers 10:2].

4 *Likkutim Ḥadashim*, ed. Benjamin Menaḥem Alter, appended to Rabbi Isaac Meir of Gur (*Ḥiddushei ha-RIM*), *Sefer ha-Zekhut* (Tel-Aviv: Pe'er, n.d.), p. 135.

Similarly, the disciples of Rav Kook credited *him* with infusing new life into the study of MaHaRaL. See Rabbi Moshe Tsevi Neriyah, *Bi-Sdeh ha-RAYaH* (Tel-Aviv, 1991), p. 190.

5 See Rabbi Gershon Ḥanokh's introduction to his father's work, *Beit Ya'akov: Bereshit*, 8d-9a. The introduction is also published separately under the title *Ha-Hakdamah ve-ha-Petiḥah*.

6 Besides references embedded in the text of *Sefat Emet* (the written record of oral discourses delivered over the years), Rabbi Judah Aryeh Leib left commentary to a few chapters of MaHaRaL's work *Netsaḥ Yisrael*; see *Sefat Emet Likkutim*, ed. Abraham Issachar Alter of Pabianice, Part Two (Piotrków,

1936), 58c-59a. According to the approbation of the author's son and successor, Rabbi Abraham Mordechai Alter of Gur (*Imrei Emet*), most of these collectanea were penned by Rabbi Judah Aryeh Leib (1847-1905) as a young man between the years 1866-1870.

7 See Rabbi Moshe Shelomo Kasher, foreword to *Derashot MaHaRaL mi-Prag* (Jerusalem, 1968), pp. 9-53; Rabbi Neriyah, *Bi-Sdeh ha-RAYaH*, pp. 182-183, 199.

8 Also known by the surname "Calabrese" after his birthplace of Calabria, Italy.

9 As stated above, Rabbi Simḥah Bunem of Pshysucha promoted the study of MaHaRaL, whereby it became a staple of the intellectual diet of various Polish schools of Ḥasidism: Kotzk, Gur, Sochatchov.

Though Rabbi Menaḥem Mendel of Lubavitch (*Tsemaḥ Tsedek*) certainly lavished praise upon MaHaRaL, referring to him as "the holy man of God" (*Derekh Mitsvotekha, Mitsvat Tefillin*, chap. 2 [18a]), it does not seem that the study of his works took hold in Lubavitch the way that it did among the Polish Ḥasidim.

(An exception would be the "*Mal'akhim*," a subsect of Lubavitch in America. The founder of the movement, Rabbi Ḥayyim Abraham Dov Baer Hakohen Levine [d. 1938], directed his disciples to the study of MaHaRaL. Their *beit midrash* in the Williamsburg section of Brooklyn is called "*Netivot 'Olam*," after the title of one of MaHaRaL's books. Levine's son, Rabbi Raphael Zalman Levine of Albany, New York, was extremely proficient in MaHaRaL's works.)

Another *beit midrash*—diametrically opposed on the issue of Zionism—where study of MaHaRaL was fostered, was Merkaz Harav in Jerusalem. There, according to the records of the *yeshivah*, Rabbi Ya'akov Moshe Ḥarlap, premier disciple of Rav Kook, taught a class in MaHaRaL.

Another student of Rav Kook, Rabbi David Cohen ("the Nazir") introduced Professor André (Asher Dov) Neher of Strasbourg to MaHaRaL. (Neher confided this to the present author, BN.) Neher, in turn, established at the University of

Strasbourg, "*Etudes Maharaliennes.*" Neher and his doctoral students went on to translate MaHaRaL's works into French. The premier volume in the series, *Le Puits d'Exil* (*Be'er ha-Golah*) was done by Neher himself (who also produced an important study of David Gans, MaHaRaL's disciple.)

Inspired by Rav Kook, Rabbi Isaac Hutner promulgated MaHaRaL in his Yeshivah Rabbi Chaim Berlin in Brooklyn.

In the Gateshead Yeshivah in England, and later in the Ponevezh Yeshivah in B'nei Berak, the *Mashgi'aḥ*, Rabbi Elijah Eliezer Dessler (author of *Mikhtav me-Eliyahu*) imparted MaHaRaL to his students.

(Recently there passed a great devotee of MaHaRaL, Rabbi Moshe Shapiro of Jerusalem, earlier a disciple of Rabbi Dessler, and later of Rabbi Hutner.)

For some of these developments, see Rabbi M.Ts. Neriyah, *Bi-Sdeh ha-RAYaH*, pp. 181-192.

To sum up, while MaHaRaL is today popular among *yeshivah* students of various stripes, this is, again, a rather recent development, and nowhere near the universal acceptance of Lurianic Kabbalah.

Inter alia, after recommending the books of MaHaRaL, Rabbi Isaac Meir of Gur "praised more the words of Rabbi Ḥayyim Vital, of blessed memory, that are in a different league, and in one line of Rabbi Ḥayyim Vital are included several discourses" (*Likkutim Ḥadashim*, p. 135).

10 In Rabbi Ḥayyim Vital, *'Ets Ḥayyim*, *Sha'ar* 30 (*Sha'ar ha-Partsufim*), chap. 1, we find "*tsurat ha-adam*" in a reference to *Zohar*, *Toledot* (I, 134b), but upon inspection, it is not an exact quote from the *Zohar*, but a paraphrase thereof. In any event, "*tsurat ha-adam*" refers to the physical body of man, comprised of its various limbs, not to any essential or metaphysical quality.

11 So according to the title page of *'Ets Ḥayyim*. See also Rabbi Ḥayyim of Volozhin's introduction to *Be'ur ha-GRA* to *Sifra di-Tseni'uta*, p. iv. The Gaon mentioned in conversation to his disciple Rabbi Ḥayyim of Volozhin that the ARI had merited "*gillui Eliyahu*" (the revelation of Elijah). See also

Samuel ben Eliezer of Kalvaria, *Darkhei No'am* (Königsberg, 1764), 96b. (The work is one of the very few to bear the formal approbation of the Vilna Gaon. See my edition of Rav Kook's commentary to the *Legends of Rabbah bar Bar Ḥannah* [New York: Orot/Kodesh, 2019], pp. 9, 17-18, n. 6.)

On the other hand, Rav Kook's premier disciple wrote: "We hold to be true that all the holy books of our rabbi MaHaRaL are the words of the Living God and were written with the appearance of a spirit from above" (Rabbi Ya'akov Moshe Ḥarlap, *Mei Marom*, vol. 1 [Commentary to Maimonides' *Eight Chapters*], Jerusalem, 1982, chap. 8, par. 18 [p. 178]).

12 Rabbi Kafaḥ surmised that some of Maimonides' remarks in the first chapter of the *Guide* were directed against the work *Shi'ur Komah*. See *Moreh ha-Nevukhim*, ed. Kafaḥ, p. 17, n. 6.

Characteristically, MaHaRaL alludes approvingly to the *Shi'ur Komah* tradition: "It is said of [man], 'for in the image of God He made man' [Genesis 9:6], for in his form (*tsurato*) there is a Godly aspect for one who knows the mysteries of wisdom (*razei ha-ḥokhmah*)" (*Tif'eret Yisrael*, chap. 4 [f. 16, col. b]). Cf. *Derekh Ḥayyim* 3:14 (f. 143, col. a).

Rav Kook made use of the term "*Shi'ur Komah*" in *Iggerot ha-RAYaH*, volume 2, Letter 473 (p. 114, n. 4).

13 See Rabbi Shelomo Eliashov, *Ḥelek ha-Be'urim*, Part One, 22c-d.

Elsewhere, I pointed out the remarkable coincidence that Vital's contemporary, MaHaRaL, offsets "*Yosher*" against the "*galgalim*," or heavenly spheres. See Rabbi Judah Löw, *Tif'eret Yisrael*, chap. 11 (f. 36, col. a—f. 38, col. a). By identifying the People of Israel (*Yeshurun*) with *Yosher*, the latter becomes the legacy of the Chosen People.

So too in the school founded by the Vilna Gaon, *Yosher* is the proper domain of Israel, and *'Iggulim* that of the Nations of the World, although by now, the trope is understood in terms of divine providence. Thus, *Yosher* represents *hashgaḥah peratit* (supervision of the individual), and *'Iggulim—hashgaḥah kelalit* (supervision of the species). See the *Likkutim* (Collectanea) published at the conclusion of Samuel Luria's edition of *Be'ur ha-GRA le-Sifra di-Tseni'uta* 38d, s.v. *Ve-ha-kav ha-hu lo' himshikho*; Rabbi Abraham Simḥah of Mstislav, *"Ma'amar be-'Inyan Shevirah ve-Tikkun,"* in *Mi-Ginzei ha-GRA u-Veit Midrasho*, ed. Kalman Redisch, p. 318; and Rabbi Yitzḥak Eizik Ḥaver, *Pitḥei She'arim*, Part One (Warsaw, 1888), *Netiv 'Iggulim ve-Yosher de-A"K*, chap. 3 (10a-11b), and *Netiv 'Olam ha-Tikkun*, chap. 12 (70b).

So too, the Ḥasidic master Rabbi Gershon Ḥanokh Leiner of Radzyn equates *'Iggulim* with *hashgaḥah kelalit* and *Yosher* with *hashgaḥah peratit*. See *Tif'eret ha-Ḥanokhi*, *Naso*, 62d (to *Zohar* III, 127b).

Out of this tradition, derive Rav Kook's two understandings of existence: causality (*"ha-havanah ha-sibbatit"*) versus ethics (*"ha-havanah ha-mussarit"*). See Mordechai Pachter, "*'Iggulim ve-Yosher—Le-Toledotehah shel Idea*" ("Circles and Straightness—A History of an Idea"), *Da'at* 18 (Winter 5747/1987), pp. 59-90; my lengthy note to *Yisrael u-Teḥiyato* (*Israel and Its Renascence*), chap. 2, in *Orot*, ed. Bezalel Naor (Maggid, 2015), pp. 468-469, n. 132; and Bezalel Naor, *The Limit of Intellectual Freedom* (Spring Valley, NY: Orot, 2011), pp. 31; 210, notes 143-144.

Yosef Avivi has pointed out the difference between the Vilna Gaon's explanation of *'Iggulim* and *Yosher*, and that of the *KaLaḤ Pitḥei Ḥokhmah* (attributed to Luzzatto). Unlike the Vilna Gaon, the *KaLaḤ*'s division is not between Israel and the nations, but between the natural scheme and that subject to the creations' deeds. See Yosef Avivi, *Kabbalat ha-GRA* (Jerusalem, 1993), pp. 90-91. It seems that Rav Kook in *Orot* (loc. cit.) has fused together elements of both the *KaLaḤ* and the Gaon. Rav Kook makes the case that Israel's providence is unique (à la Gaon), while claiming that in Israel, the two tracks of *'Iggulim* and *Yosher*, causality and ethics (à la *KaLaḤ*), somehow come together.

That Rav Kook is indebted to the *KaLaḤ* is clear from his repeated use of the term *"shalshelet ha-sibbatit"* ("causal chain"). Besides equating *'Iggulim* with *"hashgaḥah kelalit"* (general supervision) and *Yosher* with *"hanhagah meforetet"* (specific supervision), the *KaLaḤ* also makes *'Iggulim* synonymous with *"hishtalshelut,"* as opposed to the *"hanhagah"* of *Yosher*. See *KaLaḤ*, *petaḥ* 13.

In response to a letter from fellow Kabbalist Rabbi Yosef Leib Zussman of Jerusalem, the Rabbi of Tiberias, Rabbi Asher Ze'ev Werner, attempted to reconcile the Gaon's teaching that *hashgaḥah peratit* is reserved for Israel, with the teaching of the Ba'al Shem Tov that individual supervision extends to all God's creatures. See Rabbi A.Z. Werner, *Bi-Ne'areinu u-vi-Zekeneinu*, appended to *Ta'am Zekenim* (Jerusalem, 1955), chap. 23 (pp. 92-94).

Inter alia, Rabbi Werner reminisces about the great respect that RIDBaZ, the Rabbi of Safed, had for Rav Kook in the summer of 1913, at the height of the *Shemitah* controversy, despite their differing halakhic opinions. Rabbi Werner himself was not convinced by Rav Kook's statement (in a letter to RIDBaZ) that based on Kabbalah, observance of *Shemitah* is only Rabbinic and not Biblical in our day. Ibid. chap. 5 (pp. 52-55). Cf. *Iggerot ha-RAYaH*, vol. 2, pp. 195-196 (Letter 555). Rabbi Werner was a Slonimer Ḥasid. His mother, Dinah née Kastelanetz, wife of Rabbi Simḥah Bunem Werner, was the sister of Rabbi Mordechai Ḥayyim Kastelanetz, the Slonimer Rebbe of Tiberias and Jerusalem.

Finally, in thinly veiled language, Rabbi Isaac Hutner refers to the Lurianic dichotomy of *'Iggulim* and *Yosher*. See *Paḥad Yitzḥak*, *Rosh Hashanah* 27:13, 15, 19, where the terms *"kav ha-hitḥadshut"* and *"'iggul ha-maḥzoriyut"* are employed in opposition.

14 This *gematria* is found in early writings of Kabbalah. See Rabbi Joseph Gikatilla's commentary to Maimonides' *Guide*, chap. 14 (31b). (See above note 1.) Gikatilla juxtaposes the verse in Psalms 44:3: "LORD, what is man (*mah adam*) that You should know him?" Rabbi Menaḥem Recanati quotes in this respect "Midrash Ruth." See *Zohar Ḥadash* (Margaliyot edition), *Midrash Ruth*, 78c: "The mystery of the thing [is] *Yod Hé Vav Hé* is called 'Adam,' and its light emanates to forty-five lights, and this is the numerical value of Adam: *MaH* (45)."

See Recanati, *Peirush ʿal ha-Torah* (Venice, 1523), *Bereshit*, s.v. *Vayyivra Elohim et ha-adam be-tsalmo*.

[15] *Partsuf* is a Greek loanword: πρόσωπον (prósōpon). In Ancient Greek, the term *prosopon* originally designated a "face" or "mask." Later, as a theological term, it took on the meaning of "person" or "persona."

[16] See *Kitvei Rabbeinu Moshe ben Naḥman*, ed. C.B. Chavel, vol. 1 (Jerusalem: Mossad Harav Kook, 1968), p. 346. Naḥmanides writes: "I know that the book is found among you" (ibid., p. 348).

See now Rabbi Elʿazar of Worms, *Sefer "Shaʿarei ha-Sod, ha-Yiḥud ve-ha-Emunah,"* ed. Joseph Dan, in *Temirin*, ed. Israel Weinstock, vol. 1 (Jerusalem: Mossad Harav Kook, 1979), p. 146.

Naḥmanides' stratagem is brilliant. Evidently, Maimonides' frontal assault on anthropomorphic conceptions of the deity deeply offended the sensibilities of the French rabbis, who considered the work *Shiʿur Komah* (perhaps part of the larger picture of *Heikhalot* literature) to represent mainstream Jewish belief. By invoking the weighty authority of Roke'aḥ, Naḥmanides proved himself an able arbiter in this dispute. See Rabbi Zadok Hakohen of Lublin, *Sefer ha-Zikhronot*, chap. 3, in *Divrei Soferim* (Lublin, 1913; photo offset B'nei Berak, 1967), 28b; quoted in Bernard Septimus, "Open Rebuke and Concealed Love: Naḥmanides and the Andalusian Tradition," in *Rabbi Moses Naḥmanides (RaMBaN): Explorations in His Religious and Literary Virtuosity*, ed. Isadore Twersky (Cambridge, Massachussets: Harvard University Press, 1983), p. 24, n. 45. See now Moshe Halbertal, *Naḥmanides: Law and Mysticism*, transl. Daniel Tabak (New Haven: Yale University Press, 2020), pp. 317-318.

The quotation from Roke'aḥ's *Shaʿar ha-Sod ve-ha-Yiḥud ve-ha-Emunah* was designed to demonstrate that one could both maintain one's allegiance to *Shiʿur Komah* (or simply *"Sefer ha-Komah,"* as it is referred to by the Roke'aḥ) and hold to a pure incorporeal belief in the deity. Roke'aḥ taught that the so-called "body of God" was not the reality but a projection, a perception of the prophet's or mystic's imagination. For an in-depth analysis of Rabbi El'azar of Worm's belief system, see Elliot R. Wolfson, *Through a Speculum That Shines: Vision and Imagination in Medieval Jewish Mysticism* (Princeton: Princeton University Press, 1997), 214ff.

Our *gematria* occurs also in Rabbi El'azar of Worms' magnum opus, *Sefer ha-Roke'aḥ*. See *Sefer ha-Roke'aḥ ha-Gadol* (Jerusalem, 1960), *Hilkhot Ḥasidut, Shoresh Kedushat ha-Yiḥud*, p. 22.

From Rabbi El'azar of Worms the *gematria* found its way into Gikatilla's commentary to the *Guide*, chap. 3 (26c). (See above note 1.) Although Idel speculates that "*gedolei ha-Kabbalah*" ("the great Kabbalists") (ibid.) refers as well to Abraham Abulafia. Abulafia incorporated this *gematria* into one of his own commentaries on the *Guide* and considered it of great importance. It stands to reason then that he bequeathed it to his erstwhile disciple Joseph Gikatilla. See Moshe Idel, "Maimonides and Kabbalah," in *Studies in Maimonides*, ed. Isadore Twersky (Cambridge, Massachusetts: Harvard University Press, 1990), pp. 62-63; and Wolfson, *Through a Speculum That Shines*, p. 222, n. 137.

17 It is assumed that the reference is to Rabbi Isaac ben Todros. See Wolfson, ibid.

18 *Ma'arekhet ha-Elohut* (Mantua, 1558), chap. 10 (144a). It should be noted that earlier, Rashi referred to the "face of Man" ("*pnei adam*") in Ezekiel's vision of the four creatures (Ezekiel 1:10, 10:14) as "*partsuf adam.*" See Rashi, *Ḥullin* 91b, s.v. *be-diyukno shel ma'alah*.

See also *b. Sanhedrin* 103b, concerning the wicked King Menasseh who fashioned an idol of four *partsufim*. In the parallel passage in *Deuteronomy Rabbah* 2:20 it is explained that Menasseh made an image of four faces (*panim*) corresponding to the four heavenly creatures that bear the throne of the Holy One, blessed be He.

19 See *b. 'Avodah Zarah* 42b, 43b: "All the faces are permitted except for the face of man (*partsuf adam*)."

Thus, the Biblical *panim* is readily rendered as the rabbinic *partsufim*.

[20] The quote from *Shi'ur Komah* reads in its entirety: "Said Rabbi Ishmael: One who knows the measure (*shi'ur*) of the Creator is assured the World to Come. And I and Rabbi Akiva guarantee this." Quoted by Ibn Ezra in his commentary to Exodus 33. See also Naḥmanides, quoting Rabbi El'azar of Worms (above note 16). Ibn Ezra viewed *Shi'ur Komah* as a *bona fide* work of antiquity (though in need of proper interpretation). See Rabbi Abraham Ibn Ezra, *Yesod Mora ve-Sod Torah*, ed. Joseph Cohen and Uriel Simon (Ramat-Gan: Bar-Ilan University Press, 2002), p. 84. The same may be said for Ibn Ezra's compatriot Rabbi Judah Halevi; see *Kuzari* IV, end par. 3. (See however the note of Yehudah Even Shmuel to his edition of *Kuzari* [Tel-Aviv: Dvir, 1972], p. 286, quoting Rabbi Nethanel Kaspi.)

[21] Anonymous, *Ma'arekhet ha-Elohut*, (Mantua, 1558), chap. 10 (142b-144a). The author is assumed to be a product of the school of Rabbi Solomon ben Abraham ibn Adret (RaShBA) of Barcelona.

[22] For a modern scientific explanation of the phenomenon of "*Partsuf Adam*," see Shaḥar Arzy and Moshe Idel, *Kabbalah: A Neurocognitive Approach to Mystical Experiences* (New Haven: Yale University Press, 2015).

[23] See *'Ets Ḥayyim* 9:8.

[24] In *Zohar Ḥadash*, knowledge of one's body is one of four types of knowledge required of a person. See *Zohar Ḥadash*, *Shir ha-Shirim*, s.v. *sha-lamah ehyeh ke-'otyah* [Song of Songs 1:7] (Margaliyot ed. 70d), and the expansion on this passage in Rabbi Yekutiel Gordon, *Mar Yenuka u-Mar Kashisha* (n.p. [Israel], 2013), pp. 21, 52-55.

[25] The signed poem first appeared in *Likkutei MOHaRaN Tinyana* (Mohilev, 1811). Rabbi David Sears produced a bilingual edition, complete with English translation, introduction and analysis: Rabbi Naḥman of Breslov, *Shir Na'im/Song of Delight* (Spring Valley, NY: Orot, 2005). See my remarks there on pp. 125-126.

[26] It seems that Rabbi Joseph Baer Soloveitchik of Boston also viewed the issue of anthropomorphism as being crucial to an

understanding of the controversy between the Jewish mystics and the medieval philosophical rationalists:

> Both Saadiah and Maimonides explained all anthropomorphic terms as being allegorical. To the *Zohar*, however, these anthropomorphic terms are revelations of God's personality.
>
> (Meir Triebitz, "Rabbi Joseph B. Soloveitchik's Lectures on Genesis, X through XIII," *Ḥakirah* 31 [Winter 2022], p. 28)

See also Triebitz's note 6 on page 29 concerning the concept of *Partsufim* and *Deus Persona*. Cf. Gershom G. Scholem, *Major Trends in Jewish Mysticism* (New York: Schocken, 1971), pp. 268-272.

An outcropping of the controversy between Maimonides and Naḥmanides concerning anthropomorphic imagery is their differing interpretations of Onkelos' many circumlocutions. Maimonides understood these as attempts to avoid in the Aramaic translation anything that would smack of anthropomorphic language. Naḥmanides set out to poke so many holes in Maimonides' theory as to render it untenable. See *Guide of the Perplexed* I, 21, 27, 48; II, 33 (Schwarz ed. p. 380); Naḥmanides, *Commentary to the Torah*, Genesis 46:1 (Chavel ed. pp. 246-252); Exodus 20:16 (Chavel ed. pp. 406-407); Rabbi Yom Tov ben Abraham Al-Sevilli (RITBA), *Sefer ha-Zikaron*, ed. Kalman Kahana (Jerusalem: Mossad Harav Kook, 1982), pp. 62-67; Rabbi Ephraim Elankawa (Al-Naqawa), *Sha'ar Kevod Adonai*, ed. Rabbi Ḥayyim Bliaḥ (Tunis, 1902), 21a-63a; Rabbi Meir ibn Gabbai, *'Avodat ha-Kodesh*, III, 28-32.

27 *Shemonah Kevatsim* 7:84. In precise Lurianic terminology, the root of Maimonides' soul is in "the left corner of the beard of *Ze'ir Anpin*" and the root of Naḥmanides' soul is in "the right corner of the beard of *Ze'ir Anpin*" (Rabbi Ḥayyim Vital, *Sha'ar ha-Gilgulim*, *hakdamah* 36). Rabbi Ḥayyim Yosef David Azulai quotes this passage in *Shem ha-Gedolim* I, s.v. *RaMBaM* and *RaMBaN*.

28 See now Rav Kook's discussion of the controversy between Crescas and Maimonides, where Maimonides opposed

positive attributes of the deity and Crescas upheld them. See *Kovets mi-Tekufat Yaffo-Schweiz*, par. 67, in *Pinkesei ha-RAYaH*, vol. 7, p. 166. Rav Kook also discussed positive versus negative attributes in his appreciation of Maimonides, "*Li-Demut Deyokno shel ha-RaMBaM*"; reprinted in *Ma'amrei ha-RAYaH*, vol. 1 (Jerusalem, 1980), pp. 113-115.

29 Moses Maimonides, *Guide of the Perplexed*, transl. M. Friedländer (2nd edition, London: Routledge & Kegan Paul, 1904; photo offset New York: Dover, 1956), I, 46 (p. 62). See Michael Schwarz's discussion of the fine points of language; *Moreh Nevukhim* (Jerusalem: Tel-Aviv University Press, 2002), vol. 1, p. 105, n. 45.

Rav Kook's nineteen-year old son, Tsevi Yehudah, turned around the simple meaning of Rabbi Yudan's statement. See his letter to Rabbi Ḥarlap, in *Tsemaḥ Tsevi*, vol. 1, Letter 9 (pp. 24-25). I translated the lengthy passage to English. See Bezalel Naor, *Navigating Worlds: Collected Essays* (New York, NY: Orot/Kodesh, 2021), pp. 426-427, n. 38.

30 *Derekh Ḥayyim* to *Avot* 3:14 (f. 143, col. a).

31 See also *Shemonah Kevatsim* 7:41 (p. 310) where Rav Kook finds a place for anthropomorphic imagery within the Lurianic cosmogony somewhere between the *Tsimtsum* and the *Reshimu* (again quoting Rabbi Yudan's famous statement, "Great is the power of prophets who liken the creature to its Creator").

32 *Shemonah Kevatsim* 7:84.

33 The exact term, "*binyan tsurat ha-adam*," occurs in the anonymous medieval work of Kabbalah, *Ma'arekhet ha-Elohut*, chap. 10 (142b).

34 See Rabbi Shelomo David Fruchthandler, *Minḥat Shelomo* (2nd edition, n.p. [Lakewood], 5782 [i.e., 2022]).

My thanks to my dear friend Rabbi Nachman Schneider for bringing this work to my attention.

35 See the "*Zikhronot*" penned by Rabbi Hutner's daughter, Rebbetsin Beruriah Hutner David, in *Sefer ha-Zikaron le-Maran Ba'al Paḥad Yitzḥak* (Brooklyn, 2014), p. 85; *Paḥad Yitzḥak: Iggerot u-Ketavim* (Brooklyn, NY, 2016), p. 46.

One notes that a disciple of Rabbi Hutner, the Kabbalist Rabbi Yisrael Eliyahu Weintraub, also makes abundant use of the term "*tsurat ha-adam*" in his esoteric writings. See *Nefesh Eliyahu*: *Hakdamot ve-Shi'urim*, *Ma'amar be-Pitḥei She'arim*, p. 15; *Hakdamot*, pp. 125-126.

In his recently released commentary to *Sifra di-Tseni'uta* (or rather to the Vilna Gaon's *Be'ur ha-GRA*), Rabbi Hutner comes out with the startling statement that "*tsurat ha-adam*" (or in Kabbalistic jargon, "*Adam Kadmon*," the macroanthropus) is the end or point of the process of the "*ḥillul*" ("emptying" or "voiding," from "*ḥalal*," the empty space). The whole point of the process of *Tsimtsum* (divine self-contraction) is to bring about the non-divine or extradivine, as it were. In man's capacity for consciousness (and presumed autonomy) there is expressed this divine will to produce an other. The process of "othering" will repeat itself once again in the myth of the creation of Eve, when Adam too will experience this excavation. (In Lurianic parlance, this is referred to as "*Nesirah*," a mystery associated with *Rosh Hashanah*.) See *Be'ur Sifra di-Tseni'uta mi-Ba'al Paḥad Yitzḥak*, pp. 97-99.

36 Rabbi Hutner named the *kollel* (institute of higher learning for married students) attached to Yeshivah Rabbi Chaim Berlin, "Gur Aryeh," after one of MaHaRaL's works. (MaHaRaL's German surname, Löw, means "Lion," as does the Hebrew "*Aryeh*.") The *kollel* was established in 1957, Rabbi Hutner's fiftieth, "Jubilee year," a year when a "man shall return to his holding" (Leviticus 25:10). See *Paḥad Yitzḥak*: *Iggerot u-Ketavim*, p. 123; *Sefer ha-Zikaron le-Maran Ba'al Paḥad Yitzḥak*, pp. 44, 76.

In 1970, when Rabbi Hutner was hijacked by terrorists to Jordan, at a public "*farbrengen*" (Ḥasidic gathering) on 18 Elul (the *Yahrzeit* of MaHaRaL), the Lubavitcher Rebbe, Menaḥem Mendel Schneerson, expressed his fervent prayer that the MaHaRaL's merit come to the aid of one who immerses himself (in Yiddish, "*kokht zikh*") in his Torah. (The allusion to Rabbi Hutner was transparent to all.)

See also Rabbi Neriyah's depiction of Rabbi Hutner's presentation of MaHaRaL in *Bi-Sdeh ha-RAYaH*, pp. 188-189.

[37] See what Rabbi Hutner wrote after visiting the grave of MaHaRaL, in *Sefer ha-Zikaron le-Maran Ba'al Paḥad Yitzḥak*, pp. 61-64.

[38] See Bezalel Naor, *Navigating Worlds: Collected Essays* (2006-2020) (New York, NY: Orot/Kodesh, 2021/5781), pp. 274-275, n. 5; 296, n. 23.

[39] The term coined by the Radzyner is *"Ilan ha-Safek,"* or in Aramaic, *"Ilana di-Sefeka"* (Tree of Doubt). See Bezalel Naor, *Navigating Worlds*, p. 274, n. 5.

[40] I have a similar question in regard to Rabbi Hutner's literary artifice, his cloaking kabbalistic ideas in rational, non-mystical language. According to his biographer, his daughter, Rebbetsin Beruriah Hutner David, this was done in emulation of MaHaRaL. See *Sefer ha-Zikaron le-Maran Ba'al Paḥad Yitzḥak*, p. 76. But might it also have been inspired by Rabbi Hutner's mentor in Jerusalem, Rav Avraham Yitzḥak Kook, who earlier adopted this stratagem of MaHaRaL, and, at least in his mature writing, presented mystical concepts in a florid, highly suggestive Hebrew, stripped of kabbalistic jargon? See *Iggerot ha-RAYaH*, vol. 2, p. 206 (Letter 569), where Rav Kook explains his wont of communicating thoughts "in a cloak of cold logic" (*"be-ma'ateh shel kerirut sikhlit"*). He observed that Rabbi Ya'akov Moshe Ḥarlap's style of writing was not sufficiently guarded.

And see Yehoshua B. Be'ery, *Ohev Yisrael bi-Kedushah*, vol. 4, pp. 57-58: "When [Rav Kook] writes things that are truly *Sitrei Torah* (Secrets of the Torah), he tries to give them a beautiful form and express them in a modern manner." This was the assessment of Alexander Ziskind Rabinowitz (AZaR), a distinguished Jaffa writer who became an acolyte of Rav Kook. It appeared in *Keter Torah* (Jerusalem, 1911), AZaR's appreciation of Rav Kook. (AZaR, a native of Lyady, Belarus, came from a ḤaBaD background. After his marriage, he lived for some years in nearby Romanova. This explains his intercession on behalf of Rabbi Moshe Tsevi Klatzkin of

Romanova. See the facsimile of Rav Kook's response in Be'ery, vol. 4, pp. 20-21. For a short biographical sketch of Rabbi Moshe Tsevi Klatzkin, see Rabbi Moshe Ze'ira, "Rabbi Eliyahu Klatzkin," in *Yeshurun*, vol. 15 [Nissan 5765], p. 751.)

For a fine understanding of Rav Kook's style of writing, see Yosef Ben Shlomo, *"Shirat ha-Ḥayyim": Perakim be-Mishnato shel Harav Kook* (Tel-Aviv: Misrad ha-Bitaḥon, 1989), pp.16-23.

*

By the way, in the multivolume series *Ze'ev Yitrof*, which otherwise emulates the style of Rabbi Hutner's *Paḥad Yitzḥak*, we find copious quotations from the *Zohar*. The author of *Ze'ev Yitrof*, Rabbi Ze'ev Hakohen Hoberman, a disciple of Rabbi Hutner, allowed himself this one significant break from his master's precedent.

While Rabbi Hutner never mentioned the *Zohar* in public (*Sefer ha-Zikaron*, ibid.), MaHaRaL does cite the *Zohar*, on occasion outright by name (*Be'er ha-Golah*, *be'er* 5 [f. 86, col. b; 95, col. a]; *Ḥiddushei Aggadot*, *Rosh Hashanah* 17b [f. 117, col. b-118, col. a]; *Bava Metsi'a* 84a [f. 34, col. a]; *Niddah* 13a [f. 152, col. b]; *Netivot 'Olam*, *Netiv ha-Perishut*, chap. 3 [f. 118, col. a]; *Netiv ha-Teshuvah*, chap. 6 [f. 166, col. a]); other times referring to it obliquely as "Midrash" or *"Midrash ha-Ne'elam"* (*Ḥiddushei Aggadot*, *Bava Batra* 15a [f. 69, col. a]; *Tif'eret Yisrael*, chap. 4 [f. 17, col. b], chap. 13 [f. 43, col. b]).

One might conceivably argue that by and large, MaHaRaL's viewpoint developed independent of the kabbalistic tradition. However, Rav Kook perceived MaHaRaL as a "closet Kabbalist." "MaHaRaL, too, is to be reckoned among the *mekubbalim*, though his style [of writing] is different than that of most of his contemporaries" (*Iggerot ha-RAYaH*, vol. 2, p. 91 [Letter 447]). See earlier, Rabbi Menaḥem Mendel Schneersohn of Lubavitch, *Derekh Mitsvotekha*, *Mitsvat Ha'amanat Elohut*, chap. 3, who refers to "Rabbi Judah Löw ben Rabbi Bezalel of Prague" as *"ha-Gaon ha-Mekubbal."*

Very early in his rabbinic career, Rav Kook became conversant with the works of MaHaRaL. See *Siḥot ha-RAYaH* (Tel-Aviv, 1979), p. 148. In the introduction (*"Midbar Kedem"*) to *Midbar Shur*, the collection of sermons delivered in his first rabbinic post of Zeimel, Rav Kook singled out for mention the *oeuvre* of MaHaRaL as an outstanding example of works of Aggadah written with deep logic (*'omek higayon*). See *Midbar Shur*, ed. Michael Herskovitz and David Landau (Jerusalem, 1999), p. 6. In *'Eyn AYaH*, Rav Kook's commentary to the *'Eyn Ya'akov* legends of the Talmud, Rav Kook simulated the language and peculiar methodology of MaHaRaL. See Yehudah Mirsky, *Towards the Mystical Experience of Modernity: The Making of Rav Kook, 1865-1904* (Boston: Academic Studies Press, 2021), pp. 192-193. Rabbi Neriyah devoted a chapter to parallels between Rav Kook's teachings and those of MaHaRaL; see *"Bi-Netivot MaHaRaL,"* in *Bi-Sdeh ha-RAYaH*, pp. 181-215.

Rabbi Hutner confided to Rabbi Neriyah: "The Rav [i.e., Rav Avraham Yitzḥak Kook] was the one who opened before me MaHaRaL of Prague!" (*Bi-Sdeh ha-RAYaH*, pp. 189, 432). In private conversation, Rabbi Hutner referred to Rav Kook as *"Der Rov."* (Heard from my dear friend, Dr. Henry Hersh, *a"h*, a blood relation both of Rabbi Isaac Hutner and of his cousin, Havah Leah Hutner, the wife of Rabbi Tsevi Yehudah Kook, through the Segal line.)

Appendix F

1 See Rabbi Moshe Tsevi Neriyah, *Siḥot ha-RAYaH* (Tel-Aviv, 1979), pp. 77-79.

While it may be a trifling matter, there is speculation that Rav Kook derived a philosophic adage from Rabbi Menashe. In an early work of his, *'Eyn AYaH*, Rav Kook seems to be quoting Maimonides when he writes, "There is no particular in intellect and no universal in sense" (*"Ein perat be-sekhel ve-ein kelal be-ḥush"*) (*'Eyn AYaH*, vol. 1, chap. 1, par. 46 [to *Berakhot* 6a]). While the tenor of the statement is certainly consistent with Maimonides' philosophy in the *Guide* (see I, 73; III, 16 and 19), nowhere does that maxim occur. However, it does approximate the (unsourced) adage in the Short Apology (*Hitnatslut Ketsarah*) that prefaces *Alfei Menashe*, Part One:

"There is no individual (man) in intellect and no species in sense" (*"Ein ish be-sekhel ve-ein min be-ḥush"*). In a later work of Rabbi Menashe, *Peiruka li-Tekanta*, the sequence is reversed: "There is no species in sense and no individual (man) in intellect" (*"Ein min be-ḥush ve-ein ish be-sekhel"*) (*Peiruka li-Tekanta*, ed. Rabbi David Kamenetsky, in *Yeshurun* 20 [Nissan 5768], p. 821).

2 This includes Isaac Barzilay's English monograph, *Manasseh of Ilya: Precursor of Modernity among the Jews of Eastern Europe* (Jerusalem: Magnes, 1999). Though Barzilay attempts a critical study, he was unable to free himself of the pervasive influence of Plungian.

Mea culpa. I myself was misled by Plungian and company when I wrote that the Gaon of Vilna distanced himself from Rabbi Menashe of Ilya because he paid a visit to Rabbi Shneur Zalman in Liozna. See the introduction to my edition of *Be'ur ha-GRA le-Sifra di-Tseni'uta* (Jerusalem, 1998), pp. 25-26.

Rabbi David Kamenetsky has exposed this supposed anecdote as one of Plungian's many fanciful fabrications. See D. Kamenetsky, *"Ha-Gaon Rabbi Menashe me-Ilya zt"l,"* *Yeshurun*, vol. 20 (Nissan 5768 [i.e., 2008]), pp. 732, n. 7; 776-778.

On the other hand, in a personal handwritten letter to Rabbi Menaḥem Mendel Schneerson, the Rebbe of Lubavitch-Brooklyn, Rabbi Pinḥas Menaḥem Alter, later the Rebbe of Gur (known as the *"P'nei Menaḥem"*), informed the Lubavitcher Rebbe of the forthcoming marriage of his son, Rabbi Shaul Alter, to a descendant of Rabbi Menashe of Ilya. A facsimile of the letter, datelined "Jerusalem, 20 Iyyar 5737 [i.e. 1977]" is available under the entries "Pinḥas Menaḥem Alter" and "Shaul Alter" at chabadpedia.co.il.

Rabbi Pinḥas Menaḥem wrote that his future *meḥutan* (in-law), the father of the bride, is descended on his mother's side from ḤaBaD Ḥasidim, the Koppelovitch and Shmutkin families, descendants of Rabbi Menashe of Ilya. He adds "that the *Tsemaḥ Tsedek* [i.e., Rabbi Menaḥem Mendel of Lubavitch] said that there is a *kabbalah* (tradition) from the *Alter Rebbe* [i.e., Rabbi Shneur Zalman of Lyady] that one may marry descendants of Rabbi Menashe of Ilya, though he was not of the Ḥasidim, as is famous."

3 *Alfei Menashe*, Part One, par. 177 (73b).

4 This striving for *peshat* was expressed especially in regard to the study of Mishnah. Rabbi Menashe had received from the Vilna Gaon that just as there is *peshat* and *derash* in the study of Scripture, so there exist levels of *peshat* and *derash* in Mishnah. Unfortunately, the *Maskilim* of Vilna, Mordechai Plungian and company, distorted this teaching of the Gaon, as transmitted by Rabbi Menashe, to promote the reformation of Talmudic Law. See Chanan Gafni, "*Peshat u-Derash ba-Mishnah: Le-Gilguleha shel Masoret mi-Beit Midrasho shel ha-GRA*" ("*Peshat* and *Derash* in the *Mishnah*: On the Metamorphosis of a Tradition from the School of R. Elijah of Vilna"), *Sidra*, vol. 22 (2007), pp. 5-19.

5 Barzilay follows suit. See Barzilay, pp. 118-122.

6 Kamenetsky, pp. 730-750.

7 Kamenetsky, pp. 741-742, n. 20.

The good standing of "Menashe ben Joseph B[en] P[orath] of Ilya" vis-à-vis the Vilna rabbinical establishment is attested to by the fact that he co-signed with Rabbi Abraham Abeleh Posweler (Dayyan of Vilna) on the *haskamah* (approbation) to a work of novellae to Talmud and *Tikkunei Zohar* by Rabbi Abraham ben Judah Leib of Khotimsk, *Maskil le-Eitan* (Vilna, 1818). In *Alfei Menashe*, Part One, par. 161 (f. 63), Rabbi Menashe records a Talmudic exchange with Rabbi Abeleh Posweler of Vilna. See Rabbi Abraham Kosman, "*Mavo' le-Sifrei R' Menashe me-Ilya Talmid ha-GRA*," *Nitsanei Arets* (publication of Merkaz Harav), no. 8 (1992), p. 16.

8 In *Toledot ha-Gaon ha-Meḥaber*, the biography of Rabbi Menashe written by his grandson, Rabbi Isaac Spalter, we are told that though both Rabbi Menashe and his student Rabbi Aryeh Leib had excellent memories, of Rabbi Menashe it was said: "There is no forgetting." And as for their greatness in Torah, "A *ḥiddush* (original thought) that Rabbi Aryeh Leib would consider the greatest of the great, Rabbi Menashe would

consider the smallest of the small." See *Alfei Menashe*, Part Two, 4d.

9 See Rav Kook's description of the city of Smorgon in his letter to his younger brother Shaul Ḥannah, who was studying there; *Iggerot ha-RAYaH*, vol. 1, Letter 5 (p. 7).

10 It should be pointed out that Rav Kook's first teacher, back in Dvinsk, Rabbi Reuven Levin (known as "Reb Reuvaleh Denaburger") was the student of Rabbi Leibeleh Shapira. Thus, two of Rav Kook's teachers were, in a spiritual sense, "grandsons" of Rabbi Menashe of Ilya (through Reb Leibeleh Shapira).

Very little survives of Reb Leibeleh Shapira's writings, so it is well-nigh impossible to gauge what influence Rabbi Menashe exerted upon him. (A descendant of Rabbi Aryeh Leib Shapira, Rabbi Ḥayyim Ya'akov Levene published at the end of his work, *Ḥil ha-Mikdash*, a letter of Torah from Rabbi Aryeh Leib to Rabbi Ḥayyim Berlin. The letter is datelined "Sunday, 17 Sivan, 5612 [i.e., 1852], Kovno." See Rabbi Ḥayyim Ya'akov Levene, *Ḥil ha-Mikdash*: *Seder Kodashim* [Jerusalem, 1937]. Rabbi Levene's mother [wife of Rabbi Aryeh Levine of Jerusalem] was the daughter of Rabbi David Shapira of Kovno, a great-grandson of Reb Leibeleh Shapira of Kovno.)

However, into the next generation, Rabbi Leibeleh's son, Rabbi Ḥayyim Abraham Shapira of Smorgon, evidently strove for *peshat*, the hallmark of Rabbi Menashe. See his suggested emendation of the text of Maimonides' *Hilkhot Teshuvah*, preserved by his student Rav Kook in *Mishpat Kohen*, no. 128 (p. 288, column a). See also Rabbi Meshel Shmuel Shapira, *He'arot ha-Shemesh* (Odessa, 1889), end chap. 4 (p. 10). Though it might be an isolated instance, it nevertheless bespeaks intellectual daring, something for which Rabbi Menashe was famous.

As for Reb Reuvaleh, he certainly impressed upon his youthful charge, Abraham Isaac Kook, a mistrust of novel interpretations not spelled out in the Talmud and *rishonim* (early authorities). See Neriyah, *Siḥot ha-RAYaH*, pp. 69-71.

But this is not exactly the quest for *peshat* by which Rabbi Menashe was distinguished.

Based on what was revealed to him by Rav Kook's younger brother, Rabbi Dov Kook, Rabbi Ḥayyim Karlinsky wrote that it was Rabbi Reuven Levin who asked that Rav Kook pay a visit to his old study partner, Rabbi Ḥayyim Abraham Shapira, in Smorgon and convey his regards. (The two had studied together in Smorgon under the latter's father, Rabbi Leibeleh Shapira.) See Neriyah, *Tal ha-RAYaH* (Tel-Aviv, 1993), pp. 228-229.

Mirsky records an oral tradition whereby Rabbi Reuven Levin himself studied under Rabbi Menashe of Ilya, but in my humble opinion, this should be viewed with circumspection. See Yehudah Mirsky, *Towards the Mystical Experience of Modernity: The Making of Rav Kook, 1865-1904* (Boston: Academic Studies Press, 2021), p. 57, n. 68. (True, Rabbi Reuven Levin was a native of Smorgon, but that in no way makes the case for him having studied under Rabbi Menashe of Ilya.)

Today, in the world of the Lithuanian *yeshivot*, Rabbi Leibeleh Shapira is known as the father of Rabbi Raphael Shapira (author of *Torat Refael*), who was married to the daughter of Rabbi Naftali Tsevi Yehudah Berlin (NeTsIV) of Volozhin, and whose daughter Lifsha was married to Rabbi Ḥayyim Soloveitchik ("Reb Ḥayyim Brisker").

Rabbi Ḥayyim Karlinsky preserved a tradition whereby his ancestor, Rabbi Ḥayyim Abraham Shapira of Smorgon, accompanied his brother, Rabbi Raphael Shapira's son-in-law Rabbi Ḥayyim Soloveitchik to the *ḥuppah*. See Neriyah, *Siḥot ha-RAYaH*, p. 84, note.

11 Neriyah, *Siḥot ha-RAYaH*, p. 78.

12 Psalms 145:9.

13 Neriyah, *Siḥot ha-RAYaH*, p. 78.

Rabbi Neriyah adduces in this regard the fragment from Rabbi Menashe's lost work *Tikkun Kelali*, preserved by his grandson, Rabbi Spalter, in the introduction to *Alfei Menashe*, Part Two; and chapter 41 of *Alfei Menashe* (see below adjacent to note 33). However, to this writer's thinking, the more apposite passage would have been that found in the grandson's biography of Rabbi Menashe (5d), a fragment of yet another work of Rabbi Menashe that has since gone missing:

> In the introduction to his book *Ha'amek She'alah* mentioned above:
>
> My main intention is directed to a single destination, namely to the *tikkun* of distancing damage and achieving the good. I do not investigate at all my own affairs and benefit, how to improve my lot. I only investigate in general, what causes the evils and corruptions that are in the world, to understand thereby the ways of collective correction (*tikkun kelali*).
>
> For I say, what am I and what is my value opposite the species of sentient life (*ha-ḥayyim ha-margishim*) and the humans (*ha-medaberim*, literally "the speakers") that are in the world?
>
> If it could be conceived that the Creator, blessed be He, would provide me, the members of my household, my relations and friends with eternal, enduring good, but there would remain in the world some corruption, namely the suffering of some sentient being (*ḥai margish*), and all the more so, a human being (*min ha-medaber*)—I would not choose this at all. It would be impossible for me to derive benefit from this. In what way am I different from all the living creatures? These are His handiwork and those are His handiwork! Certainly this is not the completion of the *tikkun* as long as there remains some sentient being (*margish*) that has not achieved its wholeness according to its level of preparation and understanding for attaining good.

14 See Rabbi David Kamenetsky, "*Sefer Peiruka li-Tekanta*," *Yeshurun* 20 (Nissan 5768 [i.e. 2008]), pp. 800-801.

[15] The term "*ḥai margish*" is recurrent in Rabbi Menashe's writings. See below adjacent to note 33 the quote from *Alfei Menashe*, Part Two, chap. 41.

[16] *Peiruka li-Tekanta*, p. 815. Italics mine—BN.

[17] So that the reader make no mistake, I wish to clarify that the term "*Tikkun Kelali*" as used by Rabbi Menashe, has nothing in common with Rabbi Naḥman of Breslov's *Tikkun Kelali*, much in vogue these days. The latter consists of the recitation of ten psalms as a way of correcting the blemish of spilled seed (*pegam ha-berit*).

As explained by Ben-Zion Katz, Rabbi Menashe's notion is actually of a "*tikkun soziali kelali*," where Rabbi Menashe advocates for social reform and puts forth an economic plan. Katz may have exaggerated when he called Rabbi Menashe, "the first Hebrew socialist," but not by much. See Ben-Zion Katz, *Rabbanut, Ḥasidut, Haskalah*, vol. 2 (Tel-Aviv: Dvir, 1958), pp. 192-193.

[18] Plungian unlawfully read into the controversial statement reformist tendencies. Rabbi David Kamenetsky has minimized the boldness of Rabbi Menashe's statement, demonstrating that it is merely a rehashing of the Mishnah in *'Eduyot* (according to the interpretation of RABaD of Posquières) which accounts for preserving the minority opinion by saying that it might one day come in handy, should a future *beit din* wish to adopt it. See *m. 'Eduyot* 1:5; Kamenetsky, pp. 741-742, n. 20.

[19] *The Legends of Rabbah bar Bar Ḥannah with the Commentary of Rabbi Abraham Isaac Hakohen Kook*, ed. Bezalel Naor (New York, NY: Orot/Kodesh, 2019), p. 14. Because of the sensitivity of the passage, when it first appeared in print in *Ma'amrei ha-RAYaH* in 1984, the editors saw fit to add qualifying words to soften the impact of the statement. Ibid.

[20] See *Iggerot ha-RAYaH*, vol. 1, p. 303 (Letter 266). (See above Appendix A adjacent to note 14.)

And see Rabbi Abraham Isaac Hakohen Kook, *Orot* (2015), transl. Bezalel Naor, *Yisrael u-Teḥiyato* (Israel and Its Renascence), chap. 21 (pp. 218-219):

> All the differing thoughts and opinions are rivulets and chambers of this supernal knowledge, "from which rooms and chambers are filled" [*Zohar* III, 136a, 289b, 296a], and which divided right and left, are united at the root of the supernal knowledge. Yet retaining its unity, that root divides laterally, "four hundred, ninety-nine and a half on this side, and four hundred, ninety-nine and a half on this side" [*Zohar* II, 27b]. They are all subsumed in the principal divine root, which by its spiritual light fills all the chambers with precious and pleasant riches. The great and pure of knowledge strive to grasp the supernal root of knowledge, which in its original unity is indivisible and waters all with its special flow. Thus, all the private chambers of the left and the right receive its qualities, and all the high and low ideas that come to be in the world are blessed with the blessing of peace. The entire cosmic orientation of all humanity and all creatures tends to rectitude and to peace, which follows upon its heels.

21 Viz. Rabbi Menashe's work, *Pesher Davar*, designed to effect a rapprochement between various stances.

22 For Rav Kook's feelings of "kinship" toward the mineral kingdom (*domem*), see Rabbi Abraham Isaac Hakohen Kook, *Orot ha-Kodesh*, ed. Rabbi David Cohen (the Nazir), vol. 2, pp. 361-364, 414-415. See now *Kovets mi-Tekufat Yaffo-Schweiz*, par. 46, in *Pinkesei ha-RAYaH*, vol. 7, p. 147.

DaTsḤaM in the Nazir's headers is the initials of *Domem* (Mineral), *Tsome'aḥ* (Vegetable), *Ḥai* (Animal), *Medaber* (literally "Speaking," i.e., Human).

Remarkably, another cosmic thinker and poetic soul, Abraham Joshua Heschel, expressed a similar sentiment: "Awe of heaven (*yir'at shamayim*) is a relationship with all of existence; it is an awareness of the beauty of all being. Inanimate things (*domemim*) also have a meaning and a fate of their own, and a necessary connection to spiritual values" (Abraham Heschel, "*Yir'at Shamayim*," in *Sefer Hashanah li-Yehudei Amerika*, vol. 6 [1942], p. 68).

[23] In Hebrew, *"ha-nefesh ha-zot she-ru'aḥ u-neshamah ḥayah."* The recipient of the letter, Rabbi Pinḥas Hakohen Lintop, himself a student of Kabbalah, would well appreciate the allusion to the four levels of the soul in ascending order: *nefesh, ru'aḥ, neshamah, ḥayah.*

[24] Cf. Psalms 93:3; *Iggerot ha-RAYaH*, vol. 1, p. 240 (Letter 184). Datelined "Jaffa, 7 Shevat, 5669 [i.e., 1909]," the letter is addressed to Rav Kook's fellow Kabbalist in Birzh, Lithuania, Rabbi Pinḥas Hakohen Lintop.

[25] *Perek Shirah* (Chapter of Song) is an anonymous work from antiquity (of uncertain provenance) which assigns to each creature a verse from the Bible. For additional references of Rav Kook to *Perek Shirah*, see *Orot ha-Kodesh*, vol. 3, pp. 227-228.

[26] The vocalized version of *Orot* (Beit El, 2004) has *"u-me-rigshei kol margish"* ("and from the feelings of every sentient being") but that does not work syntactically. Be that as it may, Rav Kook's phraseology is highly reminiscent of Rabbi Menashe of Ilya's sensitivity to "every sentient being" (*"kol ḥai margish"*). See above note 15.

[27] *Orot*, ed. Bezalel Naor (Jerusalem: Maggid, 2015), *Orot ha-Teḥiyah*, chap. 69 (p. 415).

[28] A term coined by psychiatrist Richard Maurice Bucke in his book, *Cosmic Consciousness: A Study in the Evolution of the Human Mind* (Philadelphia, 1901). Lately, Ken Wilber has much advanced this evolutionary theory.

[29] See above note 25. At the beginning of *Perek Shirah* occurs the *"beraita"* quoted by Rav Kook: "Rabbi Eliezer says: 'Whoever delves into this *Perek Shirah* every day, I attest that he is assured the World to Come.'" The medieval philosopher Rabbi Joseph Albo records a slightly different version: "Whoever *recites Perek Shirah* every day, is assured the World to Come.'" See Albo, *Sefer ha-Ikkarim*, III, 1.

[30] *Yisrael* is interpreted as two words: *Shir El* (the Song of God). See below.

[31] Rabbi Abraham Isaac Hakohen Kook, *Orot ha-Kodesh*, vol. 2, pp. 444-445 (with emphases provided by the editor, Rabbi David Cohen, "the Nazir"); *Shemonah Kevatsim* 7:112.

The terms "*shir pashut, shir kaful, shir meshulash, shir meruba*'" ("a simple song, a twofold song, a threefold song, a fourfold song") are taken from the Introduction to *Tikkunei Zohar*. In context, the terms refer to the letters of the Tetragrammaton, as well as to the ten *sefirot*. ("A simple song" refers to *Keter*; "a twofold song" refers to *Ḥokhmah* and *Binah*; "a threefold song" refers to *Ḥesed*, *Gevurah* and *Tif'eret*; "a fourfold song" refers to *Netsaḥ*, *Hod*, *Yesod* and *Malkhut*.) The permutation *Yisrael—Shir El* is from the continuation of the Introduction to *Tikkunei Zohar*. See *Tikkunei Zohar* with the commentary of the Vilna Gaon (Vilna, 1867), 4a. And see the endnotes of the Editor of *Orot ha-Kodesh*, vol. 2, p. 608.

[32] Hebrew-Aramaic, "*Tsa'ar ba'alei ḥayyim de-'oraita*" (*b. Shabbat* 128b, [154b]; *Bava Metsi'a* 32b-33a).

In the introduction to *Peiruka li-Tekanta* (p. 803), Rabbi Menashe argues against the notion that one need not pay heed to the suffering of the "*margishim*" (sentient beings, i.e., animals) for they were created ony for the benefit of the "*medaberim*" (literally "speakers," i.e., humans). If that were the case, reasons Rabbi Menashe, we would have to suspect "that perhaps man too was created for the needs of intelligent, sentient worlds, stripped of all materiality."

Apropos this discussion, there is a fascinating passage in the writings of Rabbi Shneur Zalman of Lyady to the effect that the present souls (of humans) are as "animals" in relation to the souls that will be revealed in the future, and that just as in the present, the soul of the animal is uplifted by the righteous who consumes it, so in the future, the present souls—reincarnated in the Leviathan and the Wild Ox (*Shor ha-Bar*)—will be uplifted by the future souls who will devour them. See *Likkutei Torah*, *Tsav*, 7c.

[33] *Alfei Menashe*, Part Two, chap. 41 (29b-c).

Appendix G

1 *Sefer ha-De'ah* (*Derushei 'Olam ha-Tohu*) (Piotrków, 1912), Part One, 57a.

2 Hosea 12:11.

3 Elsewhere, I have dealt with Rabbi Zadok Hakohen's theory that the images of the *Zohar* and later, Lurianic Kabbalah, were indeed seen in prophetic (or rather, near-prophetic) visions, a perspective which might very well have come out of the *KaLaḤ Pitḥei Ḥokhmah* attributed to Luzzatto. Where Rabbi Zadok differs with RaMḤaL, is in his rejection of the notion that these visions are *meshalim* in need of rational interpretation.

Why Rabbi Zadok does not mention Luzzatto by name is a thorny issue. As I stated on previous occasions, I would tend to chalk it up to Rabbi Zadok suspecting RaMḤaL of Sabbatian heresy. (By the same token, Rabbi Ḥayyim Yosef David Azulai [ḤYDA] does not include Luzzatto, the man or his work, in his bibliography, *Shem ha-Gedolim*. This is readily explained by a passage in Azulai's travelog, *Ma'agal Tov*, where he reports the diatribe against Luzzatto that he came across, *Gilgul Meḥilot*, and that for a period of three months, he supped at the Sabbath table of Rabbi Jacob Belilius, a member of the Venetian rabbinic tribunal and the "Grand Inquisitor" that passed judgment on Luzzatto. Azulai sojourned in Venice in the year 1754.)

See Rabbi Zadok Hakohen, *Sefer ha-Zikhronot*, appended to *Divrei Soferim* (Lublin, 1913), 30c, 31b-c, 34a-b, 35a-b; Rabbi Ḥayyim Yosef David Azulai, *Ma'agal Tov*, ed. Aharon Freimann (Berlin—Jerusalem: Mekitsei Nirdamim, 1921-1934; photo offset Jerusalem, 1983), p. 9; Bezalel Naor, *Kana'uteh de-Pinḥas* (Spring Valley, New York, 2013), pp. 59-62; idem, *Maḥol la-Tsaddikim* (Monsey, New York and Jerusalem: Orot and Makhon Ramhal, 2015), pp. 133-134.

4 *Sefer ha-De'ah*, Part One, 57a.

5 *Sefer ha-De'ah*, Part One, 57a-b. See the *Leshem*'s earlier invective against RaMḤaL (specifically *KaLaḤ Pitḥei Ḥokhmah*, *petaḥ* 8), ibid. 42d-43a. In the last of his works to be published, *Ḥelek ha-Be'urim* (Jerusalem, 1935), Part One,

3b-c, while not mentioning RaMḤaL by name, Rabbi Eliashov once again inveighs against those who would attribute the Lurianic metaphors to *mar'eh ha-nevu'ah* (prophetic vision) or *mashal* (parable).

Rabbi Yosef Leib Bloch (later *Rosh Yeshivah* of Telz) related that when he visited Rabbi Eliashov in his home in Shavel, he was treated to his host's oral objection to RaMḤaL's theory of "*mar'eh ha-nevuah.*" See Rabbi Y.L. Bloch, *Shi'urei Da'at*, vol. 1 (Jerusalem: Feldheim, 1976), p. 163.

According to an oral tradition transmitted by Rabbi Ya'akov Moshe Ḥarlap to his disciple Rabbi Yosef Leib Zussman, the original wording of the *Leshem* concerning RaMḤaL was even harsher, but as Providence would have it, Rav Kook happened through the door of the *Leshem*'s residence precisely as he was penning the denunciatory lines (this occurred on Rosh Ḥodesh Adar in the year 1898) and convinced him to tone down his invective. See Rabbi Y.L. Zussman, *Mi-Beḥirei Tsaddikaya* (Jerusalem, 2007), pp. 172-173.

In a work of thought, first published in 1945, Rabbi Ḥarlap justifies RaMḤaL's use of the term "*hanhagah*" (plural, "*hanhagot*"). See *Mei Marom* (on Maimonides' *Shemonah Perakim*) (photo offset Jerusalem, 1982), chap. 8, par. 17 (pp. 176-177).

Recently, Alon Shalev has written on the controversy between the *Leshem* and Luzzatto, and Rabbi Isaac Hutner's complex relation to the latter. See Alon Shalev, *Orthodox Theology in the Age of Meaning: The Life and Works of Rabbi Isaac Hutner* (Hebrew), Ph.D. dissertation, Hebrew University, Jerusalem, 2020.

A disciple of Rabbi Hutner, the Kabbalist Rabbi Yisrael Eliyahu Weintraub justified the approach of Luzzatto despite the *Leshem*'s criticism. See *Nefesh Eliyahu: Hakdamot ve-Shi'urim, Ma'amar be-Pitḥei She'arim*, pp. 41-42, note 106.

Inter alia, the philosopher Solomon Maimon (1753-1800) recounted that in his youth, when he attempted to provide a rational, non-literal explanation of the Kabbalah's imagery, he was rebuffed by the Kabbalists:

> But by this method of explanation I brought upon myself much ill-feeling. For the Kabbalists maintain that the Kabbalah is not a human, but a divine, science; and that, consequently, it would be a degradation of it, to explain its mysteries in accordance with nature and reason. The more reasonable, therefore, my explanations proved, the more were the Kabbalists irritated with me, inasmuch as they held that alone to be divine which had no reasonable meaning. Accordingly I had to keep my explanations to myself. I brought with me to Berlin an entire work, which I wrote on the subject, and I still keep it as a monument to the struggle of the human mind after perfection, in spite of all the hindrances placed in its way.
>
> (*The Autobiography of Solomon Maimon*, translated from the German by J. Clark Murray [London: The East and West Library, 1954], p. 78)

Maimon's work on Kabbalah, *Ma'aseh Livnat ha-Sapir*, has been preserved in manuscript. See my discussion of the opus in Bezalel Naor, *Maḥol la-Tsaddikim*, pp. 99-103.

6 *KaLaḤ Pitḥei Hokhmah, petaḥ* 6-8.

7 In his scathing critique of the *Leshem*'s premier volume, *Hakdamot u-She'arim* (Piotrków, 1908), Rabbi Pinḥas Lintop noticed that evidently neither RaMḤaL nor *Pitḥei She'arim* merited mention in that work. See *Kana'uteh de-Pinḥas*, ed. Bezalel Naor (Spring Valley, New York, 2013), p. 25, adjacent to note 114.

In his unpublished work, *Pardes ha-Yahadut*, a historical survey of the development of Kabbalah, Rabbi Lintop observed that both the books of the "Gaon of Rozhinoy and Tiktin" (i.e., Rabbi Isaac Ḥaver) and the books of the "Gaon of Kratinga" (i.e., Rabbi Aryeh Leib Lipkin) were based on the Kabbalah of "the Godly Kabbalist RaMḤaL." Quoted in *Kana'uteh de-Pinḥas*, p. 119, n. 67.

8 *Yahel 'Or* (Vilna: Romm, 1882). Formerly, the manuscript was entitled *Hadrat Kodesh.*

For a detailed description of Rabbi Naftali Herz Halevi's literary output, see Eliezer Baumgarten, "*Halakhah, Kabbalah u-Madda' be-Sifriyato shel Harav Naftali Herz Halevi,*" *Cathedra* 135 (Nissan 2010), pp. 89-130; and idem, "*Ḥadshanut ve-Shamranut ba-Kabbalah shel R' Naftali Herz Halevi,*" *Da'at* 79-80 (2015), pp. 205-219. In the latter article, Baumgarten points out some ideological differences between Rabbi Shelomo Eliashov and Rabbi Naftali Herz Halevi (pp. 214-219).

9 See *KaLaḤ Pitḥei Ḥokhmah, petaḥ* 7 (p. 35 in Spinner edition): "And this is the secret of what they said: *Malkhut* is 'the hand of the prophets.'" And see *petaḥ* 9 (pp. 39-40) that *Malkhut* is responsible for the imaginative visions.

10 *Mikhtevei Ba'al ha-Leshem*, in preface to Rabbi Immanuel Ḥai Ricchi, *Mishnat Ḥasidim* with commentary by Rabbi Naftali Herz Halevi, *Kesef Mishneh*, ed. Shmuel Ya'akov Feffer (New York: Makhon ha-GRA, 2006), vol. 1, pp. 49-50 (second letter).

11 Today, Šiauliai, Lithuania.

12 See *KaLaḤ Pitḥei Ḥokhmah, petaḥ* 13 regarding *'Iggulim* and *Yosher*; and *petaḥ* 24 regarding *Tsimtsum*.

13 See *Mikhtevei Ba'al ha-Leshem*, pp. 54, 56 (third letter), 59 (fourth letter).

14 *Likkutei ha-GRA* in *Be'ur ha-GRA le-Sifra di-Tseni'uta*, ed. Samuel Luria (Vilna, 1882), 38b, s.v. *Sod ha-Tsimtsum*. See likewise *Siddur ha-GRA*, ed. Rabbi Naftali Herz Halevi (Jerusalem, 1896-1898; photo offset Jerusalem, 1971), Part One, *Imrei Shefer*, 5b, 7a, 27a, 59b-60b, 73a, 82a.

Employing this trope of "lights" and "vessels" (will and ability), Rabbi Naftali Herz will arrive at a revolutionary reading of the phenomenon of the "shattering of the vessels" (*shevirat ha-kelim*). See below note 19.

*

A twentieth-century student of Kabbalah who adopted these codes (*'or—keli/ratson—yekholet*) attributed to the Vilna Gaon, was Rabbi Dr. Israel Shabtai Ratner. See his *Le-'Or ha-Kabbalah* (Kefar Ḥabad: Abraham Zioni, 1961), pp. 32, 38, 104-106.

I met Ratner once in his apartment in Jerusalem. He explained that he had stopped teaching Kabbalah. (He volunteered that he was a chemist by profession.) After our brief meeting, as he escorted me to the door, he took leave of me with these sphinxlike words: "There is one who has a pocket but has no coins; there is another who has coins but no pocket." I believe he was alluding to the kabbalistic metaphor of *orot ve-kelim*, lights and vessels.

15 *Mikhtevei Ba'al ha-Leshem*, p. 51. The *Leshem* revisits this theme in the fourth letter (p. 59).

16 Rabbi Shelomo Eliashov, *Ḥelek ha-Be'urim*, Part One, 5b. The indefatigable researcher Yosef Avivi upholds the attribution of the *Likkut* to the Vilna Gaon; see Avivi, *Kabbalat ha-GRA* (Jerusalem, 1993), Introduction, p. 27.

17 Rabbi Naftali Herz wrote two commentaries to the *Siddur*. *Sha'ar Naftali* is restricted to the mechanics, the "nuts and bolts" of Kabbalah. *Imrei Shefer*, on the other hand, hangs flesh on the bare bones of the Kabbalah. It is there that the talk of "prophetic visions" found to be offensive by the *Leshem* occurs; there the type of conceptualization so abhorred by the *Leshem* takes place.

See Rabbi Yisrael Eliyahu Weintraub's reservations concerning *Imrei Shefer*, in *Nefesh Eliyahu: Hakdamot ve-Shi'urim, Mikhtavim*, p. 31, note 5.

18 *Siddur ha-GRA*, Part One, *Imrei Shefer*, 3b. "Prophetic vision" (*mar'eh ha-nevu'ah* or *mar'eh ha-nevu'i*) à la Luzzatto is a recurrent theme; see *Imrei Shefer*, 4a, 11a, 14b, 46a-b, 49b-50a. The discussion of *mar'eh ha-nevu'ah* in 62b may also be of peripheral interest.

19 Ibid. 59b-60b, 73a, 82a-b.

Though Rabbi Naftali Herz, a staunch *mitnaged* (opponent to Ḥasidism), would find the juxtaposition abhorrent, there is a point at which his theology coincides with the "religious determinism" (to use Joseph Weiss' term) of Rabbi Mordechai Yosef Leiner of Izbica (author of *Mei ha-Shilo'aḥ*).

20 In the third letter to Rabbi Naftali Herz (pp. 45-46), the *Leshem* invokes the necessity of reticence concerning recondite matters.

[21] My hunch is that the "father" of this theology is MaHaRaL of Prague. In the Second Introduction to *Gevurot Hashem*, he lay down the groundwork for what he called "the natural order" (*"seder ha-teva'"*) versus "the miraculous order" (*"seder ha-nissim"*).

Earlier, the great Kabbalist, Rabbi Moses ben Naḥman (Naḥmanides)—who was prone to occasional Maimonidean lapses—wrote extensively on the domains of the natural and the miraculous. See most recently, 'Oded Yisraeli, *"Le-Toledot Torat ha-Hashgaḥah shel ha-RaMBaN," Da'at* 90 (2020): 83-107.

[22] *Lev Melakhim* to 1 Kings 7:21.

It would appear that in this respect at least, Malbim parted ways with his teacher of Kabbalah, Rabbi Tsevi Hirsch Eichenstein of Zydaczów. In language remarkably similar to that of the *Leshem*, Rabbi Tsevi Hirsch lashed out against authors who would reduce the *Idrot* and Lurianic *partsufim* to parable (*mashal*) in need of unpacking. See Rabbi Tsevi Hirsch Eichenstein of Zydaczów, *Sur me-Ra' va-'Aseh Tov* (alternatively titled, *Hakdamah ve-Derekh le-'Ets Ḥayyim*) (Jerusalem, 1997), pp. 78-79. It would be convenient to assume that the unnamed nemesis is in fact Luzzatto. (See Isaiah Tishby, *"Darkhei hafatsatam shel kitvei kabbalah le-RaMḤaL be-Polin u-be-Lita," Kiryat Sefer* 45 [1970], p. 153, n. 127.) Yet elsewhere, Rabbi Tsevi Hirsch spells out his displeasure with a recent work of ḤaBaD Ḥasidism, *Sha'ar ha-Yiḥud* (Kopyst, 1820)! See *Sur me-Ra' va-'Aseh Tov*, footnote to p. 117.

Rabbi Tsevi Hirsch's nephew and disciple, Rabbi Isaac of Komarno, did outrightly attack Luzzatto's works, *Ḥoker u-Mekubal* and *KaLaḤ Pitḥei Ḥokhmah* for their philosophical bent. See Bezalel Naor, *Maḥol la-Tsaddikim*, pp. 190-191, n. 134.

[23] *Pitḥei She'arim*, Part One, *Netiv 'Iggulim ve-Yosher de-A"K*, chap. 3, *Beit Netivot*, note 8 (10b).

[24] *Hakdamot u-She'arim, Sha'ar* 6, chaps. 3-4 (21c-22d), 10-11 (31d-33b) (where the *'or makif* is equated with the *'or ha-ganuz*, "the hidden light"); *Sefer ha-De'ah*, 46d; *Ḥelek ha-*

Be'urim, Part One 8c-d (par. 18) (once again equating the *'or makif* with the *'or ha-ganuz)*, 13d-14a (par. 7), 24c-d (par. 2).

25 *Ḥelek ha-Be'urim*, Part One, 19d (par. 3). See earlier *Likkutei ha-GRA*, 37c, s.v. *sod gimmel reishin.*

26 The barest philological analysis betrays Luzzatto's profound influence upon the *Leshem*. For example, *"ha-kavvanah ha-takhlitit"* ("the ultimate intention") of *KaLaḤ Pitḥei Ḥokhmah* (Jerusalem, 1987), *petaḥ* 92 (p. 254) shows up often in the writings of the *Leshem*. The *Leshem* makes extensive use of the term *"ha-kavvanah ha-takhlitit"* in *Sefer ha-Kelalim* (Mishor Adumim: Aharon Barzani and Sons, 2010), *Kelalei Hitpashtut ve-Histalkut, kelal* 15, *'anaf* 11 (pp. 184-186); and in *Ḥelek ha-Be'urim*, Part One, 22d-23b.

Regarding Luzzatto's teleology, the "Nazir" records that Rav Kook agreed to include two quotes from *KaLaḤ Pitḥei Ḥokhmah* (*petaḥ* 131 and 30) as mottoes to the section of *Orot ha-Kodesh* entitled *"Hit'alut ha-'Olam"* ("The Elevation of the World"). See *Orot ha-Kodesh*, vol. 2, p. 513; and Rabbi David Cohen, *Kol ha-Nevu'ah*, p. 308, n. 453.

And regarding Luzzatto's theodicy, the "Nazir" speculated that Luzzatto read Leibniz's book by that name, *Théodicée* (1710). See *Kol ha-Nevu'ah*, p. 307, n. 452.

27 Yosef Avivi, *Zohar RaMḤaL* (Jerusalem, 1997). See earlier Rabbi Ḥayyim Friedlander's Introduction to Rabbi Moshe Ḥayyim Luzzatto, *Da'at Tevunot* (2nd edition, Tel-Aviv, 1975), pp. 19-20.

28 *b. Berakhot* 7a. Quoted by the *Leshem* in *Ḥelek ha-Be'urim*, Part One, 22d.

29 A rabbinic takeaway from the Book of Job reads: "The end of a man is death, and the end of a beast is slaughter, and all stand ready for death..." (*b. Berakhot* 17a).

30 *b. Bava Batra* 15a.

31 Statement of Rabbi Yannai in *m. Avot* 4:15.

32 Avivi has stressed that this historiosophy was the unique contribution of Luzzatto, not to be found in Lurianic Kabbalah. According to Avivi's findings, this novel approach first occurred to Luzzatto in 1731. Prior to that date, Luzzatto

still operated within the traditional kabbalistic scheme (viz. *hanhagat ha-mishpat*). See Avivi, *Zohar RaMḤaL*, pp. 119, 121, 204-207.

33 The term is of Talmudic origin; see *b. Berakhot* 10a.

34 *Ḥelek ha-Be'urim*, Part One, 22c-23b, 24c-d (par. 2), 28d (par. 20).

35 *Ḥelek ha-Be'urim*, Part One, 23a.

36 *Ḥelek ha-Be'urim*, Part One, 28d (par. 20).

37 *b. Pesaḥim* 50a. Quoted in Rabbi Naftali Herz Halevi's *Imrei Shefer*, 3b. See the context in which it is quoted: "But in the future, we shall recognize a higher governance, and then we shall see clearly that all was but absolute good." Halevi also quotes there from *b. Berakhot* 60b: "All that God does is for good."

38 *b. Berakhot* 55b.

39 Rabbi Jacob of Marvège, *She'elot u-Teshuvot min ha-Shamayim*, ed. Rabbi Reuven Margaliyot (Jerusalem: Mossad Harav Kook, n.d.), no. 3 (pp. 44-48). Rabbi Margaliyot's introduction to the work merits study. Of halakhic interest is the lengthy discussion in Rabbi Ḥayyim Yosef David Azulai's *Shem ha-Gedolim*, Part One, s.v. *Rabbeinu Ya'akov he-Ḥasid.*

In the fourth part of Rabbi Ḥayyim Vital's *Sha'arei Kedushah* (long suppressed), there are numerous recipes for *she'elat ḥalom.* See *Sha'arei Kedushah*, Part Four, in *Ketavim Ḥadashim me-Rabbeinu Ḥayyim Vital* (Jerusalem: Ahavat Shalom, 1988), pp. 4 (par. 9), 6 (par. 1), 7 (par. 3), 8 (par. 4). However, as pointed out by Rabbi Ya'akov Moshe Hillel in his introduction, this part, unlike Part Three of the work, should not be viewed as Lurianic transmission, rather as Vital's own survey of various medieval authors (including the controversial Abraham Abulafia).

Scholem noted that there are literally hundred of recipes for *she'elat ḥalom.* See *Major Trends in Jewish Mysticism*, pp. 103, 374 n. 76.

40 Leor Holzer, *Empty Space and Rabbi Ḥasdai Crescas' Influence over the European and Lurian Physics* (Hebrew) (Jerusalem: Hebrew University, 2010).

The Making of Rav Kook

[1] For example, in his commentary to *Berakhot* 12b, Rabbi Stern cites R[abbi] M[oshe] D[essau]'s introduction to Maimonides' *Millot ha-Higayon*; see *Zekher Yehosef* (Warsaw, 1859, photo-offset New York, 1991), 8d.

[2] As Mirsky notes, some of Yanover's explanations of *Tanya* are recorded in Rabbi Abraham Tsevi Brudno's *Kuntres Likkutim Be'urim* (Jerusalem, 1922). Brudno, a ḤaBaD Ḥasid, married the daughter of a *gevir* (wealthy man) of Grieva by the name of Aronowitz and resided there for some time before assuming the rabbinate of Kupishok. See Brudno's *Ḥesed le-Avraham*, Part 1 (Jerusalem, 1928), p. 1, regarding Rabbi Meir Simḥah Kohen of Dvinsk; and his introduction to *Meginei Avraham* (Jerusalem, 1926).

[3] Heard from Rabbi Yosef Soloveichik of Jerusalem (son of Rabbi Aharon Soloveichik of Chicago).

[4] See the Mal'akh's letter to Rabbi Asher Zelig Margulies of Jerusalem in the anonymous collection *Otsar Iggerot Kodesh* (Brooklyn, 1988), p. 86 (Letter 85).

[5] See Yosef Yitzḥak Lifshitz, *Eḥad be-Khol Dimyonot* (*One God, Many Images: Dialectical Thought in Ḥasidei Ashkenaz*) (B'nei Berak: HaKibbutz HaMe'uḥad, 2015).

[6] See, e.g., Rabbi Isaac of Volozhin, *Peh Kadosh*, ed. Dov Eliach (Jerusalem 1995), pp. 44-45, 369-370.

[7] *Iggerot ha-RAYaH*, vol. 1, p. 99 (Letter 89).

[8] Rabbi Abraham Azulai, *Ḥesed le-Avraham* 3:12.

(Continuation of note 19 on page 136)

Elsewhere, Rav Kook writes that only someone of the spiritual stature of Rabbi Abahu (*b. Niddah* 24b) would have the ability to channel the volatile achronic light into the world of order and sequence. In that passage, Rav Kook (drawing on Lurianic imagery) describes the descent from the vast expanse of the unordered to the constricted orderly world as "orphaning." See *Siddur 'Olat Re'iyah,* vol. 1 (Jerusalem, 1939), p. 152, s.v. *Abaye havah mesader seder ha-ma'arakhah;* and my rendition in *The Koren Rav Kook Siddur* (Jerusalem, 2017), pp. 79-81.

Bibliography

Abraham ben Judah Leib of Khotimsk. *Maskil le-Eitan*. Novellae to Talmud and *Tikkunei Zohar*. Vilna, 1818.

Abraham ibn Ezra. *Yesod Mora ve-Sod Torah*. Ed. Joseph Cohen and Uriel Simon. Ramat-Gan, 2002.

Abraham Simḥah of Mstislav. "*Ma'amar be-'Inyan Shevirah ve-Tikkun*." In *Mi-Ginzei ha-GRA u-Veit Midrasho*. Ed. Kalman Redisch. Lakewood, 1999.

Abraham, son of Elijah Gaon of Vilna. *Tirgem Avraham*. Ed. Elijah Landau. Jerusalem, 1896.

Abulafia, Abraham. *Imrei Shefer*. Ed. Amnon Gross. Jerusalem, 1999.

Adret, Solomon ben Abraham ibn. (RaShBA). *Ma'amar 'al Yishmael*. Ed. Bezalel Naor. Spring Valley, NY, 2008.

Agnon, Shmuel Yosef. *A Book That Was Lost and Other Stories by S.Y. Agnon*. Ed. Alan Mintz and Anne Golomb Hoffman. New York, 1995.

_____. *Ve-Hayah he-'akov le-mishor*. Jaffa, 1912.

Albo, Joseph. *Sefer ha-'Ikkarim*. Warsaw, 1877. Photo offset Jerusalem, 1960.

Alter (Rothenburg), Isaac Meir, of Gur (*Ḥiddushei ha-RIM*). *Likkutim Ḥadashim*. Ed. Benjamin Menaḥem Alter. Appended to *Sefer ha-Zekhut*.

_____. *Sefer ha-Zekhut*. On Pentateuch. Tel-Aviv, n.d.

Alter (Rothenburg), Judah Aryeh Leib, of Gur (*Sefat Emet*). Comments to MaHaRaL, *Netsaḥ Yisrael*. In *Sefat Emet Likkutim*. Ed. Abraham Issachar Alter of Pabianice. Part Two. Piotrków, 1936.

Arzy, Shaḥar and Idel, Moshe. *Kabbalah: A Neurocognitive Approach to Mystical Experiences*. New Haven, 2015.

Altschuler, Aharon Meir. See Lipkin, Aryeh Leib.

Anonymous. (Misattributed to Abraham of Granada). *Berit ha-Menuḥah*. Ed. ʿOded Porat. Jerusalem, 2016.

Anonymous. (Misattributed to Perets Hakohen). *Maʿarekhet ha-Elohut*. Mantua, 1558.

Anonymous. (Misattributed to Aaron Halevi of Barcelona). *Sefer ha-Ḥinnukh*. Venice, 1523.

Asher ben David. *Sefer ha-Yiḥud*. In Daniel Abrams. *R. Asher ben David: His Complete Works and Studies in His Kabbalistic Thought*. (Hebrew). Los Angeles, 1996.

Ashkenazi, Tsevi. *She'elot u-Teshuvot Ḥakham Tsevi*. Amsterdam, 1712.

Avivi, Yosef. *Kabbalat ha-GRA*. Jerusalem, 1993.

_____. *Kabbalat ha-RAYaH*. 4 vols. Jerusalem, 2018.

_____. *Zohar RaMḤaL*. Jerusalem, 1997.

Azriel of Gerona. *Peirush ʿEser Sefirot ʿal Derekh She'elah u-Teshuvah*. Printed together with *Derekh Emunah* of Meir ibn Gabbai. Ed. Naḥman Abraham Goldberg. Berlin, 1850.

Azulai, Abraham. *Ḥesed le-Avraham*. Lvov, 1863. Photo offset Israel, 1968.

Azulai, Ḥayyim Yosef David. *Ma'agal Tov*. Travelog. Ed. Aharon Freimann. Jerusalem, 1934. Photo offset Jerusalem, 1983.

______. *Nitsutsei Orot*. Glosses to *Zohar*. Vilna, 1882. (Title *Nitsutsei Orot* first appears in Vilna Romm edition.)

______. *Shem ha-Gedolim*. Bibliography. Two parts. Warsaw, 1876.

Bacharach, Naftali. *'Emek ha-Melekh*. Amsterdam, 1648.

Baḥya ben Asher ibn Ḥalawa. Commentary to Torah. Ed. C.B. Chavel. 3 vols. Jerusalem, 1967-1968.

Baḥya ibn Paquda. *Ḥovot ha-Levavot* (*Duties of the Heart*). Translated from Arabic to Hebrew by Judah ibn Tibbon. First Edition. Naples, 1489.

Bartholomew, Craig G. *The God Who Acts in History: The Significance of Sinai*. Grand Rapids, Michigan, 2020.

Barukh of Kosov. *'Amud ha-'Avodah*. Chernovits, 1863.

______. *Yesod ha-'Emunah*. Ed. Ya'akov Ilowitch. Monsey, 2007.

Barzilay (Eisenstein), Isaac. *Manasseh of Ilya: Precursor of Modernity among the Jews of Eastern Europe*. Jerusalem, 1999.

Baumgarten, Eliezer. "*Ḥadshanut ve-Shamranut ba-Kabbalah shel R' Naftali Herz Halevi*." *Da'at* 79-80 (2015), pp. 205-219.

______. "*Halakhah, Kabbalah u-Madda' be-Sifriyato shel Harav Naftali Herz Halevi*." *Cathedra* 135 (Nissan 2010), pp. 89-130.

Be'ery, Yehoshua B. *Ohev Yisrael bi-Kedushah*. Biography of Rav Kook. 5 vols. Tel-Aviv, 1989.

Benamozegh, Elijah. *Spinoza et la Kabbale*. Jerusalem, 1988. (Photo offset of *L'Univers Israelite*, Paris 1864).

Benayahu, Meir. *Toledot ha-ARI*. Jerusalem, 1967.

Ben Porat, Menashe. See Menashe of Ilya.

Ben Shlomo, Yosef. *"Shelemut ve-Hishtalmut be-Torat ha-Elohut shel Harav Kook." Iyyun* 33 (Tevet-Nissan 1984), pp. 289-309.

_____. *"Shirat ha-Ḥayyim": Perakim be-Mishnato shel Harav Kook*. Tel-Aviv, 1989.

Berdichevsky, Micah Joseph. Various articles in *HaMisdaronah*. Ed. Ḥayyim Hirschensohn. Jerusalem, 1888.

Bloch, Yosef Leib. *Shi'urei Da'at*. 2 vols. Jerusalem, 1976.

Bonfil, Robert. "New Information on Rabbi Menaḥem Azariah da Fano and his Age." (Hebrew). In *Studies in the History of Jewish Society in the Middle Ages and in the Modern Period* (Jacob Katz *Festschrift*). Ed. E. Etkes and Y. Salmon. Jerusalem, 1980. pp. 98-135.

Brenner, Yosef Ḥayyim. *Ha-Aḥdut*, 1914, no. 9.

_____. *Me-'Ever li-Gevulin* (play). London, 1907.

Brudno, Abraham Tsevi. *Ḥesed le-Avraham*. Part 1. Jerusalem, 1928.

_____. *Kuntres Likkutim Be'urim*. On *Tanya*. Jerusalem, 1922.

_____. *Meginei Avraham*. Jerusalem, 1926.

Bucke, Richard Maurice. *Cosmic Consciousness: A Study in the Evolution of the Human Mind*. Philadelphia, 1901.

Cohen, David (the Nazir). *Kol ha-Nevu'ah: Ha-Higayon ha-'Ivri ha-Shim'i*. Jerusalem, 1979.

Cordovero, Moses. *Elimah Rabbati*. Lvov, 1881.

_____. *Ma'ayan 'Eyn Ya'akov* (*Ha-Ma'ayan ha-Revi'i mi-Sefer Elimah*). Ed. Bracha Sack. Be'er Sheva, 2009.

_____. *'Or Yakar*. Commentary to *Zohar*. Ed. Meir Elbaum. 20 vols. Jerusalem, 1962-1995.

_____. *Shi'ur Komah*. Warsaw, 1883.

Danziger, Yeraḥmiel Yisrael Yitzḥak, of Alexander. *Yismaḥ Yisrael*. Lodz, 1911-1912.

De la Rosa, Ḥayyim. *Torat Ḥakham*. Salonika, 1848.

Dov Baer of Mezritch. *Maggid Devarav le-Ya'akov*. Brooklyn, 1986.

_____. *'Or Torah*. On Pentateuch. Koretz, 1804.

Eichenstein, Tsevi Hirsch, of Zydaczów. *Sur me-Ra' va-'Aseh Tov*. (Alternatively titled, *Hakdamah ve-Derekh le-'Ets ha-Ḥayyim*). Lemberg? Zolkiew? 1832. Jerusalem, 1997.

Elankawa (Al-Naqawa), Ephraim. *Sha'ar Kevod Adonai*. Ed. Ḥayyim Bliaḥ. Tunis, 1902.

El'azar of Worms (Roke'aḥ). *Sefer ha-Roke'aḥ ha-Gadol*. Jerusalem, 1960.

_____. *Sha'arei ha-Sod, ha-Yiḥud ve-ha-Emunah*. Ed. Joseph Dan. In *Temirin*. Ed. Israel Weinstock. vol. 1. Jerusalem, 1979.

Eliashov, Shelomo. Author multivolume series entitled *Leshem, Shevo ve-Aḥlamah*:

_____. *Hakdamot u-She'arim*. Piotrków, 1908.

_____. *Ḥelek ha-Be'urim*. Commentary to Vital's *'Ets Ḥayyim*. Two parts. Jerusalem, 1935, 1948.

_____. *Mikhtevei Ba'al ha-Leshem*. Ed. Shmuel Ya'akov Feffer. In Immanuel Ḥai Ricchi. *Mishnat Ḥasidim*. New York, 2006.

_____. *Sefer ha-De'ah (Derushei 'Olam ha-Tohu)*. Piotrków, 1912.

_____. *Sefer ha-Kelalim*. Jerusalem, 1924. Mishor Adumim, 2010.

Elijah Gaon of Vilna. *Aderet Eliyahu*. Commentary on Pentateuch. With supercommentary of Rabbi Yitzḥak Eizik Ḥaver, *Be'er Yitzhak*. Ed. Samuel Luria. Warsaw, 1887. Photo offset Jerusalem, 1980.

_____. *Be'ur ha-GRA* to *Sifra di-Tseni'uta*. Ed. Jacob Moses of Slonim. Vilna and Horadna, 1820. Ed. Samuel Luria. Vilna, 1882. Ed. Bezalel Naor. Jerusalem, 1998.

_____. *Be'ur ha-GRA* to *Tikkunei Zohar*. Vilna, 1867.

_____. *Megillat Ruth 'im Peirush ha-GRA*. Jerusalem, 1896.

_____. *Sefer Yetsirah 'im Peirush ha-GRA*. Ed. Samuel Luria. Warsaw, 1884.

_____. *Siddur ha-GRA*. Ed. Naftali Herz Halevi (Weidenbaum). With commentaries *Sha'ar Naftali* and *Imrei Shefer* by Halevi (Weidenbaum). 2 vols. Jerusalem, 1896, 1898. 1 vol. Photo offset Jerusalem, 1971. Appended *Zeh ha-Shulḥan*, Part Three, by Serayah Deblitzki.

_____. *Yahel 'Or*. Commentaries to Zohar. (Formerly titled *Hadrat Kodesh*). Ed. Naftali Herz Halevi (Weidenbaum). Vilna, 1882.

Eliyahu, Ayala. "From *Kitab al-hada'iq* to *Kitab al-dawa'ir*: Reconsidering Ibn al-Sid al-Batalyawsi's Philosophical

Treatise." *Al-Qantara* 36:1 (January-June 2015), pp. 165-198.

Epstein, Yitzḥak Eizik Halevi, of Homel. *Ḥannah Ariel.* 3 vols. Israel, 2019.

Ezra of Gerona. Commentary to Song of Songs. In *Kitvei Rabbeinu Moshe ben Naḥman*. Ed. C.B. Chavel. vol. 2.

Fano, Menaḥem Azariah da. *Pelaḥ ha-Rimon.* Commentary to *Pardes Rimonim* of Moses Cordovero. Venice, 1600.

Friedman, Shamma Yehudah. "*Tselem, Demut ve-Tavnit.*" *Sidra* 22 (2007), pp. 89-152.

Gabbai, Meir ibn. *'Avodat ha-Kodesh.* Jerusalem, 1973. Photo offset of Warsaw 1891.

_____. *Derekh Emunah*. First edition Padua 1563. With *Questions* of Azriel of Gerona. Berlin, 1850.

Gabirol, Solomon ibn. *Tikkun Middot ha-Nefesh*. Translated from Arabic to Hebrew by Judah ibn Tibbon. Ed. Ḥayyim Pollak. Pressburg, 1896.

Gafni, Chanan. "*Peshat u-Derash ba-Mishnah: Le-Gilguleha shel Masoret mi-Beit Midrasho shel ha-GRA*" ("*Peshat* and *Derash* in the *Mishnah*: On the Metamorphosis of a Tradition from the School of R. Elijah of Vilna"). *Sidra*, vol. 22 (2007), pp. 5-19.

Gans, Mozes Heiman. *Memorbook*. Baarn, 1977.

Gikatilla, Joseph. Commentary to Maimonides' *Guide*. Appended to Isaac Abravanel. *She'elot le-he-Ḥakham Rabbi Shaul Hakohen*. Venice, 1574.

_____. *Sha'arei Tsedek*. Riva di Trento, 1561.

Ginzburg, Simon. *Rabbi Moshe Ḥayyim Luzzatto u-V'nei Doro.* Collection of letters and documents. 2 vols. Tel-Aviv, 1937.

Golding, Joshua L. "Maharal's Conception of the Human Being." *Faith and Philosophy* 14, 4 (October 1997), pp. 444-457.

Goldstein, Alec. *A Theology of Holiness.* NewYork, 2018.

Goldstein, Naḥman, of Tcherin. *Rimzei ha-Ma'asiyot.* Printed at the end of Naḥman of Breslov's *Sippurei Ma'asiyot.* Lemberg, 1902.

Gordon, Yekutiel. *Mar Yenuka u-Mar Kashisha.* n.p. [Israel], 2013.

Gross, Benjamin. *Yehi 'Or.* On MaHaRaL's *Ner Mitsvah.* Jerusalem, 1995.

Habermann, A.M. *"Sha'arei ḤaBaD."* In *'Alei 'Ayin* (Salman Schocken Jubilee Volume). Jerusalem, 1948-1952.

Halbertal, Moshe. *Naḥmanides: Law and Mysticism.* Transl. Daniel Tabak. New Haven, 2020.

Ḥarlap, Ḥayyim Zevulun. *Be'er Ḥayyim.* n.p., 1995.

Ḥarlap, Ya'akov Moshe. *Iggerot Marom.* Ed. Ya'ir Ḥarlap. Beit El, 2020.

______. *Mei Marom.* vol. 1. Commentary to Maimonides' *Eight Chapters.* Jerusalem, 1945. Photo offset Jerusalem, 1982.

______. *Mei Marom.* vol. 5. *Nimmukei ha-Mikra'ot.* 2nd edition. Jerusalem, 1981.

______. *Mei Marom*, vol. 8. *Bereshit.* Jerusalem, 1994.

______. *Mei Marom*, vol. 17. *Shi'ur Komah.* Jerusalem, 2010.

_____. *Mei Marom*. vol. 18. *Razi Li*. Jerusalem, 2012.

_____. *Mei Marom*. vol. 20. *Iggerot Kodesh*. Jerusalem, 2021.

_____. *Tovim Me'orot*. Jerusalem, 1920.

Ḥaver (Wildman), Yitzḥak Eizik. *Afikei Yam*. Jerusalem, 1994.

_____. *Be'er Yitzhak*. Supercommentary to Elijah Gaon of Vilna, *Aderet Eliyahu*.

_____. *Berit Yitzḥak*. Ed. Samuel Luria. Warsaw, 1888.

_____. *Pitḥei She'arim*. Two parts. Warsaw, 1888. Photo offset Tel-Aviv, 1964.

Ḥayyim of Volozhin. *Nefesh ha-Ḥayyim*. Ed. Yissachar Dov Rubin. B'nei Berak, 1989.

Ḥazan, Abraham ben Naḥman Halevi, of Tulchin. *Be'ur ha-Likkutim*. Jerusalem, 1989.

Heilperin, Menaḥem Menkhin. *Hagahot u-Be'urim*. Commentary to Vital's *'Ets Ḥayyim*. Warsaw, 1891.

Herrera, Abraham Cohen. *Puerta del Cielo*. Transl. from Spanish to Hebrew by Isaac Aboab da Fonseca. *Sha'ar ha-Shamayim*. Amsterdam, 1655.

Heschel, Abraham Joshua. *Der Shem ha-Meforash: Mensch*. Poems. Warsaw, 1933. Translated from Yiddish to English by Morton Leifman. *The Ineffable Name of God: Man*. New York, 2004.

_____. *"Yir'at Shamayim." Sefer Hashanah li-Yehudei Amerika*. vol. 6 (1942).

Holzer, Leor. *Empty space and Rabbi Ḥasdai Crescas' Influence over the European and Lurian Physics*. (Hebrew). M.A. Thesis. Hebrew University. Jerusalem, 2010.

Hurwitz, Aharon Halevi, of Staroshelye. *'Avodat Halevi.* Lemberg, 1861. Photo offset Jerusalem, 1972.

Hutner, Isaac. *Be'ur Sifra di-Tseni'uta mi-Ba'al Paḥad Yitzḥak.* Ed. Shelomo Carlebach and Aharon Y. Cohen. n.p., n.d. (2022?)

_____. *Minḥat Shelomo.* Ed. Shelomo David Fruchthandler. 2nd edition. n.p. [Lakewood], 2022.

_____. *Paḥad Yitzḥak: Iggerot u-Ketavim.* Brooklyn, NY, 2016.

_____. *Paḥad Yitzḥak: Kuntres Ve-Zot Ḥanukkah.* New York, 1989.

_____. *Paḥad Yitzḥak: Sha'ar Yeraḥ ha-Eitanim* (*Rosh Hashanah*). New York, 2003.

_____. *Sefer ha-Zikaron le-Maran Ba'al Paḥad Yitzḥak.* Brooklyn, 2014.

Idel, Moshe. Arzy, Shaḥar and Idel, Moshe. *Kabbalah: A Neurocognitive Approach to Mystical Experiences.* New Haven, 2015.

_____. "Maimonides and Kabbalah." In *Studies in Maimonides.* Ed. Isadore Twersky. Cambridge, Massachusetts, 1990. pp. 31-80.

_____. "Multilingual Gematriot in Abraham Abulafia and Their Significance: From the Bible to Text to Language" (Hebrew). In *Nit'e Ilan: Studies in Hebrew and Related Fields Presented to Ilan Eldar.* Jerusalem, 2014. pp. 193-223.

Isaac ben Ḥayyim, of Volozhin. *Peh Kadosh.* Commentary to Torah. Ed. Dov Eliach. Jerusalem 1995.

Ish-Shalom, Benjamin. *Rabbi Abraham Isaac Kook—Between Rationalism and Mysticism.* (Hebrew). (Tel-Aviv, 1990.

Jacob Joseph ben Judah, of Ostroh. *Rav Yeivi.* Ostroh, 1808. Brody, 1874.

Jacob of Marvège. *She'elot u-Teshuvot min ha-Shamayim.* Ed. Reuven Margaliyot. Jerusalem, n.d.

Judah Halevi. *Kuzari.* Hebrew translation from the Arabic. Yehudah Even Shmuel (Kaufman). Tel-Aviv, 1972. Yosef Kafaḥ. Kiryat Ono, 2013.

Kahn, Matithyahu. *"Ha-Ein Sof ve-ha-Gevul, ve-ha-Sheleimut ve-ha-Hishtalmut."* Unpublished manuscript.

Kamenetsky, David. *"Ha-Gaon Rabbi Menashe me-Ilya zt"l." Yeshurun*, vol. 20 (Nissan 5768/2008), pp. 729-799.

Kaplan, Avraham Eliyahu. *Be-'Ikvot ha-Yir'ah.* Jerusalem, 1960.

Kasher, Moshe Shelomo. Foreward to *Derashot MaHaRaL mi-Prag.* Jerusalem, 1968.

Katz, Ben-Zion. *Rabbanut, Ḥasidut, Haskalah.* 4 parts in 2 vols. Tel-Aviv, 1956, 1958.

Kohut, Alexander. *Aruch Completum.* 8 vols. Vienna, 1878–1892.

Kook, Abraham Isaac Hakohen. *'Arpilei Tohar.* Ed. Yitzḥak Shilat (Greenspan). Jerusalem, 1983.

_____. *"Da'at Elohim."* In *'Ikvei ha-Tson.*

_____. *'Eyn AYaH.* Commentary to *'Eyn Ya'akov* (Legends of the Talmud). Ed. Ya'akov Filber. 4 vols. (Vols. 1-2: *Berakhot.* Vols. 3-4: *Shabbat.*) Jerusalem, 1987-2000.

_____. *Iggerot ha-RAYaH*. Ed. Tsevi Yehudah Hakohen Kook. 3 vols. (Vol. 1: 1888-1910. Vol. 2: 1911-1915. Vol. 3: 1916-1919.) Jerusalem, 1985. Ed. Ya'akov Filber. Vol. 4: 1920-1925. Jerusalem, 1984.

_____. *Iggerot la-RAYaH*. Ed. Benzion Shapira. Jerusalem, 1990.

_____. *'Ikvei ha-Tson*. Jerusalem, 1906.

_____. *Kevatsim mi-Ketav Yad Kodsho*. Ed. Boaz Ofen. 3 vols. Jerusalem, 2006-2018.

_____. *The Legends of Rabbah bar Bar Ḥannah*. Bilingual Hebrew and English. Ed. and transl. Bezalel Naor. New York, 2019.

_____. *Li-Nevukhei ha-Dor*. Ed. Shaḥar Raḥmani. Tel-Aviv, 2014.

_____. *Ma'amrei ha-RAYaH*. vol. 1. Ed. Elisha Langenauer and David Landau. Jerusalem, 1980. vol. 2. Ed. Elisha Aviner (Langenauer). Jerusalem, 1984.

_____. *Metsi'ot Katan*. Ed. Harel Cohen. Jerusalem, 2018.

_____. *Midbar Shur*. Ed. Michael Herskovitz and David Landau. Jerusalem, 1999.

_____. *Mishpat Kohen*. Jerusalem, 1985.

_____. *Mussar Avikha*. Jerusalem, 1985.

_____. *Orot*. Ed. Tsevi Yehudah Hakohen Kook. Jerusalem, 1920. Expanded edition with added material. Jerusalem, 1950. With vocalization of Hebrew text. Beit El, 2004. With English translation by Bezalel Naor. Jerusalem, 2015.

_____. *Orot ha-Kodesh*. Ed. David Cohen. vols. 1-3. Jerusalem, 1985. vol. 4. Jerusalem, 1990.

_____. *Orot ha-RAYaH*. Ed. Tsevi Yehudah Hakohen Kook. Collected poems. Jerusalem, 1969.

_____. *Orot ha-Teshuvah.* Ed. Tsevi Yehudah Hakohen Kook. Jerusalem, 1924.

_____. *Pinkesei ha-RAYaH.* 7 vols. Jerusalem, 2008-2021.

_____. *Rav A.Y. Kook: Selected Letters.* Ed. and transl. Tzvi Feldman. Ma'aleh Adumim, 1986.

_____. *Shemonah Kevatsim.* 2nd edition. 2 vols. Jerusalem, 2004.

_____. *Shemu'ot RAYaH.* Vol. 1. *Bereshit.* Ed. Kalman Eliezer Frankel. Jerusalem, 1939. Vol. 2. *Shemot.* Ed. Ḥayyim Yeshayahu Hadari. Jerusalem, 2015. Vol. 3. *Vayyikra, Bamidbar, Devarim.* Ed. Aryeh Hendler. Israel, 2022.

_____. *Siddur 'Olat Re'iyah.* Vol. 1. Weekdays. Jerusalem, 1939. Vol. 2. Sabbath and Festivals. Jerusalem, 1949.

_____. *The Koren Rav Kook Siddur.* Transl. and adapted Bezalel Naor. Jerusalem, 2017.

_____. *"Zer'onim."* In *Ha-Tarbut ha-Yisraelit.* Ed. Alexander Ziskind Rabinowitz and Tsevi Yehudah Hakohen Kook. Jaffa, 1913.

_____. *Zivḥei RAYaH.* On Tractate *Ḥullin.* Jerusalem, 1924. Reprinted in *Mishpat Kohen.*

Kook, Tsevi Yehudah Hakohen. *Li-Netivot Yisrael.* Collected essays. Vol. 1. Tel-Aviv, 1967. With vowel points. Ed. Harel Cohen. Beit El, 2002. Vol. 2. Jerusalem, 1979.

_____. *Li-Sheloshah be-Ellul.* Biographical sketches of Abraham Isaac Hakohen Kook. 2 vols. Jerusalem, 1938, 1947. Photo offset Jerusalem, 1978.

_____. *Shemoneh Iggerot (Eight Letters from Rabbi Zvi Yehuda Kook about Historiosophy, Philosophy,*

Theology and Zionism). Hebrew and German. Ed. Ḥagay Shtamler. Jerusalem, 2021.

_____. *Tsemaḥ Tsevi.* Collected letters. Vol. 1 (5667-5679/1907-1919). Jerusalem, 1991.

Kosman, Abraham. "*Mavo' le-Sifrei R' Menashe me-Ilya Talmid ha-GRA.*" *Nitsanei Arets* (publication of Merkaz Harav), no. 8 (1992).

Lazarus-Yafeh, Ḥava. *Intertwined Worlds: Medieval Islam and Bible Criticism.* Princeton, New Jersey, 1992.

Leiner, Gershon Ḥanokh, of Radzyn. *Ha-Hakdamah ve-ha-Petiḥah.* New York, 1950. [= Introduction to Ya'akov Leiner, *Beit Ya'akov*].

_____. *Sod Yesharim: Rosh Hashanah.* Warsaw, 1902.

_____. *Tif'eret ha-Ḥanokhi.* Commentary to *Zohar.* Warsaw, 1900. Photo offset New York, 1974.

Leiner, Mordechai Yosef, of Izbica. *Mei ha-Shilo'aḥ.* Vol. 1. "Vienna," 1860. vol. 2. Lublin, 1922.

Leiner, Ya'akov, of Izbica and Radzyn. *Beit Ya'akov.* Vol. 1. Genesis. Warsaw, 1990. Vol. 2. Exodus. Lublin, 1903. Vol. 3. Leviticus. Lublin, 1937.

Leon, Moses de. *Ha-Nefesh ha-Ḥakhamah.* Basel, 1608.

Levin, Ḥayyim Abraham Dov Baer. (Published anonymously.) *Otsar Iggerot Kodesh.* Brooklyn, 1988.

Levene, Ḥayyim Ya'akov. *Ḥil ha-Mikdash: Seder Kodashim.* Jerusalem, 1937.

Liebes, Esther. "*Cordovero ve-ha-ARI—Beḥinah meḥudeshet shel mythos mitat malkhei Edom.*" In *Ma'ayan 'Eyn Ya'akov le-Rabbi Moshe Cordovero* (*Ha-Ma'ayan ha-Revi'i mi-Sefer Elimah*). Ed. Bracha Sack. Be'er Sheva, 2009.

Liebes, Yehuda. *Studies in the Zohar.* Albany, 1993.

_____. *"Zemirot li-Se'udot Shabbat she-Yisad ha-ARI ha-Kadosh." Molad* 4 (1972), pp. 540-555.

Lifshitz, Ḥayyim. *Shivḥei ha-RAYaH.* Jerusalem, 1979. Photo offset Jerusalem, 1995.

Lifshitz, Yosef Yitzḥak. *Eḥad be-Khol Dimyonot* (*One God, Many Images: Dialectical Thought in Ḥasidei Ashkenaz*). Israel, 2015.

Lintop, Pinḥas Hakohen, of Birzh. *Kana'uteh de-Pinḥas.* Ed. Bezalel Naor. Spring Valley, NY, 2013.

Lipkin, Aryeh Leib. (Published anonymously.) Ed. Aharon Meir Altschuler. *Kelalei Hatḥalat ha-Ḥokhmah.* Warsaw, 1893.

Lipkin, Israel, of Salant. *'Or Yisrael.* Ed. Isaac Blaser of St. Petersburg. Vilna, 1900.

Lorberbaum, Menachem. *Lifnei Heyot ha-Ḥasidut* (Before Ḥasidism). Jerusalem, 2022.

Löw, Judah (MaHaRaL) of Prague. *Be'er ha-Golah.* London, 1964.

_____. *Derekh Ḥayyim.* Commentary on *Avot.* London, 1961.

_____. *Gevurot Hashem.* London, 1954.

_____. *Ḥiddushei Aggadot.* London, 1960.

_____. *Ner Mitsvah.* B'nei Berak, 1972.

_____. *Netivot 'Olam.* London, 1961.

_____. *Netsaḥ Yisrael.* London, 1957.

_____. *Tif'eret Yisrael.* London, 1955.

Luria, Solomon. *Yam shel Shelomo.* Tractate *Bava Kamma.* Prague, 1616-1618.

Luzzatto, Moshe Ḥayyim. *Adir ba-Marom*. Ed. Yosef Spinner. Part One. Jerusalem, 1990. Part Two. Jerusalem, 1988. Ed. Mordekhai Chriqui. Jerusalem, 2018.

_____. *Da'at Tevunot*. Ed. Ḥayyim Friedlander. 2nd edition. B'nei Berak, 1975.

_____. *Iggerot Pitḥei Ḥokhmah va-Da'at*. In *Sha'arei RaMḤaL*. Ed. Ḥayyim Friedlander. B'nei Berak, 1989.

_____. (attributed to). *KaLaḤ Pitḥei Ḥokhmah*. Koretz, 1785. Ed. Yosef Spinner. Jerusalem, 1987.

Maimon (Fishman), Yehudah Leib. *Igrot Harav Maimon*. vol. 1 (5656-5680/1896-1920). Ed. Bick, Yosifon, Frankel and Reich. Jerusalem, 1979.

Maimon, Solomon. *Lebensgeschichte von ihm selbst geschrieben*. Berlin, 1792. Translated to English by J. Clark Murray. *The Autobiography of Solomon Maimon*. London, 1954.

_____. *Giv'at ha-Moreh*. Commentary to *Moreh Nevukhim*. Sulzbach, 1828. Published anonymously.

Maimonides, Abraham. *Ma'amar 'al ha-Derashot ve-'al ha-Aggadot*. Ed. Moshe Maimon. Monsey, NY, 2020.

Maimonides, Moses.

_____. (Attributed to). *Be'ur Millot ha-Higayon*. With commentary by Moses Mendelssohn. (Mendelssohn's commentary first published anonymously.) Frankfort on Oder, 1761.

_____. *The Guide for the Perplexed*. English translation from the Arabic. M. Friedländer. London, 1904; photo offset New York, 1956.

_____. *Moreh Nevukhim*. Hebrew translation from the Arabic. Yosef Kafaḥ. Jerusalem, 1977. Michael Schwarz. 2 vols. Jerusalem, 2002.

Malbim (Wisser), Meir Leibush. *Yemei Kedem*. Commentary to Chronicles. Warsaw, 1874.

Margaliyot, Reuven. *Nitsotsei Zohar.* Notes to *Zohar.* Published in margins of *Zohar*. 3 vols. 4th edition, corrected with additions. Jerusalem, 1964.

Margi, Ya'akov. *Emet le-Ya'akov.* Commentary to *Zohar.* In *Sefer ha-Zohar 'im Peirush Emet le-Ya'akov.* 10 vols. Jerusalem, 2021.

_____. *Peirush 'al ha-Idra Zuta Kadisha,* Vienna, 1887.

Medina, David de. *Ru'aḥ David ve-Nishmat David*. Commentary to *Idra Rabba* and Song of Songs. Salonika, 1747.

Meir, Jonatan. "Longing of Souls for the *Shekhina*: Relations between Rabbi Kook, Zeitlin and Brenner." (Hebrew). In *The Path of the Spirit*: *Eliezer Schweid Jubilee Volume* (*Jerusalem Studies in Jewish Thought*, vol. 19, 2005, 2), pp. 771-818.

Menashe ben Yosef, of Ilya. *Alfei Menashe*. Part One. Vilna, 1822. Part Two. Ed. Yitzḥak Spalter. Vilna, 1905.

_____. *Peiruka li-Tekanta*. Ed. David Kamenetsky. In *Yeshurun*, vol. 20 (Nissan 5768), pp. 800-825.

_____. *Pesher Davar*. Vilna, 1807. Reprinted in *Kiryat Arba'*. Jerusalem, 1995.

Mendelssohn, Moses. *Morgenstunden oder Vorlesungen über das Dasein Gottes*. Berlin, 1785.

Mirsky, Yehudah. *Rav Kook: Mystic in a Time of Revolution.* New Haven, 2014.

_____. *Towards the Mystical Experience of Modernity: The Making of Rav Kook, 1865-1904*. Boston, 2021.

Nahir, Ehud. *"Ha-Ḥut ha-meshulash: Ma'arekhet ha-yaḥasim ha-mitpataḥat bein Brenner, ha-RAYaH Kook ve-ha-RZYH Kook." Oreshet* 9 (2020), pp. 107-144.

_____. *Tikkun: Ha-'Etgar ha-Spinozi be-Kitvei Harav Kook* (*"Tikkun": The Spinozian Challenge in Rav Kook's Writings*). Ph.D. dissertation. Bar-Ilan University. Ramat Gan, 2017.

Naḥman of Breslov. *Likkutei MoHaRaN Tinyana*. Mohilev, 1811.

_____. *Rabbi Nachman's Stories* (*Sippurey Ma'asioth*). Ed. Aryeh Kaplan. n.p., 1983.

_____. *Shir Na'im/Song of Delight*. Ed. and transl. David Sears. Spring Valley, New York, 2005.

Naḥmani, Amihud. *Pirkei Reḥovot*. New York, 1962.

Naḥmanides, Moses. *Commentary to Job*. Ed. Judah Leib Friedman. Israel, 2018.

_____. *Commentary on the Torah*. Ed. C.B. Chavel. Vol. 1. Genesis, Exodus. Jerusalem, 1959. Vol. 2. Leviticus, Numbers, Deuteronomy. Jerusalem, 1960.

_____. *Kitvei Rabbeinu Moshe ben Naḥman*. Ed. C.B. Chavel. 2 vols. Jerusalem, 1963-1964.

Naor, Bezalel. "Ascent and Descent in the Yom Kippur Rite (From the Ḥasidic Thought of Izbica-Radzyn)." In Naor, *From a Kabbalist's Diary: Collected Essays.*

_____. *Ba-Yam Derekh: Netivot ba-Talmud.* Jerusalem, 1983.

_____. *From a Kabbalist's Diary: Collected Essays.* Spring Valley, New York, 2005.

_____. *"Gilgulei ketav-yad 'Adir ba-Marom' le-RaMḤaL she-hayah be-ba'alut mishpaḥat ha-GRA," Sinai, Tishrei-Ḥeshvan* 5759 [1998], pp. 53-62.

_____. *Kana'uteh de-Pinḥas*. See Lintop, Pinḥas.

_____. *The Limit of Intellectual Freedom*. Spring Valley, New York, 2011.

_____. *Maḥol la-Tsaddikim*. Monsey, New York and Jerusalem, 2015.

_____. *Navigating Worlds: Collected Essays*. New York, 2021.

_____. *Post-Sabbatian Sabbatianism*. Spring Valley, New York, 1999.

_____. "Rabbi Naḥman's *Shir Na'im* as a Reply to Maimonides." In Naor, *Navigating Worlds*.

_____. *When God Becomes History: Historical Essays of Rabbi Abraham Isaac Hakohen Kook*. New York, 2016.

_____. *"Zedonot na'asot ke-zakhuyot be-mishnato shel Harav Kuk." Sinai* 93 (1983), pp. 78-87. Re-issued in Naor, *Ba-Yam Derekh*. And in *'Ofer ha-Ayyalim*. Ed. Dani Kokhav (Koch). Jerusalem, 1994.

Nathan of Gaza. *Sefer ha-Beri'ah*. Ed. Leor Holzer. Jerusalem, 2019.

Neriyah, Moshe Tsevi. *Bi-Sdeh ha-RAYaH*. Tel-Aviv, 1991.

_____. *Ḥayyei ha-RAYaH*. Tel-Aviv, 1983.

_____. *Siḥot ha-RAYaH*. Tel-Aviv, 1979.

_____. *Tal ha-RAYaH*. Tel-Aviv, 1993.

Nieto, David. *Della Divina Providencia, ó sea Naturalezza Universal, ó Natura Naturante*. London, 1704.

Pachter, Mordechai. "'*Iggulim ve-Yosher—Le-Toledotehah shel Idea*" ("Circles and Straightness—A History of an Idea"). *Da'at* 18 (Winter 5747/1987), pp. 59-90.

Papo, Eliezer. *Pele' Yo'ets*. Constantinople 1825. Bucharest 1860.

Plungian, Mordechai. *Ben Porat*. Biography of Rabbi Menashe of Ilya. Vilna, 1858.

Popkin, Richard. "Spinoza, Neoplatonic Kabbalist?" In *Neoplatonism and Jewish Thought*. Ed. Len E. Goodman. Albany, 1992. pp. 387-409.

Rabinowitz, David Yitzḥak Eizik, of Skolya. *Mekor ha-Berakhah*. On the Commandments. vol. 1. Brooklyn, 1967.

Rabinowitz, Zadok Hakohen, of Lublin. *Divrei Soferim*. Lublin, 1913.

_____. *Likkutei Ma'amarim*. In *Divrei Soferim*.

_____. *Peri Tsaddik*. Ḥasidic discourses on Torah. 5 vols. Lublin, 1901-1934.

_____. *Sefer ha-Zikhronot*. In *Divrei Soferim*.

Ratner, Israel Shabtai. *Le-'Or ha-Kabbalah*. Kefar Ḥabad, 1961.

Recanati. Menaḥem. Commentary to Torah. Venice, 1523.

Ricchi, Immanuel Ḥai. *Mishnat Ḥasidim*. First Edition Amsterdam, 1727. With commentary *Kesef Mishneh* by Naftali Herz Halevi (Weidenbaum) of Jaffa. Ed. Shmuel Ya'akov Feffer. 2 vols. New York, 2006.

Rivkin, Moshe Dov Baer. *Ashkavta de-Rabbi*. Memoir of last days of Rabbi Shalom Dov Baer Schneersohn of Lubavitch. Brooklyn, 1953.

_____. *Tif'eret Zion*. Talmudic lectures. New York, 1975.

Rosen-Zvi, Ishay. *Demonic Desires: "Yetzer Hara" and the Problem of Evil in Late Antiquity.* Philadelphia, 2011.

_____. "Two Rabbinic Inclinations? Rethinking a Scholarly Dogma." *Journal for the Study of Judaism* 39 (2008), pp. 1-27.

Sa'adyah ben Yosef al-Fayyumi. *Peirushei Rabbeinu Sa'adyah Gaon 'al ha-Torah.* Ed. Yosef Kafaḥ. Jerusalem, 1963.

Safran, Bezalel. "Maharal and Early Hasidism." In *Ḥasidism: Continuity or Innovation?* Ed. Bezalel Safran. Cambridge, Massachusetts, 1988.

Safrin, Isaac Judah Jeḥiel, of Komarno. *'Assirit ha-'Eifah.* Commentary to *Torat Kohanim* (*Sifra*). Lemberg, 1849.

_____. *Heikhal ha-Berakhah.* Commentary to Torah. 5 vols. Lemberg, 1869.

Saks, Jeffrey. "A Portrait of Two Artists at the Crossroads: Between Rav Kook and S.Y. Agnon." *Tradition* 49:2 (2016), pp. 32-52.

Samuel ben Eliezer of Kalvaria. *Darkhei No'am.* Kabbalistic commentary to the Legends of Rabbah bar Bar Ḥannah. Königsberg, 1764.

Schneersohn, Joseph Isaac, of Lubavitch. *Sefer ha-Siḥot 5701.* Brooklyn, NY, 1964.

Schneersohn, Menaḥem Mendel, of Lubavitch. *Derekh Mitsvotekha* (*Ta'amei ha-Mitsvot*). Poltava, 1911.

Schneerson, Isaac Dov Baer, of Lyady. *Siddur 'im Peirush MaHaRID.* 2 vols. Berdichev, 1913. Photo offset Kefar Ḥabad, 1991.

Scholem, Gershom G. *Major Trends in Jewish Mysticism.* New York, 1971.

Septimus, Bernard. "Open Rebuke and Concealed Love: Naḥmanides and the Andalusian Tradition." In *Rabbi Moses Nahmanides (RaMBaN): Explorations in His Religious and Literary Virtuosity*. Ed. Isadore Twersky. Cambridge, Massachusetts, 1983. pp. 11-34.

Shalev, Alon. *Orthodox Theology in the Age of Meaning: The Life and Works of Rabbi Isaac Hutner*. (Hebrew). Ph.D. dissertation. Hebrew University. Jerusalem, 2020.

Shapira, Meshel Shmuel. *He'arot ha-Shemesh*. Odessa, 1889.

Sherman, Moshe. "The 1934 Diary of Oscar Z. Fasman, Journey to Europe and the Land of Israel." *Ḥakirah* 30 (Winter 2021).

Shilo, Elḥanan. *Ha-Kabbalah bi-Yetsirat S.Y. Agnon*. Ramat Gan, 2011.

Shneur Zalman of Lyady. *Likkutei Torah*. Ḥasidic discourses to Leviticus, Numbers, Deuteronomy, and Song of Songs. Vilna, 1904. Photo offset Brooklyn, 1972.

_____. *Siddur 'im DAḤ [=Divrei Elohim Ḥayyim]*. New York, 1971. Photo offset of Zhitomir, 1863 and Warsaw, 1867.

_____. *Tanya*. Vilna, 1937. Photo offset Brooklyn, 1966.

_____. *Torah 'Or*. Ḥasidic discourses to Genesis, Exodus, and Esther. Vilna, 1899. Photo offset Brooklyn, 1972.

Shneuri, Dov Baer, of Lubavitch. *Sha'ar ha-Yiḥud*. Kopyst, 1820.

_____. *Torat Ḥayyim, Bereshit*. Brooklyn, 1993.

Shu'aib, Joshua ibn. *Derashot Rabbi Joshua Ibn Shu'aib*. Ze'ev Metzger. Jerusalem, 1992.

Shuchat, Raphael B. "The Historiosophy of the Vilna Gaon and the Influence of Luzzatto on Him and His Disciples." (Hebrew). *Da'at* 40 (1998), pp. 125-152.

Silman, Yochanan. "Psychology in the Teachings of Rabbi Israel Lipkin (Salanter)." (Hebrew). *Bar-Ilan* 11 (1973), pp. 291-292.

Soloveitchik, Joseph Baer, of Boston. *Halakhic Man*. Authorized translation of *"Ish ha-Halakhah"* by Lawrence Kaplan. Philadelphia, 1983.

_____. *"Ish ha-Halakhah."* In *Talpiyot* 1 (1944), pp. 651-735. Ed. Samuel Mirsky.

Soloveitchik, Joseph Baer, of Brisk. *Beit Halevi* on Genesis and Exodus. Warsaw, 1884.

Spinoza, Benedict de. *A Theologico-Political Treatise*. Transl. R.H.M. Elwes. New York, 1951.

Spira, Tsevi Elimelekh, of Dynów. *Hagahot* (glosses) to Tsevi Hirsch Eichenstein of Zydaczów, *Sur me-Ra' va-'Aseh Tov: Hakdamah ve-Derekh le-'Ets ha-Ḥayyim*. Jerusalem, 1997.

_____. *Igra de-Pirka*. Lemberg, 1858.

Stern, Yosef Zechariah. *Zekher Yehosef*. Warsaw, 1859. Photo offset New York, 1991.

Strauss, Leo. *Spinoza's Critique of Religion*. Transl. E.M. Sinclair. Chicago, 1997.

Tchernowitz, Chaim (*Rav Tza'ir*). *Masekhet Zikhronot: Partsufim ve-Ha'arakhot* (*Book of Memoirs: Portraits and Appraisals*). New York, 1945.

Teich, Samuel. *Otsar Emet 'al Mo'adei ha-Shanah: Purim*. Brooklyn, 1979.

Tishby, Isaiah. "*Darkhei hafatsatam shel kitvei kabbalah le-RaMḤaL be-Polin u-be-Lita.*" *Kiryat Sefer* 45 (5730/1970), pp. 127-154.

_____. *Paths of Faith and Heresy: Essays in Kabbalah and Sabbateanism.* (Hebrew). Jerusalem, 1994.

Tsemaḥ, Ya'akov. *Kol be-Ramah.* Commentary to *Idra Rabba.* Ed. Eliyahu Attiah. Jerusalem, 2001.

Tsiyoni, Menaḥem. Commentary to Torah. Cremona, 1560.

Tyrer, Ḥayyim, of Tchernowitz. *Sha'ar ha-Tefillah.* Warsaw, 1874.

_____. *Sidduro shel Shabbat.* Warsaw, 1876. Photo offset Jerusalem, 1955.

Vital (Calabrese), Ḥayyim. *'Ets Ḥayyim.* Tel-Aviv, 1975. (Photo offset of Warsaw, 1891). With commentary of Menaḥem Menkhin Heilperin. Appended glosses of Rabbi Yitzḥak Berman.

_____. *Ketavim Ḥadashim me-Rabbeinu Ḥayyim Vital.* Jerusalem, 1988.

_____. *Likkutei Torah.* Vilna, 1880.

_____. *Sefer ha-Likkutim.* Jerusalem, 1913.

_____. *Sha'arei Kedushah.* With notes of Rabbi Ze'ev Wolf Ashkenazi. Jerusalem, 1926. And with vocalization of the Hebrew text. Israel, 2005.

_____. *Sha'arei Kedushah,* Part Four (from manuscript). In *Ketavim Ḥadashim me-Rabbeinu Ḥayyim Vital.*

_____. *Sha'ar ha-Gilgulim.* With commentary *B'nei Aharon* of Shim'on Agasi. Jerusalem, 1990.

_____. *Sha'ar ha-Kelalim.* Printed in beginning of *'Ets Ḥayyim.*

Weidenbaum, Naftali Herz Halevi, of Jaffa. *Siddur ha-GRA*. See Elijah Gaon of Vilna.

_____. *Kesef Mishneh*. Commentary to *Mishnat Ḥasidim*. See Ricchi, Immanuel Ḥai.

Weintraub, Yisrael Eliyahu. *Nefesh Eliyahu: Hakdamot ve-Shi'urim*. n.p. [Israel], 2012.

Wellhausen, Julius. *Prolegomena zur Geschichte Israels* (*Prolegomena to the History of Israel*). Second edition. Berlin, 1883.

Werner, Asher Ze'ev. *Bi-Ne'areinu u-vi-Zekeneinu*. Kabbalistic responsa. Appended to *Ta'am Zekenim*. Jerusalem, 1955.

Wolfson, Elliot R. *Through a Speculum That Shines: Vision and Imagination in Medieval Jewish Mysticism*. Princeton, 1997.

Wolfson, Harry Austryn. *Crescas' Critique of Aristotle: Problems of Aristotle's* Physics *in Jewish and Arabic Philosophy*. Cambridge, Massachusetts, 1929.

_____. *The Philosophy of Spinoza: Unfolding the Latent Processes of His Reasoning*. Vol. 1. New York, 1969.

Yaffe, Samuel Ashkenazi. *Yefeh To'ar*. Commentary to *Bereshit Rabbah*. Venice, 1597-1606.

Yisraeli, 'Oded. "*Le-Toledot Torat ha-Hashgaḥah shel ha-RaMBaN*." *Da'at* 90 (2020), pp. 83-107.

Yom Tov ben Abraham Al-Sevilli (RITBA). *Sefer ha-Zikaron*. Ed. Kalman Kahana. Jerusalem, 1982.

Yosef Ḥayyim of Baghdad (*Ben Ish Ḥai*). *Benayahu*. Ed. Yeshu'ah Salem. 3 vols. Jerusalem, 1990.

_____. *Rav Pe'alim*. Halakhic and Kabbalistic responsa. 4 vols. Jerusalem, 1901-1912.

Zacuto, Moses. *Peirush ha-RaMaZ la-Zohar*. Ed. Yitzḥak Naḥum. 6 vols. Jerusalem, 1998-2005.

Ze'ira, Moshe. "Rabbi Eliyahu Klatzkin." *Yeshurun*, vol. 15 (Nissan 5765/2005), pp. 745-797.

Zeitlin, Aharon. *Bein Emunah la-'Omanut*. vol. 1. Tel-Aviv, 1980.

_____. *Ha-Metsi'ut ha-Aḥeret*. Tel-Aviv, 1967.

Zeitlin, Hillel. *"Ha-Kav ha-Yesodi ba-Kabbalah shel Harav Kook." HaTzofeh, Erev Rosh Hashanah* 5699 (1938).

_____. *Sifran shel Yeḥidim*. Jerusalem, 1979.

_____. *"Tefillot." HaTekufah* (Tel-Aviv), vol. 12 (Tammuz-Ellul 5681/1921).

Zussman, Yosef Leib. *Mi-Beḥirei Tsaddikaya*. Jerusalem, 2007.

הספר הזה מוקדש
לעילוי נשמת

הרב יצחק ברוך
ב״ר אריה ז״ל

מראשוני המוסמכים לרבנות על ידי
ישיבת רבינו יעקב יוסף
אם הישיבות בארה״ב

הנעים קולו כש״ץ בקהילות שונות

רופא אומן לרפואת הנפש

מסר נפשו לחינוך יוצאי חלציו
וגידלם שיהיו עובדי ה׳ עוסקים בתורה ובמצוות

נלב״ע ג׳ תשרי תשע״ח
תנצב״ה

הספר הזה מוקדש
לעילוי נשמת

מרת רבקה
ב"ר נחמן ז"ל

רוח הבריות נוחה בתפארת מידותיה והליכותיה
בזהירות בכשרות ובאמונה יסדה ביתה וחינכה בניה
קיבלה מאביה שמסר נפשו לשמירת שבת ומצותיה
הרבתה להיטיב לזולתה בסבר פנים יפות במאור פניה

בתמידות הגבילה צרכיה והרחיבה חסדיה וצדקותיה

נהנו ממנה עצה ותושיה ורבים נתמכו בהלואותיה
חגרה בעוז מתניה לעזר צאצאיה ונכדיה
מסירות לבבה עבורם רבה ועצומה כל ימי חייה
נזדככה ביסורים בעד משפחתה תליץ יושר מליצותיה

נלב"ע כ"ב אדר תשפ"א
תנצב"ה

www.ingramcontent.com/pod-product-compliance
Lightning Source LLC
Chambersburg PA
CBHW072114050526
44107CB00098BA/182
9798888940020